SCOTTISH
BOTHY
WALKS

Scotland's 28 best bothy adventures

GEOFF ALLAN

WILD THINGS PUBLISHING

SCOTTISH BOTHY WALKS

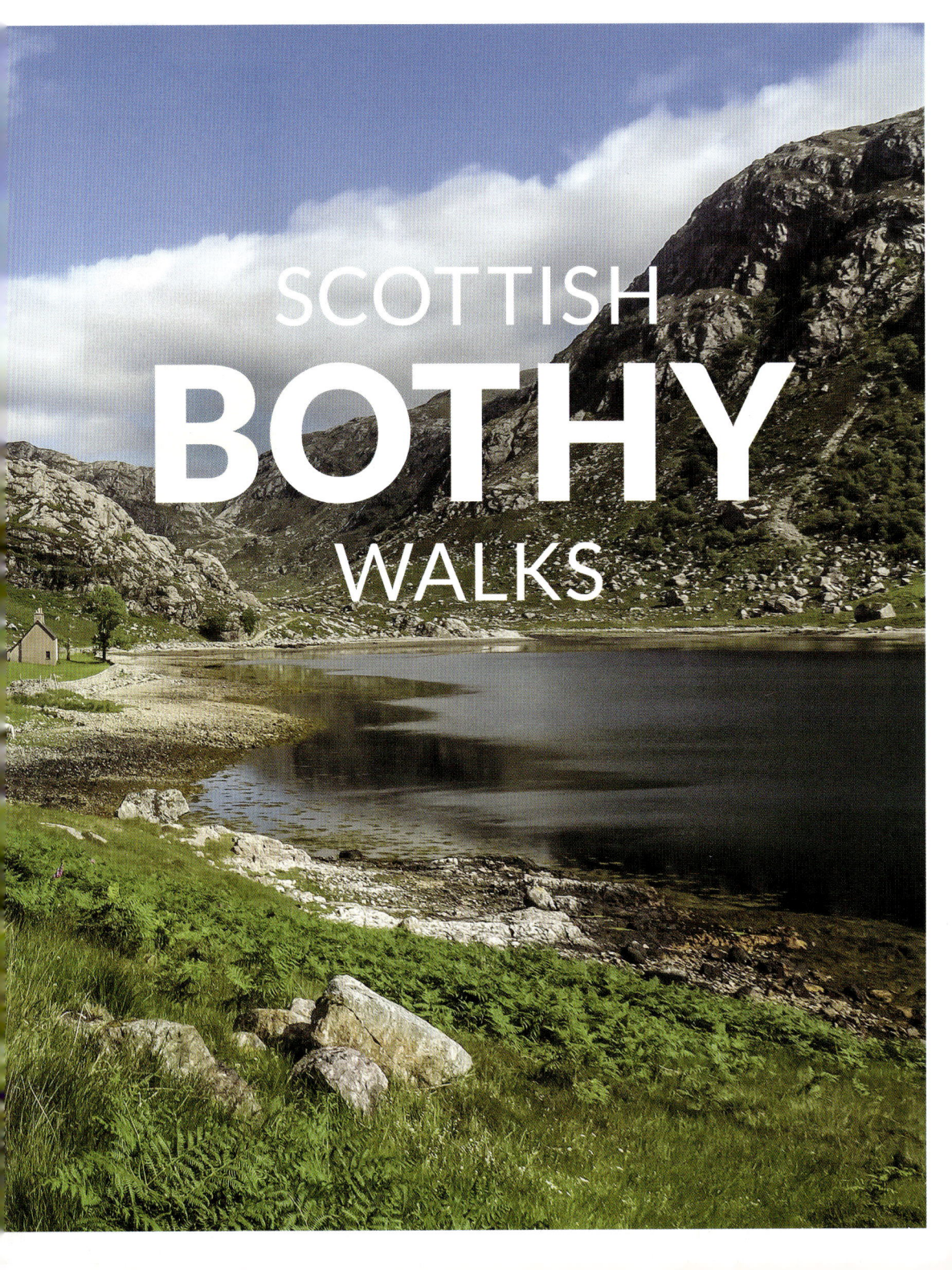

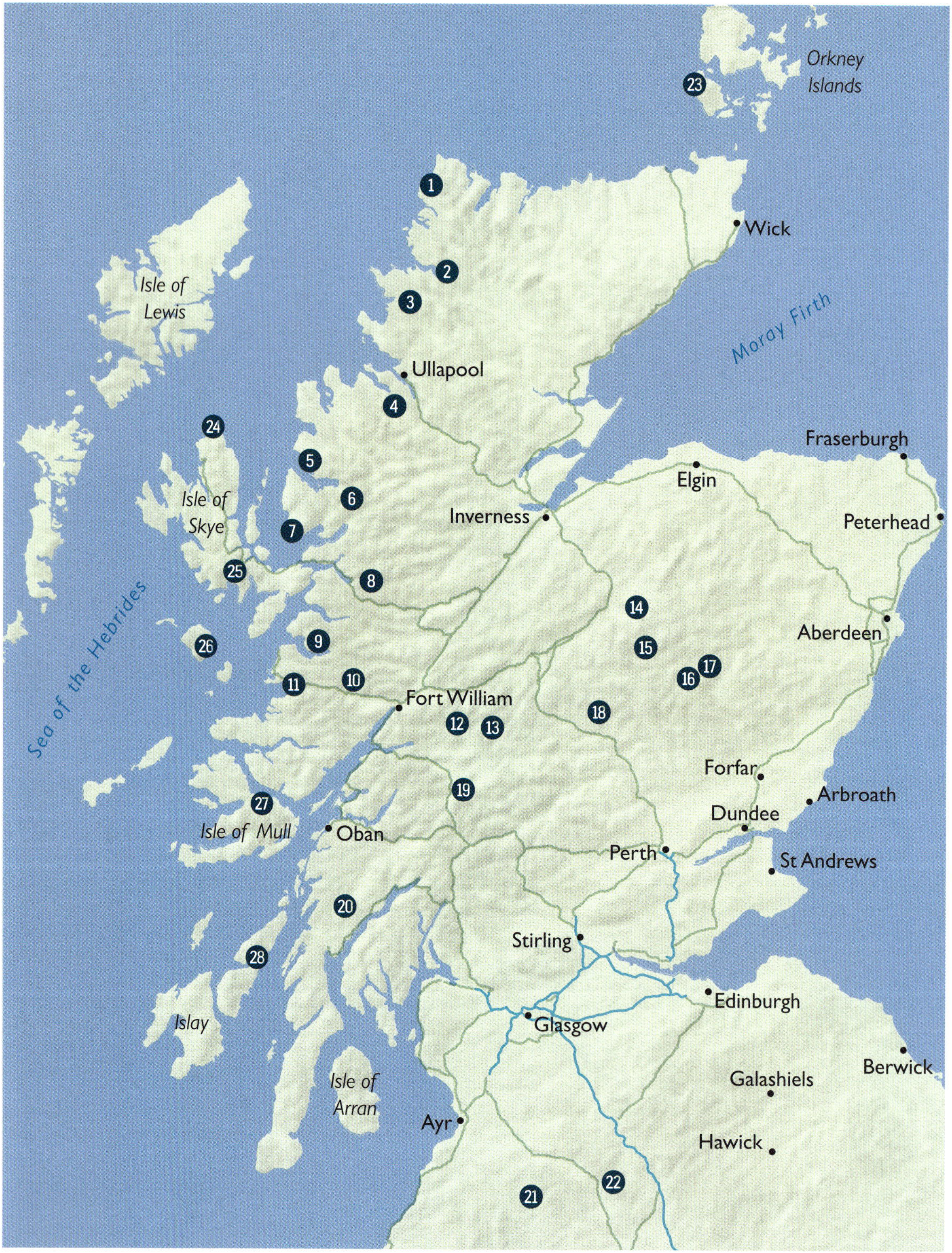

Orkney Islands
Wick
Moray Firth
Isle of Lewis
Ullapool
Fraserburgh
Elgin
Peterhead
Isle of Skye
Inverness
Aberdeen
Sea of the Hebrides
Fort William
Forfar
Arbroath
Dundee
Isle of Mull
Oban
Perth
St Andrews
Stirling
Edinburgh
Islay
Glasgow
Berwick
Galashiels
Isle of Arran
Ayr
Hawick
1
2
3
4
5
6
7
8
9
10
11
12
13
14
15
16
17
18
19
20
21
22
23
24
25
26
27
28

CONTENTS

Table of Walks 6
Introduction 9
Bothies & bothying 13
How to use this guide 16
Clothing & other essentials 18
Safety 20

NORTHERN HIGHLANDS

01. Sandwood Bay & the bothies at
    Strathchailleach & Strathan 24
02. Beinn Leòid from Kylestrome
    visiting Glendhu & Glencoul 32
03. Suilven & Suileag Bothy from
    Glencanisp Lodge 42
04. Beinn Dearg Mòr & Shenavall Bothy 50

NORTH WEST HIGHLANDS

05. Mesolithic Cave & Shell Midden
    beyond Craig Bothy in Torridon 62
06. Coire Fionnaraich Bothy & a circuit of
    Maol Chean-dearg 68
07. Uags Bothy &
    the Applecross Peninsula 76
08. Beinn Fhada & Camban Bothy 82

WESTERN HIGHLANDS

09. Knoydart & the Rough Bounds via
    Sourlies Bothy 92
10. Streap & Gleann Dubh-lighe Bothy 104
11. Peanmeanach Bothy &
    the Ardnish Peninsula 112

CENTRAL HIGHLANDS

12. Overnight at Staoineag Bothy 120
13. A Ben Alder crossing from Rannoch to
    Corrour station 126

EASTERN HIGHLANDS

14. Meall a' Bhuachaille & Ryvoan Bothy 136
15. Ben Macdui visiting Bob Scott's Bothy &
    Hutchison Memorial Hut 142
16. Callater Stables & Loch Kander 152
17. Lochnagar from Balmoral &
    Gelder Shiel Stables 158
18. Beinn Dearg &
    Allt Scheicheachan Bothy 166

SOUTH WEST HIGHLANDS

19. Beinn a'Chreachain &
    Beinn Achaladair via Gorton Bothy 174
20. Kilneuair by Loch Awe to Carron Bothy 182

SOUTHERN SCOTLAND

21. Clennoch Bothy &
    Cairnsmore of Carsphairn 190
22. Kettleton Byre & Scaw'd Law 196

THE ISLANDS

23. Burnmouth Cottage, Rackwick Bay &
    The Old Man of Hoy 204
24. The Lookout & Rubha Hunish on Skye 210
25. New Camasunary Bothy,
    the 'Bad Step' & Loch Coruisk 216
26. Dibidil Bothy & the Rùm Cuillin 224
27. Beinn Talaidh &
    Tomsleibhe Bothy, Mull 234
28. Jura's remote coastal bothies Cruib &
    Ruantallain 240

APPENDIX

Munros, Corbetts & Grahams 250
Gaelic glossary 251
Bibliography 252
Copyright & Acknowledgements 256

NO.	NAME	DISTANCE	WALKING TIME	TOTAL ASCENT
01	Sandwood Bay & the bothies at Strathchailleach & Strathan	22km/14 miles	7.5-9.5 hours (over 2 days)	520m
02	Beinn Leòid from Kylestrome visiting Glendhu & Glencoul	36km/22.5 miles	11-14 hours (over 3 days)	1200m
03	Suilven & Suileag Bothy from Glencanisp Lodge	19km/12 miles	6-8 hours	836m
04	Beinn Dearg Mòr & Shenavall Bothy	25km/15.5 miles	8-10 hours	1530m
05	Mesolithic Cave & Shell Midden beyond Craig Bothy in Torridon	12km/7.5 miles	4-5 hours	154m
06	Coire Fionnaraich Bothy & a circuit of Maol Chean-dearg	19km/12 miles	6-7 hours	713m
07	Uags Bothy & the Applecross Peninsula	11km/7 miles	4-5 hours	169m
08	Beinn Fhada & Camban Bothy	25.75km/16 miles	8-10 hours	1234m
09	Knoydart & the Rough Bounds via Sourlies Bothy	44km/27.25 miles	14-17 hours (over 2 days)	1790m
10	Streap & Gleann Dubh-lighe Bothy	17.5km/11 miles	6-8 hours	1197m
11	Peanmeanach Bothy & The Ardnish Peninsula	11km/7 miles	4-5 hours	187m
12	Overnight at Staoineag Bothy	17km/10.5 miles	5-6 hours (over 2 days)	100m
13	A Ben Alder Crossing from Rannoch to Corrour Station	30km/18.5 miles	9-11 hours (over 2 days)	750m
14	Meall a' Bhuachaille & Ryvoan Bothy	9km/5.5 miles	4.5-5.5 hours	570m
15	Ben Macdui visiting Bob Scott's Bothy & Hutchison Memorial Hut	32km/20 miles	10-12 hours	1440m
16	Callater Stables & Loch Kander	19m/12 miles	6-8 hours	790m
17	Lochnagar from Balmoral & Gelder Shiel Stables	21km/13 miles	6-8 hours	1089m
18	Beinn Dearg & Allt Scheicheachan Bothy	29km/18 miles	9-11 hours	1377m
19	Beinn a'Chreachain & Beinn Achaladair via Gorton Bothy	25.5km/15.5 miles	8-10 hours	1300m
20	Kilneuair by Loch Awe to Carron Bothy	17km/10.5 miles	5-6 hours	727m
21	Clennoch Bothy & Cairnsmore of Carsphairn	18km/11 miles	6-7 hours	890m
22	Kettleton Byre & Scaw'd Law	12km/7.5 miles	3.5-4.5 hours	590m
23	Burnmouth Cottage, Rackwick Bay & The Old Man of Hoy	11km/7 miles	4-5 hours	190m
24	The Lookout & Rubha Hunish on Skye	4km/2.5 miles	3-4 hours	93m
25	New Camasunary Bothy, the 'Bad Step' & Loch Coruisk	29km/18 miles	10-12 hours	670m
26	Dibidil Bothy & the Rùm Cuillin	20.5km/13 miles	10-12 hours	1900m
27	Beinn Talaidh & Tomsleibhe Bothy, Mull	18km/11 miles	5-6 hours	748m
28	Jura's remote coastal bothies Cruib & Ruantallain	27km/17 miles	9-12 hours (over 3 days)	140m

TABLE OF WALKS

SUMMITS	NAVIGATION	TERRAIN	DIFFICULTY
	Straightforward	Challenging	Straightforward
Beinn Leòid (Corbett), 792m	Challenging	Challenging	Challenging
Caisteal Liath (Corbett), 731m	Easy	Straightforward	Straightforward
Beinn Dearg Mòr (Corbett), 906m	Straightforward	Challenging (steep climb)	Challenging
	Easy	Easy	Easy
	Straightforward	Easy	Straightforward
	Easy	Easy	Easy
Beinn Fhada (Munro), 1032 m; Sgùrr a' Dubh Doire (Munro Top), 962m	Challenging	Straightforward	Challenging
	Straightforward	Straightforward	Challenging
Meall an Uillt Chaoil, 844m; Stob Coire nan Cearc, 887m; Streap (Corbett), 909m; Streap Comhlaidh, 898m	Straightforward	Straightforward/ Challenging	Straightforward/ Challenging
	Easy	Easy	Straightforward
	Easy	Easy	Straightforward
	Easy	Challenging	Challenging
	Easy	Easy	Easy
Ben Macdui (Munro), 1309m; Stob Coire Sputan Dearg (Munro Top), 1249m; Sròn Riach (Munro Top), 1113m	Challenging	Straightforward/ Challenging	Challenging
	Easy	Straightforward	Straightforward
Lochnagar/Cac Carn Beag (Munro), 1115m; Cac Carn Mòr, 1150m	Straightforward	Straightforward	Straightforward/ Challenging
Beinn Dearg (Munro), 1008m	Straightforward	Straightforward	Challenging
Beinn a'Chreachain (Munro), 1081m; Meall Buidhe (Munro Top), 978m; Beinn Achaladair (Munro), 1038m; South Top, 1002m	Straightforward	Straightforward	Challenging
	Easy	Easy	Straightforward
Cairnsmore of Carsphairn (Corbett), 797m; Beninner (Donald Top), 710m	Straightforward	Straightforward	Straightforward
Scaw'd Law (Donald), 663m; Little Scaw'd Law, 594m; Glenleith Fell (Donald Top), 612m–quick detour from route	Easy	Easy	Easy
	Easy	Easy	Easy
	Easy	Easy (one short scramble)	Easy
	Easy	Hard (serious rock traverse)	Challenging
Askival (Corbett), 812m; Ainshval (Corbett), 781m; Trollabhal (Graham), 702m; Sgùrr nan Gillean (Corbett Top), 764m; Hallival, 723m.	Challenging	Hard (ridge scramble)	Challenging
Beinn Talaidh (Graham), 761m	Easy	Straightforward	Straightforward
	Challenging	Challenging	Challenging

APPROACHING THE 'BAD STEP' ON SKYE (WALK 25)

INTRODUCTION

Bothy Walks is a natural companion to my first book, *The Scottish Bothy Bible*. In this volume, I showcase some of the best bothies in the country, setting out a range of short hikes, mountain climbs and multi-day expeditions using these unique shelters as a focal point. Over the last two years I have eagerly retraced my steps around the bothy network, checking out routes for inclusion here, and adding a raft of new images to my photographic archive. My aim has been to tempt you out into Scotland's rugged and beautiful landscape, whatever your level of ability. The walks range from a stroll along the cliffs above Rackwick Bay to the Old Man of Hoy on the Orkney Archipelago, to a challenging traverse of the 'Bad Step' on Skye. As well as including all the essential technical details, each entry offers a taste of what makes the area special, from its unique geology, wildlife and flora, to the intriguing history and culture of its people. And there are a few personal reminiscences along the way...

Even after more than 30 years spent exploring Scotland's nooks and crannies, I still feel a surge of anticipation and delight when I see a bothy in the distance, even if I have visited it many times before. My adventures into the bothy world began during my student days in the late-1980s, when I became an enthusiastic member of the Edinburgh University Mountaineering Club. By my second year of study, I was bothy secretary for the club hut, Glenlicht House, tucked away beneath the mountains of Kintail, and had begun to seek out bothy locations. At the time, these were closely guarded secrets, held only by a knowledgeable few. One of my first discoveries was the Mountain Bothies Association (MBA) bothy at Camban (described in Walk 8), which sits on the lonely pass between Glen Affric and Gleann Lichd. I vividly remember staring up at the mist-laden Munros surrounding the bothy, not quite believing that this isolated refuge was free to use by anyone who had the wherewithal to get there. Soon I had acquired a prized copy of the MBA bothy grid references (finally published online by the MBA in 2009), and stumbled upon Irvine Butterfield's 1972 *Survey of Shelters in Remote Mountain Areas of the Scottish Highlands*. This treasure trove of information became the basis of my own precious bothy list, and inspired an even greater passion to travel around the country.

Through my love affair with bothies I have developed an intimate personal relationship with the Scottish Highlands, a bond that has only intensified since the autumn of 2011, when I hit upon the idea of producing a countrywide bothy guide. Without the use of a car, it took five years to complete the survey and research all the background material – the vast majority of fieldwork undertaken using my trusty bike and public transport. With the luxury of time, I have been lucky enough to rediscover the country at a slower pace and get a deeper feel for the history that has played out across the landscape over millennia. *The Scottish Bothy Bible* was finally published in March 2017 and went on to win UK Travel Guidebook of the Year.

Much thought has been invested in choosing the walks and bothies in this guide. The selection represents my absolute favourite bothy locations with the most memorable and beautiful approaches. You will find routes that not only range over the whole of Scotland, but also are suitable for a broad spectrum of fitness levels and experience. I have included a mix of day walks and multi-day adventures, and have been conscious not to create itineraries that are too complex or that replicate suggestions in other Scottish walking books. All the day walks return to the same location, whether circular or there-and-back, so there is no requirement for two cars or an anxious hitch-hike to retrieve a vehicle. It is also important to emphasise that each bothy is a worthy objective in itself, as well as a base from which to climb mountain tops or explore additional places of interest. On a *dreich* morning or a lazy sunny afternoon I have often set out to visit a bothy just to have a look around. Happiness comes from the satisfaction of having a simple objective combined with the opportunity to venture off the beaten track.

Creating *The Scottish Bothy Bible* was a life-changing experience for me, and I hope *Scottish Bothy Walks* will encourage even more people out into the hills. Enjoy the descriptions of the walks and the photographs that accompany them. Hopefully they will inspire you to make your own journeys and build lasting relationships with the bothies and mountains that I know and love.

CROSSING THE PARPH, SOUTH OF CAPE WRATH (WALK 1)

STRATHCHAILLEACH BOTHY (WALK 1)

BOTHIES & BOTHYING

'A simple shelter in remote country for the use and benefit of all who love being in wild and lonely places'.

Definition from the MBA members' handbook

Scotland's bothies are a loose collection of shepherds' cottages, estate houses and abandoned crofts that have been saved from ruin and renovated. They form a network of basic shelters located throughout the country's most remote and uninhabited regions. Freely available for anyone to use as a lunch stop, or to stay in overnight, bothies have been used by mountaineers and stravaigers for well over a hundred years and become integral to Scotland's outdoor culture.

In very simple terms, there are many derelict properties scattered across the Scottish landscape because of the waves of depopulation that began in the mid- to late-18th century and did not ease until after World War II. The initial driving force behind the exodus was a process of forced evictions known as the 'Highland Clearances'. People then continued to abandon their communities when harvest failures led to illness and famine, with many leaving for the industrial heartland that grew rapidly in Lowland Scotland through the Victorian era.

The term bothy derives from the Gaelic *bothan* (via the Old Irish *both*) meaning hut, and originally described rough-and-ready accommodation provided by landowners for farm labourers or estate workers. More recently the term has become synonymous with an idea of sanctuary and shelter. This cultural transition began in the 1930s, with the rise in popularity of hillwalking among the urban populations of Glasgow, Edinburgh and Aberdeen. Short of money, but with more leisure time on their hands, groups of mainly young men used these partly derelict cottages as places to congregate and sleep for free during hard-earned weekends. In some cases this practice was clandestine, but increasingly, various estates gave their tacit consent.

The rural exodus following World War II left an increasing number of farmhouses unoccupied, and walkers simply started using them as somewhere to stay overnight. By the 1960s, however, the fabric of many of these properties began to suffer through misuse and lack of maintenance. A few were cared for by climbing clubs, but the remainder received little attention. I strongly believe the bothy tradition in its current form would not have endured without the invention of the MBA, which came into existence in 1965. Bernard Heath, a keen cyclist and hillwalker was inspired by a chance remark in a bothy book suggesting the establishment of a club to keep bothies in good repair. He and a few of his friends decided to restore the ruins of Tunskeen Farm in Galloway, and the following November a group of like-minded individuals gathered in nearby Dalmellington village hall where the Mountain Bothies Association was born. During the next five decades the MBA extended its renovation work across the country, as well as taking over the upkeep of many bothies maintained by various climbing clubs. Today there are over 80 MBA bothies in Scotland as

PEANMEANACH BOTHY (WALK 11)

INSIDE STRATHCHAILLEACH BOTHY (WALK 1)

well as 21 in England and Wales. In 2015, when the organisation celebrated its 50th anniversary, it received The Queen's Award for Voluntary Service – the highest accolade for a voluntary group in the UK.

WHAT TO EXPECT

Bothies come in many shapes and sizes, but the most common configuration is the classic two-roomed cottage referred to by its Scots term, but and ben. The 'but' referring to the kitchen and living room, and the 'ben' the bedroom. Accommodation is very rudimentary, and in almost all cases there is no gas, electricity, tap, or toilet. You should expect only a wind- and waterproof building that offers somewhere dry to sleep. If you are staying overnight, you will need to carry in all the equipment you would normally take camping, plus candles and, if there is a fireplace, fuel to burn. As a bare minimum, bothies will have a table and a couple of chairs, but many also have sleeping platforms and stoves. Water comes from a nearby stream and, although some bothies have latrines or loos, answering calls of nature will involve a walk and the use of a spade.

Bothies can look romantic, but in reality they can be cold, dusty, damp, and pretty dark. Yet in the evening, with the fire blazing, candles burning, hot food on the table and a glass of wine at your elbow, the place is transformed. Some (myself included) just like to go 'bothying' – setting off for the weekend without any other objective in mind – and many bothies have been adopted as a home from home. Evenings can be peaceful or convivial, so respect other users as well as the bothy itself. Each shelter has at least one dedicated MBA maintenance officer who volunteers their services to look after the fabric of the building and when major renovations are required, the MBA organises work parties. I would wholeheartedly recommend joining the MBA to support all their good work.

LOCATING BOTHIES

Bothies differ from other systems of mountain huts and refuges around the world in a number of subtle and distinctive ways. Because only a very small number have been purpose-built, the location of the majority is fairly random. They are not necessarily close to a particular peak or spaced at equal distances along a recognised long-distance walk. Neither are they tied to any specific National Park. They are found right across the country, some in very remote places that are rarely visited. Another intriguing element is the past reticence about advertising the network. Except in a very few cases, the word bothy has not been printed on any OS maps; only the name of the building. And on the ground there are few signposts to point the way. As I explain in the next section, you cannot rely on this guide alone, but in combination with the right OS map you should be able to find your way with ease.

HOW TO USE THIS GUIDE

There are 28 walks in this book covering all of the eight different geographical areas of Scotland. All levels of ability are catered for, from short excursions to longer hikes, from walks that focus on a single peak, whether Munro, Corbett or Graham (definitions in Appendix p250) to multi-day expeditions. Alongside each walk description the relevant maps are listed. The 1:25,000 OS Explorer maps are particularly recommended because the Gaelic names of geographical features such as streams and rock outcrops are not necessarily printed at 1:50,000 scale. All the day walks and four out of the six multi-day expeditions start and end at the same location with minimal road walking. The two other multi-day routes start and end at train stations. All details are summarised in the table of walks. The book uses the convention of distances in miles, and height in metres.

STAY SAFE

Carry a first-aid kit, survival blanket and whistle (often incorporated on straps of modern outdoor rucksacks).

Leave a route description and expected return time with a friend.

Never rely solely on a mobile phone or GPS.

Know your fitness limitations and choose appropriate walks.

Scrambling experience is required on walks graded 'Hard'. Do not take unnecessary risks.

Always carry an ice axe in winter and know how to use it; crampons will also be needed on summits in icy conditions.

DIRECTIONS & TIMINGS

Each description includes a directions summary and a simple sketch map. Waymarkers are plotted on the maps and cross-referenced in the directions with numbered circles. Grid references of significant features such as path junctions, footbridges and river crossings are included. The Information section gives additional advice and suggestions, an overview of the location as well as details of features and risks. The estimated walk times given assume good summer conditions and err on the generous side but depend on fitness levels (and the number of stops). Double the time for winter conditions and after heavy rain.

MAPS & NAVIGATION

None of these walks should be attempted without the relevant OS 1:50,000 (or 1:25,000 if recommended) map and compass. Popular mountain areas and long-distance routes are also covered by Harvey Maps. It is possible to download OS maps onto your smartphone, as a useful additional reference. Do not go out on your own if you are not confident about your map-reading and navigational skills.

DOWNLOADABLE DIRECTIONS

Directions, maps and GPX files for the routes in this book can be accessed online using the last two words of the relevant chapter introduction text e.g. Walk 1 is at http://www.wildthingspublishing.com/bothywalks/wrathtrail

WALKING GRADES

There are three main categories for Terrain, Navigation and Difficulty: Easy, Straightforward, and Challenging. For two walks, the 'Bad Step' on Skye (Walk 25) and the Rùm Cuillin (Walk 26), a fourth category for terrain – Hard – applies. Typically the routes have a simple bothy walk in (along a track or well-defined path) and then the possibility of a more strenuous onward objective.

TERRAIN

Easy Follows a clearly identifiable path/track
Straightforward Paths are visible, continuous and reasonably easy to follow but cross short sections of boggy, rough or rocky ground.
Challenging Walk involves sections following faint trails or pathless terrain that can be particularly rough or boggy, plus potentially hazardous river crossings.
Hard Scrambling ability plus a good head for heights required.

NAVIGATION

Easy Minimal navigation required
Straightforward Navigation skills needed to cross open hillsides and tops of mountains
Challenging Particularly difficult navigation across plateaus or ridges, especially in mist.

DIFFICULTY

These overall gradings take into account the length of the walk, remoteness, and potential obstacles en route. Some walks designated **Straightforward** would be graded **Easy** if it were not for their length.

CLOTHING & OTHER ESSENTIALS

Even in summer you need to keep warm so mid-layers and a waterproof jacket are essential. Footwear should be comfortable, supportive and have good grip. Do not underestimate how much food and water you will need and remember to take any personal medication you require, including reserves in case of illness or delay. If walking as part of a group, make sure your companions are aware of any medical condition you may have, such as diabetes, and how to deal with it if problems occur.

WHEN TO GO

My most frequent visits to the Highlands are in the spring and early summer before the midge season, and then mid-September and October when the biting beasties have abated. Peak tourist season is July and August, when there is glorious colour and long days but the midges will be at their height, and tourist numbers swell. Although the stalking season officially runs from 1st July to mid-February, in practice peak stag-stalking takes place from mid-August to mid-October. Access to the hills is restricted during these times, but most bothies remain open and available for use. In winter, the days may be shorter but the atmosphere is very different with far fewer people, a slower pace of life and much less traffic the further north you go.

WEATHER

Scotland's weather can be very changeable and difficult to predict. Beyond the source observations of the Met Office, there are a number of useful websites and apps I refer to for forecasts with pretty accurate results. These include BBC Weather, XCWeather, and WillyWeather, which also provides information about tides and phases of the moon. For summit walks, essential summaries are provided by the Mountain Weather Information Service (MWIS), which produces forecasts for eight different mountain areas across the UK; five in Scotland. Even if you are armed with the most comprehensive forecast, you must be aware that the overhead conditions can change suddenly, reducing visibility on summits. The forecast temperature applies to sea level; on average this drops between 7–10 degrees centigrade for every 1000m climbed. As for realistic expectations, if you get two days of sunny weather out of seven you are winning.

BEASTIES WITH A BITE

Midges Consistently the bane of summer in Scotland, midges breed near water or marsh and swarm relentlessly on the unwary, particularly in the evenings and early mornings when the wind has dropped. They start to appear with unerring regularity from the beginning of June. The most effective protection I have found is Avon's Skin So Soft (available at some enlightened backpacking stores) though there are various other creams or sprays on the market containing differing amounts of DEET (diethyltoluamide), the most common active ingredient in insect repellents.

Ticks A particular problem in areas where there are high numbers of deer or sheep and when walking through bracken or long grass. Ticks are difficult to dislodge once embedded and are best removed with tweezers or a specialist tick remover (the Lifesystems one is effective), making sure you remove the head in the process. Wearing long trousers rather than shorts is a simple strategy that can narrow your chances of picking them up. Some ticks carry Lyme disease, a debilitating condition recognisable by a characteristic bullseye rash at the sight of the bite. Early symptoms include tiredness, fever, muscular pain and achy joints. However, removing infected ticks within 36 hours seriously reduces the risks of catching the disease.

Adders Britain's only venomous snake and a not uncommon sight, sunning themselves in open moorland, woodland edges and heaths. They are unlikely to bother you unless you bother them, and most people who are bitten were handling them at the time. Be aware of their presence in summer. I almost stepped on one once, which certainly wasn't a good move. A bite can cause dizziness, vomiting and a painful swelling.

KIT CHECK

For overnight bothy essentials you will need everything you would take camping plus candles and some fuel to burn such as coal or briquettes. There may be some wood and peat at remote bothies.

Waterproof jacket and overtrousers

Hat and gloves

Outdoor trousers

Fleece, t-shirts (syntheti'technical tees' wick away sweat and dry quickly, unlike cotton) and two mid-layers (thermals for winter)

Two or three pairs of specialist walking socks, one kept in the car

Sturdy boots that provide ankle support

Gaiters

Water bottle

Map, map case and compass

Head torch

Walking poles

SAFETY

Plan your route within the capability of the least experienced members of your party. Avoid the mindset which assumes that if something goes wrong, someone else will come to your aid – whether another party on the hill or a Mountain Rescue Team. Only call out the Mountain Rescue Service when you are in genuine need of assistance. If you are in any doubt about your own competence or, more crucially, that of the weakest or least experienced member of a group, make plans conservatively.

If you are new to walking, it is important to appreciate that many accidents or difficult situations arise late in the day or on the way down from a mountain. You are more likely to make navigation errors or take bad decisions near the very end of a route, owing to tiredness, hunger or rushing get to your destination. Use common sense in bad weather and do not push on to a summit. On days with a marginal weather forecast always be flexible in your plans: the hills will still be there another day.

IN AN EMERGENCY

If the unexpected happens and one of your party gets injured, the first instinct is, understandably, to start flapping and make rash decisions. Try to stay calm and assess the situation rationally. The basic first aid procedure follows a simple acronym ABC: checking airways, breathing and circulation. Make the casualty as comfortable as possible, and, if unconscious, put them in the recovery position. Try and work out your exact position and consider whether to seek help, which may involve one of the party walking out if you cannot get a mobile signal. Telephone 999 and ask for the Police and Mountain Rescue, and be ready to explain the situation in detail, starting with the grid reference.

RIVER CROSSINGS

Rivers in spate are one of the most important things to be aware of when out walking in Scotland, and it is wise to treat fast-flowing water higher than knee-deep with extreme caution. In periods of thaw or heavy rainfall, the level of rivers and even small streams can rise alarmingly quickly. When encountering a swollen burn, the most obvious solution is to walk upstream to where you can cross more safely. If you are in a quandary, it is better to contemplate turning back rather than putting yourself in danger. A worst-case scenario could be to successfully cross one swollen stream and then come up against another further on that you judge to be impassable, and on your return discover that the first is running higher than before! If you are intent on crossing a swollen stream, look for a stretch of water that is wide and shallow, with

COIRE ACHALADAIR (WALK 19)

perhaps only the final step into a fast-flowing channel. Be patient and assess the situation as calmly as you can – wading a fast-flowing river can be a more unnerving experience than you might expect. Plot your route carefully and resist any temptation to run. Where you are able, walk diagonally upstream across the channel, treading carefully and focus on the point where you are going to climb onto the far bank. Walking poles are very useful.

RIGHT TO ROAM

Scotland enjoys some of the most liberal access rights in the world, and the 'right to roam' is ingrained in the Scottish psyche. Although considered common law, the right was only reinforced in statute by the Land Reform (Scotland) Act of 2003. The key thing is to act responsibly and with due consideration of others, whether landowners or those enjoying their free time in the countryside. Be aware that landowners have a legal duty not to put up fences, walls or signs that prevent people from crossing their land, but you are advised to keep to paths and tracks where possible. This is especially important during the stag-stalking season (the most active time is early August to mid-October). When you are heading on to higher ground during this time, you are advised to use the 'Hillphones service' (details can be found on www.outdooraccess-scotland.scot). This enables walkers and climbers to find out where deer stalking is taking place, and to plan their trips accordingly. Information is also often posted at popular parking spots, and your co-operation is appreciated.

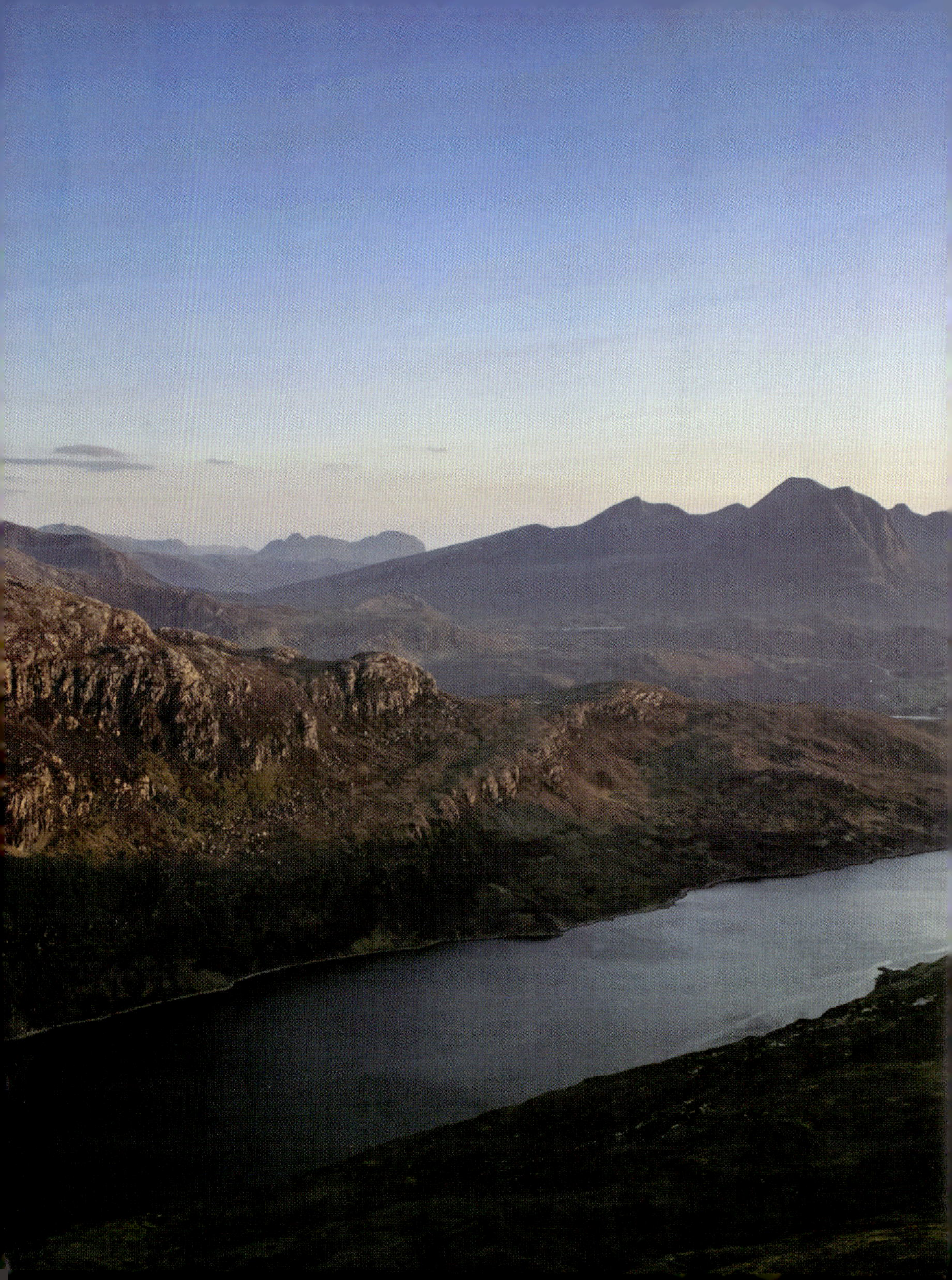

NORTHERN HIGHLANDS

WALKING IN TO SANDWOOD BAY

WALK 1

SANDWOOD BAY & THE BOTHIES AT STRATHCHAILLEACH & STRATHAN

Two-day expedition to Scotland's far north-western corner, combining sensational Sandwood Bay with visits to two of Scotland's most remote and picturesque bothies.

Exposed to the hypnotic rhythm of the North Atlantic swell, Sandwood is the jewel among the unspoiled bays of Scotland's precious coastal fringes. Yet this dynamic, sweeping stretch of platinum-blonde sand, high dunes, and rugged cliff, with a distinctive sea stack at its southern end, remains remarkably untouched. Footprints are the only marks left at the turn of each tide. Owned by the John Muir Trust since 1993, the mile and a half of strand has become better known of late, but is never crowded and retains its wild feel.

Inland lies the Parph, a remote, trackless expanse of peat and upland moor that is home to two special bothies, each with a fascinating story. Strathchailleach (Valley of the Old Woman), to the north-east, lays claim to be the last permanently inhabited building in the UK without any piped water, gas or electricity, and was occupied as recently as 1996. Strathan, to the south, had temporary residents in 2000 when a couple moved in with the intention of setting up a working croft, only to be evicted four months later. Those inspired to travel so far north and undertake this truly remarkable journey – unique in Britain – will always treasure the memory.

Day 1. It is a fair step to Sandwood and on to Strathchailleach, but if you are lucky with the weather, bothy walk-ins don't get much better than this. ❶ From the car park at Blairmore, a well-maintained track threads its way through common grazing land, past a series of fetching lochans all the way to the bay. As the trail contours round Druim na Buainn, the dunes come

INFORMATION

MAPS: LR 9 Cape Wrath, Explorer 446 Durness & Cape Wrath.
START/END GRID REF: NC 195 601. John Muir car park at Blairmore: toilets and drinking water on site. Donations welcome.
DISTANCE: 22.5km/14 miles
DAY 1: 10.5km/6.5 miles
TIME: 3.5–4.5 hours
DAY 2: 12km/7.5 miles
TIME: 4–5 hours
TOTAL ASCENT: 520m
HIGHEST POINT: 230m
NAVIGATION: Straightforward
TERRAIN: Challenging. Tracks, faint trails, open moor.
DIFFICULTY: Straightforward
PUBLIC TRANSPORT: Scottish Citylink service 961/Stagecoach Highland service 61 Inverness-Ullapool. Durness Bike Bus (01463 419160) and The Durness Bus (01971 511223) Group booking bus service. North West Community Bus Association's service 890 Ullapool to Kinlochbervie (01971 521054).
SPECIAL NOTES: Both bothies are open all year round. Sandwood Bay is a nature reserve owned and managed by the John Muir Trust. Keep dogs under control to avoid disturbing free-roaming sheep and ground-nesting birds.

WALK 1 SANDWOOD BAY & THE BOTHIES AT STRATHCHAILLEACH & STRATHAN

enticingly into view, while cliffs to the north of the bay snake away up to Cape Wrath. On a clear day you can just glimpse the lighthouse on the promontory, a bright white speck on the horizon. Before it was built in 1828, the coastline was notorious for shipwrecks and locals still tell of the ghostly mariner who roams the strand on stormy nights.

❷ From here, you are irresistibly drawn down to the wide expanse of sandy shoreline stretching away into the distance, the sound of the waves a constant presence. Walking out to the breakers, the monumental stack, Am Buachaille (the Herdsman), makes its presence felt, with the rocky outcrop, Am Balg, visible a little further out. Alongside the sand, a huge dune system has built up over millennia, evidence of the wind's immense power in this exposed location. Even on a sun-kissed afternoon there is always a hint of a breeze, while in winter, hurricane-force gales whip in from the Atlantic. Home to ground-nesting dunlins and ringed plovers, the sand is held in check by marram grass. Beyond, a carpet of rare machair leads back to freshwater Sandwood Loch.

Striding up to the north end of the beach, you reach the brackish outflow from the loch, a wide channel that is easily crossed in dry conditions but in times of spate is more of a challenge and best tackled close to the shore. Few visitors venture this far, and you may have the rest of the beach to yourself. ❸ Once up through the broken rocks to the clifftop, it is tempting to plough straight across the moor towards Lochan nan Sac, then onto the Strathchailleach, hidden between the peat hags. However, easier terrain is found on a vague path along the southern bank of the Strath Chailleach, which meanders round to the bothy, though it adds another half a mile to the walk. From late spring, pink lousewort and round leaf orchids can be found among tall cotton grass and prostrate juniper. And if you are keen, there is a chance to wild swim in one of the numerous pools.

Strathchailleach Bothy is a tiny stone cottage with a low facade, and most need to stoop before stepping over the threshold into the world of hermit James MacRory-Smith. Known locally as Sandy, he was a cantankerous old soul, who lived here without running water, gas or electricity for 32 years, before ill health forced him to leave in 1996. The interior's most distinctive feature is a series of simple frescoes he painted over the years, some with astrological themes. Although his home-made bellows have been removed and the kitchen area is now a two-person dormitory, as you sit in front of a slow-burning peat fire (from the ample supplies cut by the generous maintenance officer), Sandy's presence is almost palpable. The few he invited into his abode might, if the mood took him, be regaled with stories of his hermit's life. Increasingly used by hikers finishing the Cape Wrath Trail as well as visitors curious to see this living museum, the bothy now boasts additional bunk beds.

Day 2. Leaving for Strathan, there is a frisson of anticipation as you envisage the route ahead across the pathless moor. ❹ Head due south over the stile in the sheep fence, climbing steadily past Lochan Beul na Faireachan, and on to the shoulder of An Grianan. It is slow-going if the

STRATHCHAILLEACH BOTHY

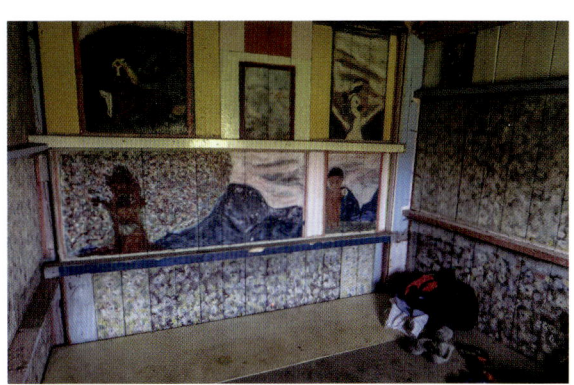

STRATHAN BOTHY

terrain is saturated, but it gets easier with altitude as the vegetation thins. ❺ From a high point, pick a line down to the valley below, crossing a number of small tributaries that funnel down to the river. It is exhilarating being in such open terrain, using your experience to measure the lie of the land, and steer a course as efficiently as possible down to the floodplain. The key point of orientation, especially in poor visibility, is the sharp meander where the V-shaped notch of the Allt a Ghleannain rushes down into the main channel. Once across this stream, a faint but increasingly obvious path leads on to the bothy at Strathan just over 500 yards further on, its bright red front door a most welcome sight. Similar in style to Strathchailleach, the bothy is set in good pastureland, the river and an old well are close by, and there is a peat bank with bricks built up to dry over the summer. No wonder this secluded spot attracted the attention of Robbie and Anne Northway, a travelling couple who quite brazenly moved in during the spring of 2000. They intended to set up a working croft, to the consternation of the MBA and local community. After four months of campaigning, and police intervention, the couple were evicted, leaving the cottage open to all once more.

After walking over from Strathchailleach through wild, trackless land, there is a reasonably clear path back to the single-track road from Kinlochbervie out to Blairmore. However, the terrain can be rather tough-going where the trail, surrounded by a swathe of waterlogged peatbog, picks its way along the shoreline of two small lochs. ❻ Once over the suspension footbridge, you follow the faint path zigzagging up the slope. At the top of the rise and looking out over the flat expanse of peatland to the coast, you can trace the inward route to Sandwood, a yellow smudge in the distance. Once past the two lochans, concentrate hard and keep the path in sight so you don't end up knee-deep in the bog! ❼ Fortunately, you can follow a line of wooden poles (quite widely spaced) heading west back to a farm track, and onto the road. The house at the roadside doesn't seem to get any closer for an inordinate amount of time, but then suddenly you are back in civilisation, elated to have achieved your goal. On the final mile back to the car park you can relax and relive the experience of a fantastic expedition. There is nothing quite like it in the whole of the UK.

Notes: The route described is split into two days. It is quite feasible to complete the circuit in one day, though this is only recommended in the summer months with long daylight hours. The terrain across the Parph can be quite unforgiving underfoot so allow additional time. The first section of the route follows the route of the Cape Wrath Trail.

DIRECTIONS

Day 1
Blairmore to Strathchailleach

1 From the John Muir Trust (JMT) car park at Blairmore head along the track signposted to Sandwood, through a gate blocking vehicular access, past a series of lochans to the bay, following the route of the Cape Wrath Trail.
6.5km/4 miles

2 Traverse the beach heading N, crossing the outflow from Sandwood Loch, which can be a hazard when in spate.
0.8km/0.5 miles

3 Ascend the broken rocks to the clifftop just beyond the outflow, then walk along the cliff to the riverbank of the Strath Chailleach at (NC 232 663). Negotiate the sheep fence and walk inland, following the meanders of the Strath Chailleach, then cut across the final section of moor to follow the faint path all the way to the bothy (NC 249 658). Alternatively from the clifftop head straight across the pathless moor ENE past Lochan nan Sac. Head on to a stile in the sheep fence (NC 244 657) and quickly reach the bothy. Although this route is half a mile shorter, it is tough-going especially if the ground is saturated.
3.2km/2 miles

Day 2
Strathchailleach to Blairemore

4 From Strathchailleach Bothy head due S, climbing over a stile on the sheep fence running parallel to the glen (NC 244 657). From the bothy door you can see the tall, wooden pole by the stile. Climb steadily up the pathless moor past Lochan Beul na Faireachan, and on to the W shoulder of An Grianan.
2km/1.25 miles

5 Pick out a route down into Strath Shinary, crossing a couple of small streams before reaching the E bank of the Abhainn an t-Srathain. Follow the river S to the sharp bend (NC 242 618), where the Allt a' Ghleannain flows into the main channel. Once across this stream, a faint but increasingly obvious path leads on to the bothy at Strathan, just over 500 yards further on (NC 247 612).
3.2km/2 miles

6 From the bothy walk down to a suspension footbridge over the Abhainn an t-Srathain, and once across turn L along the bank for 200 yds. Then pick up a path zigzagging up the slope onto the open moor. Skirt round the northern shore of two lochs following a boggy path. (Hard going in saturated conditions.)
3.2km/2 miles

7 At the S end of the second loch, Loch Mòr a' Chraisg (NC 224 603), look for a faint path that follows a line of wooden poles set at wide intervals and then on to the track marked with a cairn (NC 212 602).
1.3km/0.75 miles

8 Continuing along the track, reach the single-track road from Kinlochbervie, turn R and follow it back to the car park at Blairmore.
2.5km/1.5 miles

WALK 1 SANDWOOD BAY & THE BOTHIES AT STRATHCHAILLEACH & STRATHAN

GLENDHU BOTHY

WALK 2

BEINN LEÒID FROM KYLESTROME VISITING GLENDHU & GLENCOUL

A three-day voyage of discovery through back-country east of Inchnadamph and Unapool, with an ascent of the remote Corbett, Beinn Leòid, from a lochside bothy base.

I have a long-held fascination with the remote territory that lies beyond the closely linked bothies at Glendhu and Glencoul – a raw, ice-scoured hinterland of gnarly Lewisian gneiss, peat bog, and rugged moor, dotted with innumerable tiny lochans. I have heard said that within its lonely confines there is a remarkable gathering of red deer during the yearly rut, listened to enthusiastic anglers wax lyrical about the quality of the fishing (streams supposedly full to bursting with brown trout!) and also stumbled upon an intriguing tale of wild-cat footprints in the snow. Climbing Beinn Leòid (Macleod's Hill), gives you an opportunity to venture into this rarely visited corner of the Highlands. Excellent stalkers' paths transport you towards the peak, but the final approach crosses wild, trackless terrain. And, as soon as you step away from the recognised waypoints, you become immersed in a world of your own.

The rock configuration underlying the topography in this region is hugely significant, forensically detailed in geological textbooks the world over. Older rocks, in this case the ancient metamorphic gneiss, were shifted over the comparatively younger Cambrian quartzite, over 400 million years ago. Over millions of years, this colossal movement – the 'Moine Thrust' which occurred across the whole of north-west Scotland – gradually pushed rocks between 50 and 70 miles from their original home. The alignment caused controversy among geologists of the Victorian era, who subscribed to the theory that newer rocks were always laid on top of older ones.

INFORMATION

MAPS: LR15 Loch Assynt, Lochinver & Kylesku, Explorer 442 Assynt & Lochinver (recommended).
START/END GRID REF: NC 218 345. Car park at Kylestrome just off the A894, 1 mile from Kylesku Bridge. Not signposted.
DAY 1: 7km/4.5 miles
TIME: 2–2.5 hours
DAY 2: 22km/13.5 miles
TIME: 7–9 hours
DAY 3: 7km/4.5 miles
TIME: 2–2.5 hours
SUMMIT: Beinn Leòid (Corbett), 792m
TOTAL ASCENT: 1200m
NAVIGATION: Challenging.
TERRAIN: Challenging. Tracks, open hillside and steep boulder field.
DIFFICULTY: Challenging. Requires confident hillcraft.
PUBLIC TRANSPORT: Scottish Citylink service 961/Stagecoach Highland service 61 Inverness-Ullapool. Durness Bike Bus (01463 419160) and The Durness Bus (01971 511223) Group booking bus services. North West Community Bus Association's service 890 Ullapool to Kinlochbervie (01971 521054).
SPECIAL NOTES: Bothies open all year. Phone Reay Forest Estate (01971 500221) if visiting during the stalking season, August 12–October 20.

WALK 2 BEINN LEÒID FROM KYLESTROME VISITING GLENDHU & GLENCOUL

The discovery added weight to then controversial ideas that the earth's crust moved over time, causing earthquakes and volcanic eruptions. Contemporary theories of plate tectonics and continental drift have become accepted only in the last few decades.

❶ Walking down by the newly refurbished estate house from Kylestrome towards the shore of Loch Glendhu, it is hard to believe that this tranquil spot was once the public highway, shown on the old one-inch map as 'a narrow class A road with passing places'. Before the eye-catching Kylesku Bridge was completed in 1984, a small turntable ferry plied its trade across the strait, with the inevitable long queues of traffic on the journey up and back from Durness. As the tarmac curves down to the old slipway, turn left onto the old pony path that winds its way inland towards the Maldie Burn. A mile from the car park, a new unmetalled road joins from the left; it was built to provide access to a hydroelectric scheme damming the powerful stream below Loch an Leathaid Bhuain. ❷ Beyond the concrete bridge over the burn, the track returns to its original stony surface, in places negotiating a precarious course between the rock face and the lochside, before Glendhu Bothy finally comes into view. Close to the bothy it is easy to spot the slanting band of quartzite with a slightly red hue, which forms a sheer cliff that slopes down to the waterside. This continues round the headland into Loch Glencoul, sandwiched between the layers of gneiss.

There are three buildings at the head of the loch: an old stalkers' cottage, a small stone stables, and the well-appointed bothy, one of the best on the MBA roster. The last full-time tenants in the main house, the Elliots, moved here from Glencoul in the 1950s, where they had been resident since before the turn of the 20th century. During the summer months, a ghillie lived upstairs in the bothy, using one downstairs room as a living room, and the other for storing the deer carcasses shot by paying guests who travelled in by boat from Kylesku. The last of the family to live at Glendhu, John Elliot and his son Willie, finally moved out a few years later, though their descendants still keep a close connection to the area.

❸ It is wise to make an early start for the following day's ascent: tackling the open hillside can take far longer than you anticipate, even in dry conditions. The crags of Taobh Granda are an imposing presence as you make your way up Gleann Dubh (Black Glen), the sun barely catching the north-facing rocks for much of the year. As the valley sides knot together in a tight, interlocking spur, the stalkers' path zigzags steeply above the cascading river, before levelling out as it reaches Lochan Cadh' Allein. ❹ Cross

LOCH GLENDHU

GLENDHU BOTHY

BEINN LEÒID FROM BEINN A' BHÙTHA

GLEANN DUBH

the Abhainn a' Ghlinne Dhuibh via a solidly built vehicle bridge, and ascend steadily below the bluffs of Cnoc a' Mhadaidh, following the path as it contours up towards the exposed upland moor. Once across Allt Poll a' Mhadaidh, which can be an obstacle in times of spate, the track rises more steeply before coming to an abrupt halt at a rather incongruously placed wooden bridge, lost in the midst of its grand surroundings.

❺ Now steel yourself for a battle through the peat hags and bog, before reaching more solid ground on the slopes of Sàil na Slataich. With some relief, the pace quickens over the gently slanting slabs to the high point of 652m. Up ahead Beinn Leòid rises serenely, guarded by a steep boulder field. Clamber through the rocks and onto the summit plateau where a stunning 360-degree panorama opens up. Looking back north, the shattered quartzite slopes of Arkle and Foinaven dominate the scene, and to the east the silvery outline of Loch Shin slips away to the horizon. The complex coires of Quinag take centre stage to the west and Ben More Assynt and Conival rear up to the south, while the tops of Suilven and Canisp are just visible above the whaleback ridge of Beinn Uidhe. And as far as the eye can see, an abundance of lochans sparkle in the sunshine.

❻ Reluctantly retreating from the summit, descend to the Bealach Beinn Leòid, quickly crossing another unnamed top, before picking your way down to the outflow of Lochan Druim nam Eithreag. Hop across the channel, and a few hundred yards further south, look out for an All Terrain Vehicle track that isn't marked on the map and seems to materialise out of thin air. It takes a considered diagonal line down through the crags above Loch an Eircill, onto another well-maintained stalkers' path. ❼ After the intensity of crossing the open moorland, it is a relief to be able to relax and just follow the track down to Loch Glencoul and Glencoul Bothy, tucked away inland from the rocky shore. As you approach sea level again, the impressive crags of the Stack of Glencoul, unseen from a higher altitude, are revealed. Suppress any urge to scramble up to the precarious summit because there is still a long way to go to reach the sanctuary of Glendhu Bothy. After a steep final descent, the path crosses the Glencoul River via a vehicle bridge and reaches the lochside, where you are treated to another fabulous vista. Glencoul Bothy, a curious extension to the main house built by the Reay Forest Estate, lies above a ring of sculpted islands. From the door you look down the length of the deep fjord towards Unapool and the satellite peaks of Quinag. Here the Elliots raised their five sons, initially using the bothy as a schoolhouse. A memorial cross to the two eldest boys who perished in World War I stands on a knoll just above the house. It was financed by the estate owner, the Duke of Westminster.

❽ After a quick pit stop, a fabulous little section of the Cape Wrath Trail offers an unforgettable finale to the walk, contouring round the headland of Aird da Loch and down to the head of Loch Glendhu. Cross back over the Glencoul River, and take the path to the left, which rises steadily above the loch, past a newly fenced area of saplings. As you gain height, there is a superb view back to the bothy,

WALK 2 BEINN LEÒID FROM KYLESTROME VISITING GLENDHU & GLENCOUL

framed beneath the steep crags of the Stack of Glencoul with the Eas a' Chùal Aluinn waterfall, the highest in the UK, a slender ribbon of white in the distant background. Approaching the highest point of the traverse, the impressive coires of Sàil Gharb and Sàil Gorm rise majestically above Kylesku, while the sinuous curves of the loch draw your eye beyond the bridge to the islands of Eddrachillis Bay. Once round the promontory, with the bothy in sight on the far shore, follow the sloping bedding plane of quartzite down through a pocket of birch woodland and along the southern tideline of Loch Glendhu, through some huge boulders. A number of these were painstakingly moved so ponies could be led along the beach, rather than cross the difficult ground above the water. Continue on to a footbridge over the Abhainn a' Ghlinne Dhuibh, and back round to the bothy. ❾ Rest up after an epic day, before leaving the following morning.

Notes: Beinn Leòid is very much off the beaten track, and it is unlikely that anyone will come to your aid if you get into trouble. The sense of remoteness concentrates the mind in a wonderfully all-consuming way and reaching the top seems a fitting reward for the battle against the terrain. This is a mountain set apart from the headline peaks surrounding it, but it offers grandstand views of them all from the summit plateau. Part of the route follows a short section of the Cape Wrath Trail between Glencoul, Glendhu and the Maldie Burn.

SOUTHERN SHORE OF LOCH GLENDHU

GLENCOUL BOTHY

DIRECTIONS

Day 1 Walk to Glendhu

1 From the car park at Kylestrome (NC 218 345), head through a gate and down a metalled road past the estate house. After half a mile, as the road curves away to the R, turn L along a track signposted to Loch Glendhu that follows the shoreline to the Maldie Burn.
3.5km/2.25 miles

2 Cross a wide vehicle bridge and continue on the stony path down the lochside to the bothy at Glendhu (NC 283 338).
3.5km/2.25 miles

Day 2 Beinn Leòid, returning via Glencoul Bothy

3 Take the path that leads from the bothy past the old stalkers' cottage to the head of the loch. Continue on up into Gleann Dubh, ignoring a path on R down to a footbridge (this is the return route for this walk). After just over a mile, the track zigzags up steeply before levelling out by Lochan Cadh' Ailein. Continue to the vehicle bridge over the Abhainn a' Ghlinne Dhuibh (NC 310 329).
3.1km/2 miles

4 Ignore a path L, and cross the bridge, ascending beneath the crags of Cnoc a' Mhadaidh to a ford over the Allt Poll a' Mhadaidh. Continue up to a wooden bridge (NC 318 320) where the path peters out.
1.8km/1 mile

5 Stride out across the peat hags and bog, and up Sàil na Slataich to the high point (652m). Drop down a few hundred yards then climb the steep boulder field to Beinn Leòid's summit and trig pillar surrounded by a stone shelter (NC 320 295).
2.75km/1.75 miles

DIRECTIONS

6 Descend SW to Bealach Beinn Leòid, up West Top (729m) and down to Loch Druim nam Eithreag. Cross the stream and after 200 yards S pick up ATV track (NC 313 276). Follow down to Loch an Eircill to a good stalkers' path (NC 308 278).
2.5km/1.5 miles

7 Head down the track that follows the Glencoul River to Loch Glencoul. Just before the shore ignore a track R (the return route to Loch Glendhu) and cross the Glencoul River by a new footbridge. The bothy is close by (NC 271 304).
4.4km/2.75 miles

8 Retrace your steps back across the bridge then take path on L rising steadily towards Aird da Loch. Round the promontory and descend to Loch Glendhu shore. Pick your way through boulders above the tideline onto the footbridge over Abhainn a' Ghlinne Dhuibh, and back round to Glendhu Bothy (The Cape Wrath Trail).
7km/4.5 miles

Day 3 Back to Kylestrome

9 Retrace the walk-in route along the N shore of the loch back to the car park.
7km/4.5 miles

WALK 2 BEINN LEÒID FROM KYLESTROME VISITING GLENDHU & GLENCOUL

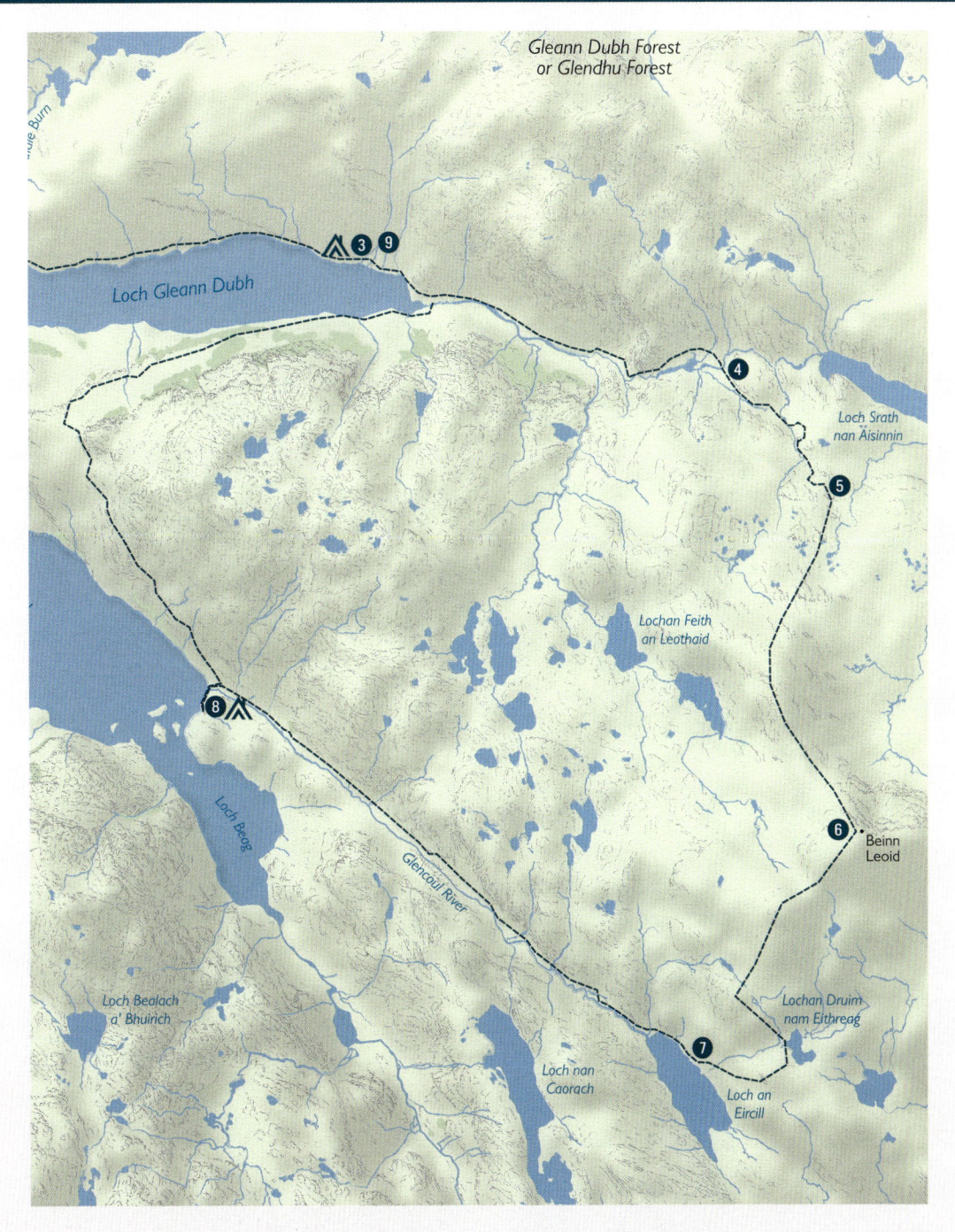

41

CAISTEAL LIATH

WALK 3

SUILVEN & SUILEAG BOTHY FROM GLENCANISP LODGE

One of the finest mountain walks in Scotland, with exceptional views from the summit dome over Assynt's other-worldly landscape of rugged peaks and ribbon lochs.

It is easy to be seduced by any of Assynt's distinctive sandstone peaks, but your gaze is irresistibly drawn to the striking monolith of Suilven (Sula Bheinn, Pillar Mountain). I always look forward to seeing the iconic sugarloaf profile on any journey north from Ullapool, tracing and retracing the lines of the summit ridge as it finally comes into view. The peak's magnetic hold has inspired much writing, poetry and song, most notably by celebrated Scottish bard Norman MacCaig whose poem 'Climbing Suilven' neatly encapsulates both the toil of ascent and thrill of summit views. Battle-scarred by successive waves of glaciation, the hills here are unique in Scotland, enshrined within Scotland's first Geopark, which was given UNESCO status in 2006. They lie above an ancient bed of Lewisian gneiss, formed over 3 billion years ago and comprising some of the oldest rocks in the world.

Although guarded by formidable, intimidating buttresses, scaling the dome of Suilven's western summit, Caisteal Liath, is far easier than it might appear. The ascent to Bealach Mòr, the low point of the mountain's saddle, avoids the major ramparts; although steep, it is relatively short and not exposed. There are a couple of challenges to negotiate on the final ridge, but nothing untoward. In contrast, Meall Meadhonach, the mountain's eastern turret, is a far more challenging proposition, requiring competent scrambling skills and best avoided unless you are a confident climber.

INFORMATION

MAPS: LR 15 Loch Assynt, Lochinver & Kylesku, Explorer 442 Assynt & Lochinver.
START/END GRID REF: NC108220 Car park 500m before Glencanisp Lodge on the road from Lochinver.
DISTANCE: 19km/12 miles
TIME: 6–8 hours. (3-5 hours from the bothy).
SUMMITS: Caisteal Liath (Corbett), 731m
TOTAL ASCENT: 836m
NAVIGATION: Easy
TERRAIN: Straightforward. Track and well-defined path. Short exposed section on summit ridge.
DIFFICULTY: Straightforward.
PUBLIC TRANSPORT: Scottish Citylink service 961/Stagecoach Highland service 61 Inverness-Ullapool. Ullapool to Lochinver: service 809 George Rapson Travel (01463 242649), service 815 Ewen's of Ullapool (01854 612966).
SPECIAL NOTES: The bothy is open all year round. Loch fishing by permit only. No dogs. For all enquiries contact the Assynt Foundation (01571 844122).

WALK 3 SUILVEN & SUILEAG BOTHY FROM GLENCANISP LODGE

Turning left out of the small fishing port and tourist hub of Lochinver, Suilven and its distant neighbour Canisp instantly announce themselves, and on a clear day they hold your attention for the entire walk in. Whatever the weather, this is an unforgettable expedition and well worth the long drive north. ❶ After just over 500 yards from the walkers' car park you pass through Glencanisp Lodge. This typical working estate is now owned by the Assynt Foundation, a community-based organisation set up in a landmark buyout of the vast 44,000-acre estate in 2005. There is one asset of particular interest: a tempting honesty shop where it is possible to stock up on extra chocolate bars, or justify an early tea or coffee. The premises are almost always unmanned, so simply add to the collection box and jot down your purchases in the notebook.

❷ Just beyond the woodshed at the far end of the estate, a signpost directs you towards the eastern shore of Loch Druim Suardalain, the far bank recently planted with saplings of birch, oak, hazel and rowan. In the summer black-throated divers and ring ouzels are often seen out on the water, while otters and pine martens are also regularly spotted. Heading left through a gate in a high deer fence the rugged, breathtaking landscape opens up. Countless outcrops of ancient Lewisian gneiss stretch into the distance, and the first of a myriad trout-filled lochans beckon you on your way. After two miles of gentle undulation on this old stalkers' path, you reach a junction marked with a small cairn and a stone boundary wall. Turn left here for Suileag Bothy, which quickly appears in view. A perfect place for a pit stop, the bothy is a long, single-storey stone building with a locked outhouse at one end. Compared to many of the bothies in the far north, the interior is pretty basic, split into two rooms by a plywood partition, but it offers welcome sanctuary and a useful base camp.

❸ Retracing your steps back to the junction, continue south-east on the track leading down and staying close to the meandering Abhainn na Clach Airigh. Soon the profile of Suilven looms closer and once across a solid footbridge you begin to get a real sense of the scale of the proposition ahead. After 750 yards a new path leads off right into the blanket peatbog. ❹ This approach route, once renowned as a laborious plod, was relaid in 2017 by the John Muir Trust and funded by a public campaign promoted by Chris Bonington. After a steady gain in altitude you pass between two small lochans, Loch na Barrack and Loch a' Choire Dhuibh, to the foot of the final climb. ❺ At first it is difficult to pick out the new zigzag route up between the rock bands, a stark contrast to the original path which left an ugly scar.

❻ A palpable sense of anticipation builds as you toil up between the boulders of Suilven's northern flank to Bealach Mòr, and the view revealed when you reach level ground does not disappoint. The sweeping profiles of Cùl Mòr, Stac Pollaidh and Ben More Coigach stretch off to the south, beyond the mesmerising curves of Fionn Loch and Loch Sionascaig, while to the north, there are tantalising glimpses of Foinaven and Ben Hope beyond Quinag's complex ridge line. The final lines of Norman MacCaig's

SUILVEN

SUILEAG BOTHY

VIEW SOUTH FROM BEALACH MÒR TO CUL MOR & STAC POLLAIDH

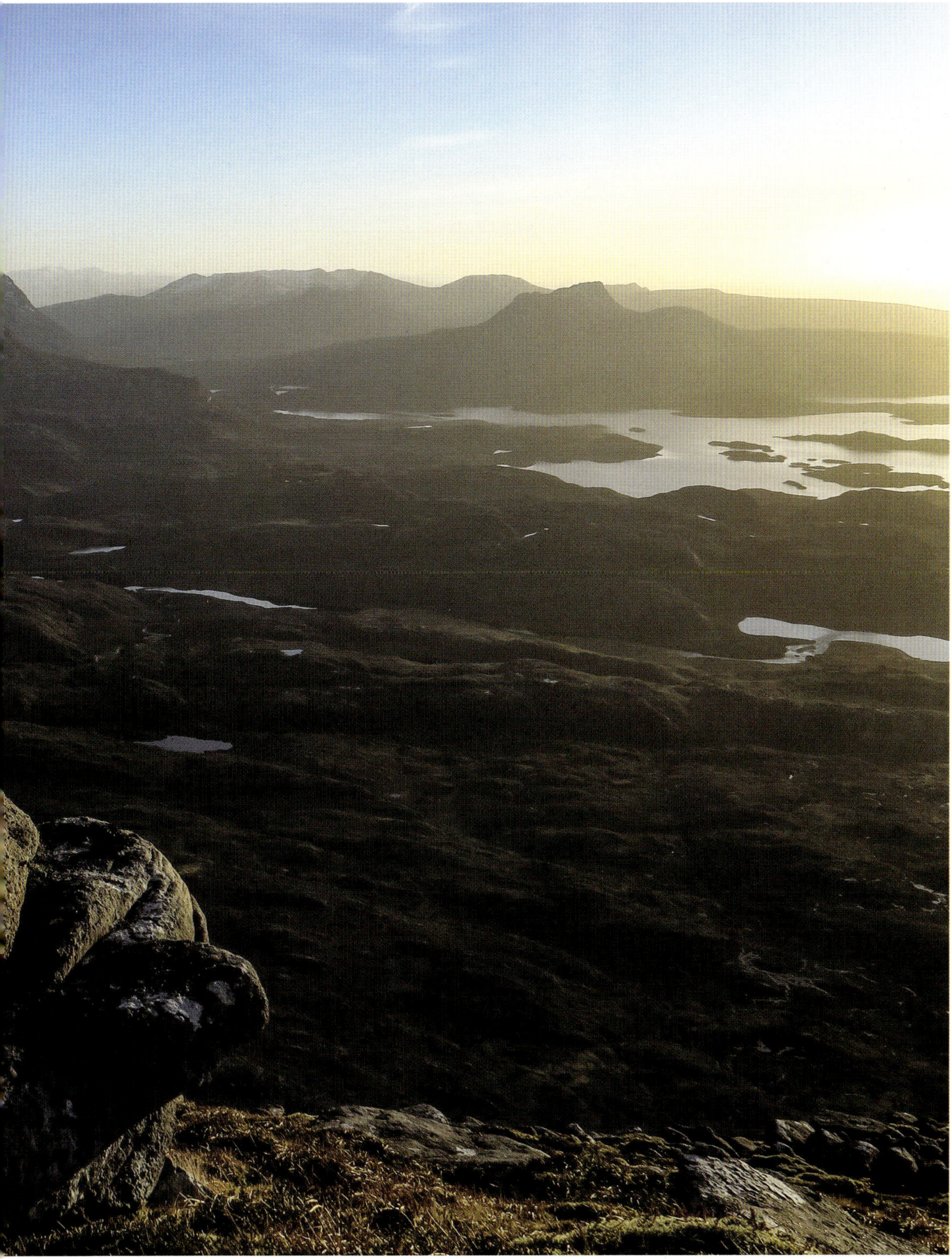

WALK 3 SUILVEN & SUILEAG BOTHY FROM GLENCANISP LODGE

SUMMIT SUILVEN

poetic account of the ascent encapsulate the experience: 'I claw that tall horizon down to this, And suddenly my shadow jumps huge miles away from me'. Turning west, an impressive and rather incongruous drystone dyke stretches down each side of the saddle, reminiscent of a piece of land art by Andy Goldsworthy. The path leads through a gap in the stonework, and up onto the summit dome, the vista of protected wilderness expanding with every stride. There are a couple of rock steps to be negotiated, but nothing too off-putting. At 731m, Suilven's highest point is lowly, relative to those of Scotland's legion of Munros, but the mountain punches well above its weight.

Notes: Although there is another fine route up to the summit from Inverkirkaig the approach to Suilven from Lochinver is the simplest and most direct, and requires very little navigation.

DIRECTIONS

❶ From the walkers' car park (NC107 220) continue along the tarmac road through the estate buildings of Glencanisp, turning R at the signpost to Loch Druim Suardalain.
1km/0.6 miles

❷ Branch L just before the shore (NC 118 220), taking the clear, well-maintained stalkers' path through a high, metalled gate, and out onto the open moor. This track traverses across the Glencanisp Forest, eventually finishing at Elphin and Ledmore Junction. After two miles you reach a junction marked with a cairn (NC 148 209). A quick detour L takes you to Suileag Bothy (NC 149 211).
3.6km/2.25 miles

WALK 3 SUILVEN & SUILEAG BOTHY FROM GLENCANISP LODGE

3 Retracing your steps, head E and continue for another mile, crossing the Abhainn na Clach Airigh by a footbridge just beyond Lochan Buidhe. 750 yards further on leave the main track (NC 167 196), and strike S towards the foot of Suilven, along the meandering, recently relaid footpath (not marked on either the 1:50,000 or 1:25,000 maps of the area).
2.4km/1.5 miles

4 Climb steadily across the moor, skirting two small lochans, before reaching the bottom of the steep slope up to Bealach Mòr.
1.5km/1 mile

5 Scale Suilven's N flank via a very steep zigzag path to Bealach Mòr (NC 158 181).
0.4km/0.25 miles

6 Turn R (W), through a gap in a drystone dyke, and up to the summit cairn of Caisteal Liath 731m (NC 153 184), scrambling carefully across a couple of exposed points.
0.5km/0.3 miles

7 Retrace your steps back to Glencanisp.

NOTES: Although there is a recognised descent down the scree slope of Suilven, returning to Inverkirkaig via Fionn Loch, it is far easier to return back down to Glencanisp the way you came. The E summit of Suilven, Meall Meadhonach is an exposed scramble from Bealach Mòr, and should not be attempted unless you have a good head for heights.

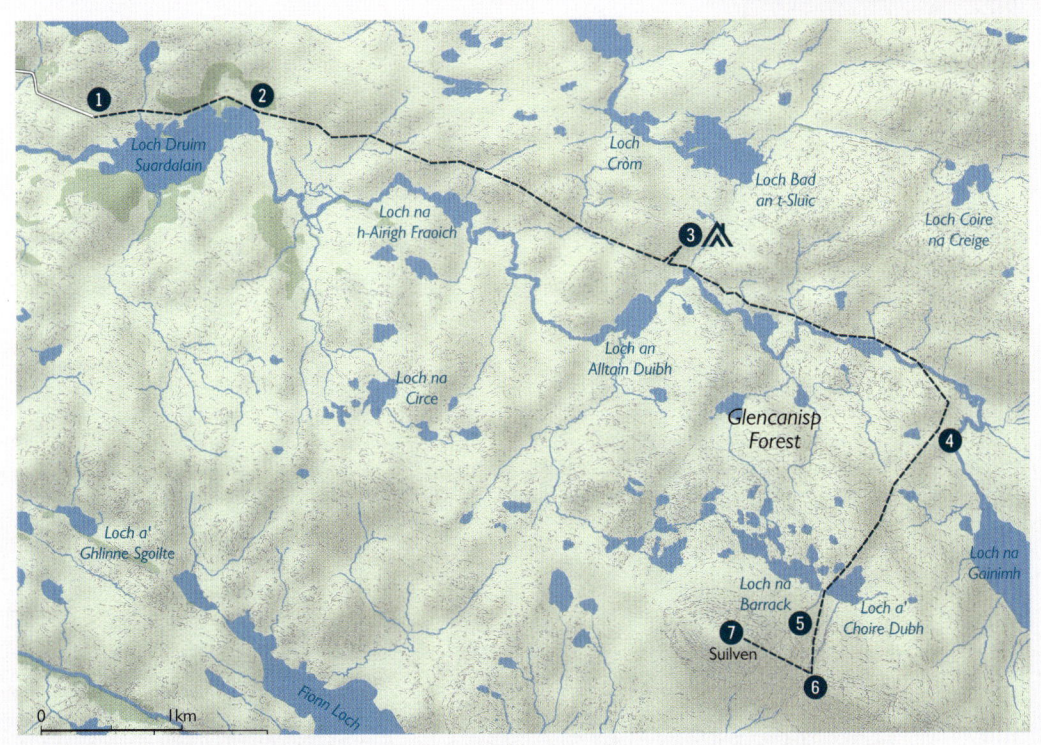

VIEW ACROSS STRATH NA SEALGA TO BEINN DEARG MÒR

WALK 4

BEINN DEARG MÒR & SHENAVALL BOTHY

An unforgettable expedition into the heart of the Great Wilderness, one of Scotland's most remote and majestic mountain regions, to claim a prized ascent of Beinn Dearg Mòr.

The iconic view of Beinn Dearg Mòr (Big Red Hill) rising up behind Shenavall is among the most familiar in the bothy world, although it is surprising how few people actually scale its airy heights. The deep, sculpted bowl of Coire nan Clach, and the towering Torridonian sandstone buttresses beneath the summit prow are incredibly beguiling, and whenever you arrive at the bothy there always seems to be someone outside looking up transfixed. The esteemed post-war guidebook writer and photographer W.A. Poucher is said to have described it as 'the perfect mountain'. However, because Beinn Dearg Mòr is classified as a Corbett rather than a Munro, it remains of subsidiary importance to most of the bagging fraternity who trek in from Dundonnell. As with Streap (described in Walk 10), given a few more metres in altitude there would be a far more defined route across its lofty ridge line.

For over a century the formidable mountain scenery of the Letterewe and Fisherfield Forests, which boast some of the most remote and impressive Munros in the country, has held a magnetic attraction for hill-walkers and stravaigers. Within this vast, uninhabited area of Wester Ross, stretching north from Loch Maree to Little Loch Broom, there are a number of superb walks, including the famous Fisherfield Six, an exacting test of stamina and determination. Another is the ascent of An Teallach, a stately mountain of the highest quality, which features some exhilarating scrambling over the pinnacles between Corrag Bhuidhe and Sgùrr Fiona. Climbing Beinn Dearg Mòr is equally dramatic and worth

INFORMATION

MAPS: LR Map 19 Gairloch, Explorer 435 An Teallach & Slioch (recommended).
START/END GRID REF: NH 114 851. Layby at Corrie Hallie on A832 'Desolation Road', 2 miles SE of Dundonnell. Limited parking.
DISTANCE: 25km/15.5 miles
TIME: 8–10 hours. 4–5 hours from bothy.
TOTAL ASCENT: 1530m
SUMMIT: Beinn Dearg Mòr (Corbett), 906m.
NAVIGATION: Straightforward
TERRAIN: Challenging. Tracks, defined path, open hillside. Climbs steep boulder-filled gully. Two serious river crossings, impassable in spate.
DIFFICULTY: Challenging. Very remote location, confident hillcraft skills required.
PUBLIC TRANSPORT: ScotRail Service from Glasgow/Edinburgh–Perth–Inverness or Citylink coach service M90/M91 Glasgow/Edinburgh–Perth–Inverness. Westerbus service 700 from Inverness to Gairloch or Laide stops at Dundonnell (01445 712255).
SPECIAL NOTES: Use of the bothy courtesy of the Gruinard Estate. Unavailable during stag-stalking, 15 September–20 October. Be prepared to camp Easter and summer months.

WALK 4 BEINN DEARG MÒR & SHENAVALL BOTHY

savouring in its own right. An ascent is certainly challenging, comprising a lengthy walk in, as well as two potentially serious river crossings, and a couple of steep, exposed sections to negotiate; but it is a truly memorable experience.

No trip to the Fisherfield Forest would be complete without paying a visit to Shenavall. A wealth of material has been written about the cottage, from accounts of the people who lived there to entries in journals and bothy books. In *Undiscovered Scotland*, renowned author and mountaineer W.H. Murray describes the bothy's early use after the last tenants left in 1941. Records of his visits are contained in a series of bothy books from the 1950s, part of an archive donated by the Scottish Mountaineering Club (SMC) to the National Library of Scotland (NLS). While browsing the collection I found a far earlier entry in an SMC journal of 1908, describing an expedition to climb An Teallach and Beinn Dearg Mòr by William Norman Ling 1873–1953 (in whose memory the Ling Hut in Torridon was named). In an age when mountaineering was the preserve of the middle and upper-middle classes, Ling hired a motor car and chauffeur to travel up to Dundonnell from the railway station at Garve. He and his compatriots then spent three days in the wilderness, staying at the cottage at Larachantivore across the Strath na Sealga from Shenavall. He mentions passing the bothy (then a working croft) on the walk out.

❶ So many adventures have begun from the lay-by at Corrie Hallie, located part way along the scenic drive to Gairloch from Braemore Junction. The verge-side Scottish Rights of Way signpost lists three daunting routes traversing this sparse wilderness – ancient byways to the far perimeter points of Kinlochewe, Poolewe and Gruinard. It is not just the summits but also the sheer beauty of the landscape that attracts visitors to this fabulous area of the Highlands. The track climbs steadily through the birch woodland of Gleann Chaorachain, before levelling out at a ford. A footbridge is close by if the water level is high. After crossing the stream, a short, steep ascent brings you to a prominent cairn overlooking Loch Coire Chaorachain, indicating the highest point on the route at 380m. ❷ A little further on, two smaller cairns mark a path branching right, which contours round the lower flanks of Sàil Liath, before descending to the bothy. Once past a low, sloping sandstone crag, you see the conical summit of Beinn a' Chlaidheimh, a lonely sentinel guarding the entry to the remote mountains beyond. Soon after, Beinn Dearg Mòr appears in all its regal grandeur, the anticipation of the climb leading you irresistibly on towards Strath na Sealga.

DESCENT TOWARDS SHENAVALL

GLEANN CHAORACHAIN

SHENAVALL BOTHY & BEINN DEARG MÒR

On arrival at Shenavall, it is worth taking a little time to assess the challenge ahead. If you are staying overnight, this can be a more leisurely process that is best left to the morning as conditions can change dramatically in a few short hours. The most direct route up Beinn Dearg Mòr climbs the obvious curving runnel that narrows to a short gully below the mountain's eastern top, and on to the summit slopes. However, a far easier option is to traverse round into the hanging coire above Gleann Na Muice Beag, which avoids all the possible scrambling obstacles. It is also vital to evaluate the strength of the current in the two rivers that drain into Loch na Sealga. These must be negotiated before any trip into the interior of Fisherfield and if they are in heavy spate, do not attempt to cross them.

❸ Leaving the bothy, take the obvious path that leads down to the banks of the Abhainn Strath na Sealga, to a point where the flow slackens to form a partial island within the meandering channel. In dry conditions, this is a relatively straightforward fording point. From the far bank, you then head directly across the peatbog towards the locked cottage at Larachantivore. Be prepared to double-back to avoid the deepest drainage channels. A wire bridge that spanned the Abhainn Gleann na Muice just below the estate building has long since washed away, and there is no obvious place to cross. The last time I ventured this way, I splashed through the river 300 yards to the north of the cottage.

Now for the ascent. Pick a line up the open slope just beyond Larachantivore, aiming for the start of the shallow grass and boulder-filled depression curving up towards the summit crest. The going is punishingly steep but the slope eases as you approach the runnel. The view back down to the graceful meanders of Strath na Sealga and across to the distinctive serrated pinnacles of An Teallach is well earned. The last couple of hundred feet before you reach the ridge are exposed, but no real scrambling ability is required.

From the dizzying heights of the eastern top of Beinn Dearg Mòr, you have the first opportunity to look down at the jaw-dropping buttresses that seem to free fall into the Coire nan Clach (Corrie of the Stones). The final ascent above the crags of Coir' an Talaimh-tholl to the summit prow is an absolute joy, finishing at a spectacular vantage point jutting out in mid-air. Out beyond the void, Loch na Sealga tapers towards Gruinard Bay and The Minch, while to the south, the route of the Fisherfield Six can be traced round from Ruadh Stac Mòr and the plateau of A' Mhaighdean, to Beinn Tarsuinn and Mullach Coire Mhic Fhearchair. This is very remote territory indeed.

WALK 4 BEINN DEARG MÒR & SHENAVALL BOTHY

❺ A faint path threads its way along the north ridge of Beinn Dearg Mòr from the summit cairn, before dropping precariously down the steep boulder field into Coire nan Clach. However, a more pragmatic option to reach the safety of Strath na Sealga is to descend to the bealach towards Beinn Dearg Beag, then follow a grassy rake down to the beautiful, heart-shaped Loch Toll an Lochain. This route is still steep, but the gradient eventually relents. An ascent of Beinn Dearg Beag is certainly worth contemplating, especially if you are staying at Shenavall, but the five-mile walk out to Corrie Hall weighs heavily if you are just out for the day. Carefully pick your way through the bluffs below the loch, to the right of the waterfalls of Allt na-Doiure Gaineamhaich, and down to the shore of Loch na Sealga. ❻ Here a stalkers' path contours above the lochside and back to the strath. Continue past the end of the loch for 500 yards, then, as the track bends away back towards Larachantivore, head directly to the riverbank. If the water level is low, you can pick your way across a wide section of the channel with a stony bed, just below the confluence of the two rivers. Feel yourself blessed if you keep your feet dry, then make a beeline for the bothy across the tussocky grass. ❼ Take a short break to refuel and one last lingering look back, then savour the experience on the long journey back to Corrie Hallie.

Notes: The route described can be undertaken in one long day walk from Corrie Hallie, or over two days if you base yourself at Shenavall. The most direct route to the top of Beinn Dearg Mòr is exposed in the upper section and requires a good head for heights. To either side there are scrambling routes East Ridge Grade 3 and Southeast Ridge Grade 1. For a less demanding ascent, contour round into Gleann Na Muice Beag and climb into the hanging coire before proceeding directly to the summit. Combining the walk with an additional ascent of Beinn Dearg Bheag adds another mile and 200m of climbing. Best tackled if you are staying at the bothy.

Beinn Dearg Mòr from Shenavall: 10.5km/6.5 miles, 876m ascent, 4.5 hours–5.5 hours (summer conditions).

NORTH RIDGE OF BEINN DEARG MÒR

BEINN DEARG BEAG & LOCH TOLL AN LOCHAIN

DIRECTIONS

① From the lay-by at Corrie Hallie, take the track signposted to Kinlochewe, Poolewe and Gruinard that climbs up Gleann Chorachain to a ford (NH 107 830). Cross the stream here or at the footbridge before ascending more steeply to the cairn overlooking Loch Coire Chorachain. If you have trouble crossing, it is unlikely that the two rivers in Strath na Sealga will be passable after reaching Shenavall, curtailing any ascent of Beinn Dearg Mòr. A little further on, two smaller cairns mark a path branching R, which contours round the lower flanks of Sàil Liath (NH 100 823).
3.2km/2 miles

② Initially the path is well maintained but starts to deteriorate on approaching the springs of the Allt a' Chlaiginn. Follow the stream down to the bothy at Shenavall (NH 066 810).
4km/2.5 miles

③ Take the obvious path from Shenavall down to the Abhainn Strath na Sealga, crossing at the meander bend (NH 061 808). From the far bank, make for the cottage at Larachantivore (NH 053 802), avoiding the deepest drainage channels. There is no obvious place to cross Abhainn Gleann na Muice; one recommended spot is 300 yards N of the cottage. In times of spate, these two rivers may be impassable.
1.6km/1 mile

④ Just beyond Larachantivore, strike directly up open hillside to an obvious shallow depression. Climb this to the summit crest, exposed for the last 200ft as it narrows to a gully. Progress to E top of Beinn Dearg Mòr, and on round to the summit prow where there is a large cairn.
2.4km/1.5 miles

⑤ Descend steeply to the bealach between Beinn Dearg Mòr and Beinn Dearg Bheag. Just beyond the lowest point, follow a grassy rake down to Loch Toll an Lochain. Skirt round to the W of the loch, before picking a way through the bluffs R of the Allt na Doire Gaineamhaich, then

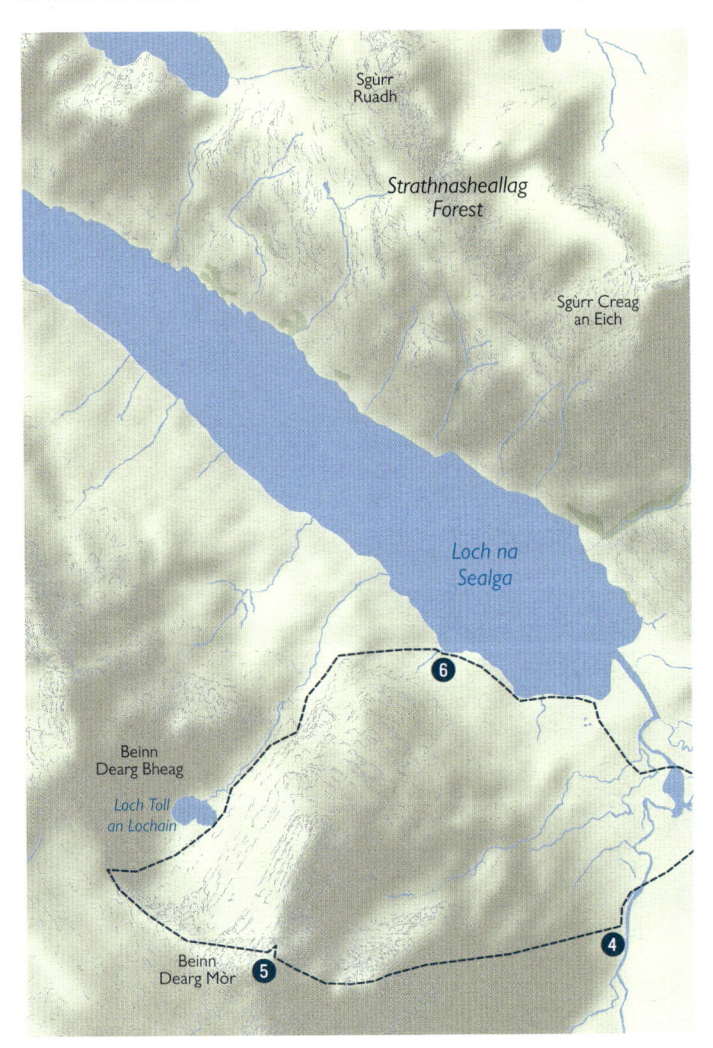

WALK 4 BEINN DEARG MÒR & SHENAVALL BOTHY

head down and round to Loch na Sealga shore (NH 042 817). **4km/2.5 miles**

6 Take the track that contours above the loch sideback to Strath na Sealga. Continue past the loch for 500 yards, and as the track curves R towards Larachantivore, walk directly to the riverbank.

If water level is low, cross a wide section of the channel just below the confluence of Abhainn Strath na Sealga and Abhainn Gleann na Muice. (If you cannot cross safely reverse the route described in section 3.) Once across, head straight to Shenavall over rough ground. **2.7km/1.7 miles**

7 Retrace your steps from the bothy to Corrie Hallie, **7.25km/4.5 miles**

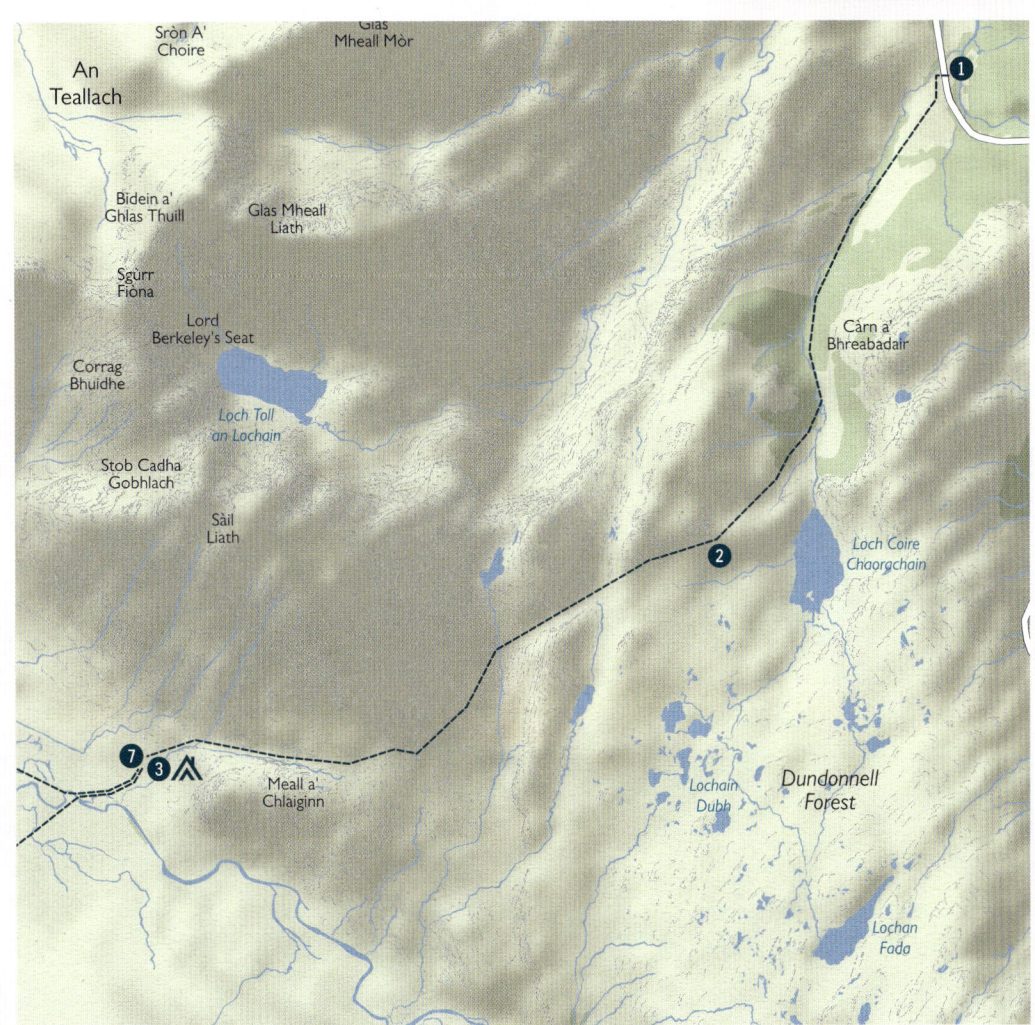

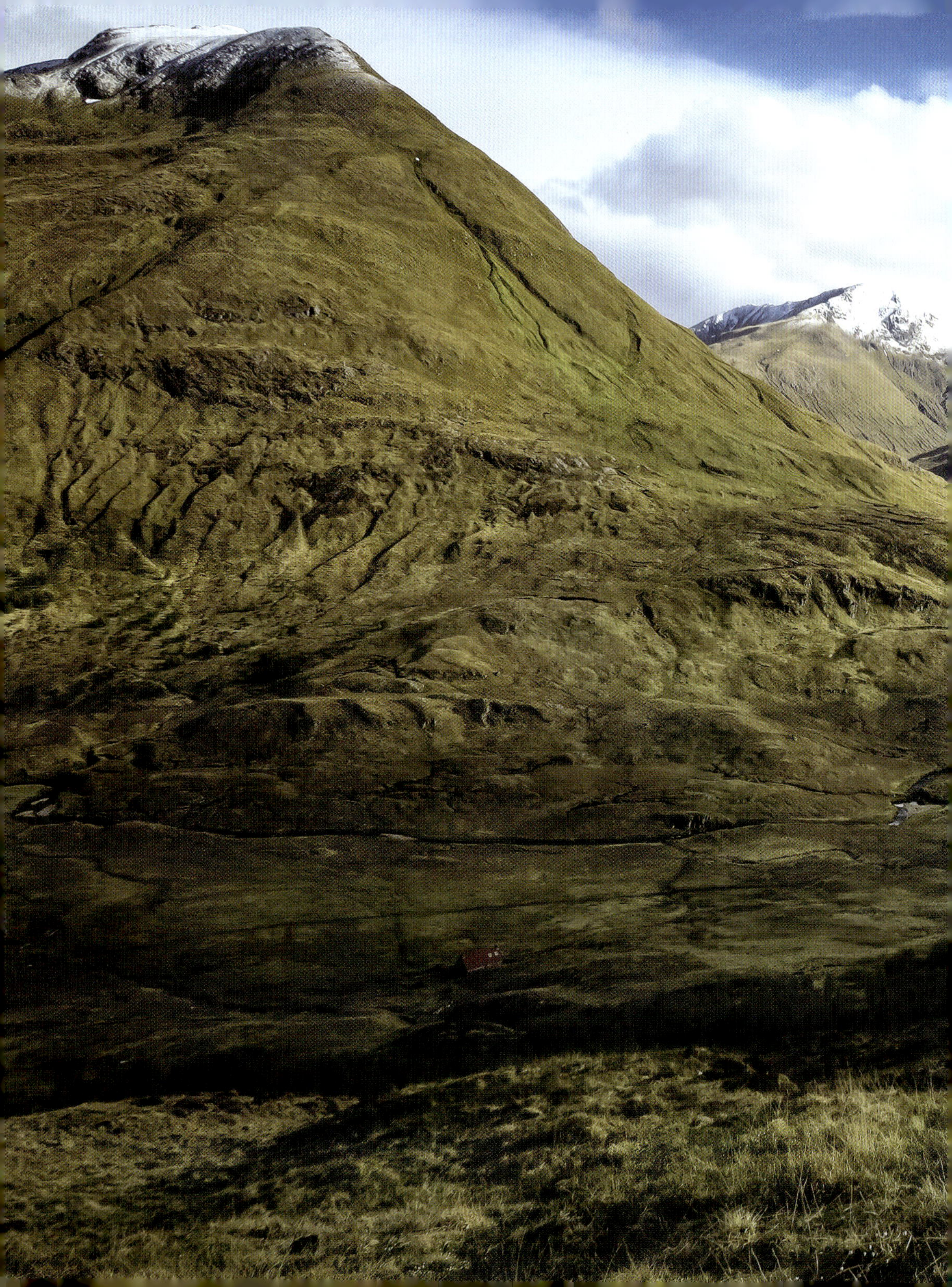

NORTH WEST HIGHLANDS

WALK IN TO CRAIG BOTHY

WALK 5

MESOLITHIC CAVE & SHELL MIDDEN BEYOND CRAIG BOTHY IN TORRIDON

A gentle day walk above the northern coast of Loch Torridon, with views over to the Applecross Peninsula and Skye.

One of the particular pleasures of roaming across even seemingly familiar places in the Highlands is the unexpected discovery of tumbledown ruins, or man-made indentations in the land. Often these are the remnants of an old shieling, croft, or the telltale ridges and furrows of runrig cultivation. But just occasionally someone stumbles upon a rare treasure, such as the remarkable Mesolithic cave beyond Craig Bothy, hidden above the remote coast west of the monumental peaks of Torridon. Located below a rocky outcrop, the cave was a place of shelter, and the small, grassy mound before the entrance is a shell midden where the remains of shellfish and other meals were discarded. In this wild and rather spooky place, you can almost feel the presence of our prehistoric ancestors, returning home after combing the beach.

The journey from Torridon village to the road end at Lower Diabaig is not for the faint-hearted. There are crazy switchbacks and first-gear slopes to negotiate, but the compensation is the spectacular scenery. Craning your neck after the first zigzag, you look up at the airy scramble along the horns of Beinn Alligin, and, from a viewpoint at the Bealach na Gaoithe (Pass of the Winds), a fantastic panorama of Maol Chean-dearg and the peaks of the Coulin Forest unfolds above the loch. Just before the final alarming hairpin down to the pier at Lower Diabaig, there is a sharp turn right onto a short, single-track road. Park with some relief, in a small lay-by close to the last house.

❶ A forlorn, collapsed signpost, its rusting way-pointer lost in a thicket of ferns, marks the start of the path to Craig

INFORMATION

MAPS: LR Map 24 Raasay & Applecross, Explorer 433 Torridon, Beinn Eighe & Liathach.
START/END GRID REF: NG 798 606. Turn sharp R at the final junction above the pier at Lower Diabaig, onto a single-track road, and park close the road end. Small car park down by the pier adds just over half a mile to the walk in (NG 797 599).
DISTANCE: 12km/7.5 miles
TIME: 4–5 hours' round trip (1.5 –2 hours' excursion from the bothy).
TOTAL ASCENT: 154m
HIGHEST POINT: 140m
NAVIGATION: Easy
TERRAIN: Easy. Well defined path all the way to the bothy, boggy trail to the cave.
DIFFICULTY: Easy
PUBLIC TRANSPORT: ScotRail service from Inverness to Kyle of Lochalsh stops at Strathcarron. DMK Motors minibus meets the train Monday to Saturday – Strathcarron to Shieldaig and Torridon village (01520 722682). No public transport on to Lower Diabaig.
SPECIAL NOTES: Bothy is open all year round, no restrictions.

WALK 5 MESOLITHIC CAVE & SHELL MIDDEN BEYOND CRAIG BOTHY IN TORRIDON

and Redpoint. Fortunately the trail itself is in very good condition, restored by the Footpath Trust. Pass through a wooden gate, and head left, contouring above the coast, through the low sandstone bluffs and slabs that are such a distinctive feature of the region. A superb seascape over Loch Torridon slowly reveals itself as you gradually gain height, the thin outline of Applecross merging seamlessly into the island of Rona and the Trotternish Peninsula on Skye. After crossing a couple of small streams you reach a large cairn on a flat shelf of rock, which marks the approximate halfway point to the bothy. From here the path slowly trends to the north, crossing one more burn by a set of stepping stones.

❷ The next stretch on to Lochan Dubh is quite boggy and indistinct; in misty conditions or poor light it is easy to lose your way for a few moments. Just beyond the lochan the trail reaches a high point above the Craig River, and you can just pick out the bothy, a little away from the eastern bank and close to a small stand of Scots pines. Carefully pick your way through a jumble of rocks before the path levels out and you reach the comfort of this rather stately cottage. The bothy is a former youth hostel and once the most remote in the country. Finally closed by the SYHA in 2003, it was resurrected as an open shelter four years later, through the initiative of the Mountain Bothies Association. Even now it is still recognisable as a hostel in all but name.

❸ After a brief stop continue on, the path descending to a wooden bridge over the fast-flowing Craig River. On the far bank pick your way through the roots of a stretch of silver birch, clinging stubbornly to the rocks above the channel, before the terrain opens up. A wild, remote stretch of coastal moorland dominates the view, continuing on to the white sands of Redpoint, just visible in the far distance. The trail noticeably deteriorates at this point, and it is heavy-going in comparison with the path from Diabaig. Persevere. At the crossing of a second stream, Coire na h-Uamha, strike uphill to a low line of sandstone cliffs, blanketed in coarse heather. There is no path, so you have to keep faith, but after five minutes you finally see the cave, formed by three enormous boulders; the grassy mound before its mouth is an intense green.

❹ If you have time before heading back to Diabaig, it is worth wandering down to the rocky beach below the bothy. Craig was once a small crofting township, and the ruins of old homesteads are visible between the birches that line the final stretch down to the coast. When the decline of herring fishing in the early 1900s made life even harsher, the last families left. If you are lucky you may see dolphins and porpoises out in the bay and, in the summer months, even a basking shark.

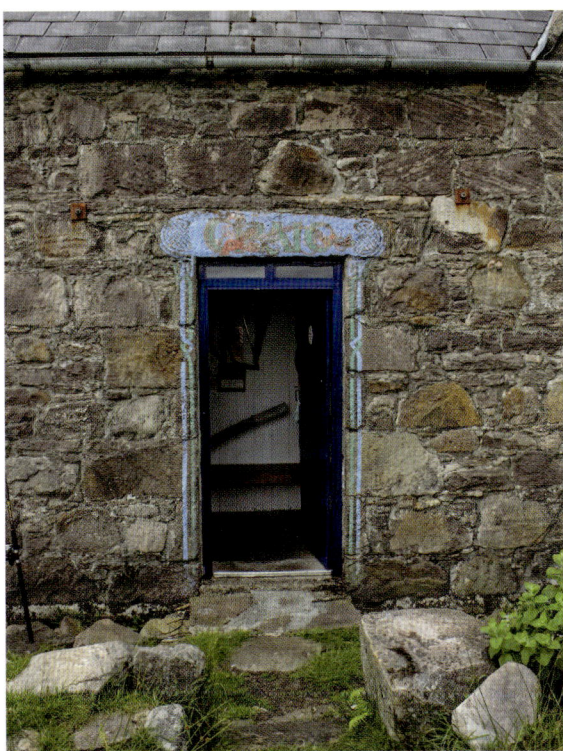

CRAIG BOTHY

WALK 5 MESOLITHIC CAVE & SHELL MIDDEN BEYOND CRAIG BOTHY IN TORRIDON

MESOLITHIC CAVE & SHELL MIDDEN

DIRECTIONS

1 From the road end pass through a wooden gate (NG 789 606), and follow a well-constructed trail heading uphill above Loch Torridon. Cross a couple of small streams by sets of stepping stones, before reaching a large cairn approximately halfway to Craig Bothy (NG 778 616).
1.75km/1 mile

2 Trend N to Lochan Dubh, fording another stream via stepping stones. Just beyond the lochan the path curves L and cuts down through crags before levelling out towards the bothy, set close to the Craig River (NG 775 639).
2.25km/1.5 miles

3 Continue N from the bothy, crossing the Craig River by a wooden bridge, then follow the N bank of the river to just above the rocky shore of Loch Torridon. Continue on for 500 yds, passing one stream, and heading inland at the second, the Coire na h-Uamha. The cave (NG 767 649) takes a little finding, but is no more the five minutes from the coastal path.
2km/1.25 miles

4 Retrace your steps back to Lower Diabaig.

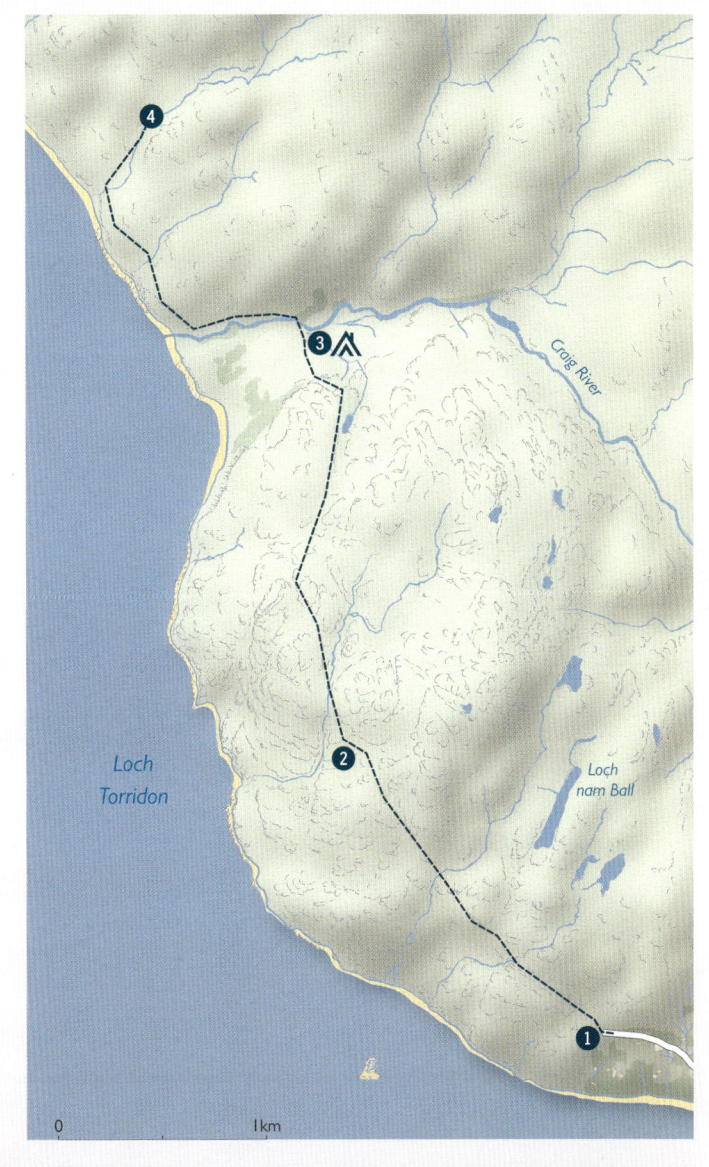

LOCH AN EOIN & MAOL CHEAN-DEARG

WALK 6

COIRE FIONNARAICH BOTHY & A CIRCUIT OF MAOL CHEAN-DEARG

Circular walk through the depths of the Coulin Deer forest, linking a series of enchanting lochans on the lower slopes of an impressive Munro.

Between Glen Carron and the Torridon Hills lies a complex glaciated region of red sandstone peaks and shattered quartzite, its coires protected by steep, sculptured walls and dotted with tranquil lochs. A number of fine stalkers' paths cut through this imposing landscape, one improbably encircling the great, bare dome of Maol Chean-dearg (literally 'bald, head-red' in Gaelic). The peak is a classic Munro tick, but the circumnavigation of its lower slopes offers privileged access to a secluded area of the North West Highlands.

❶ The route starts at the scattering of houses at Coulags, five miles north-east of the pretty west-coast village of Lochcarron. Heading up the farm track look out for a small cairn and a waymarker which directs you down a steep path, left of the boundary fence and cattle grid of a farm cottage. Pick your way through a handful of silver birch trees, along the terrace above the wide channel of the Fionn-abhainn, and quickly join the hydro access road that sweeps in from the right. ❷ A couple of hundred yards further on, just before a vehicle bridge, a helpful public footpath sign guides you onto a recently improved section of the original stalkers' path, which winds its way up into the glen. After a mile of gentle climbing the new dam comes into view, immediately followed by a slender footbridge. Cross to the far bank and continue on, past a memorial plaque set in a stone slab, and up to Coire Fionnaraich Bothy. This atmospheric old stalkers' cottage has retained much of its original wooden interior, and is a very comfortable place to spend the night. The first tenant was employed here as stalker and watcher in 1913.

INFORMATION

MAPS: LR 25 Glen Carron & Glen Affric, Explorer 429 Glen Carron & West Monar.
START GRID REF: NG957 451 Lay-by on N side of A890, just W of bridge at Coulags, 5 miles NE of Lochcarron.
DISTANCE: 19km/12 miles
TIME: 6–7 hours. 4–5 hours from the bothy.
TOTAL ASCENT: 713m
HIGHEST POINT: 587m
NAVIGATION: Straightforward. Basic map-reading skills required in misty conditions.
TERRAIN: Easy. Track and well defined paths. One simple river crossing. Ascent to high mountain pass.
DIFFICULTY: Straightforward.
PUBLIC TRANSPORT: ScotRail service from Inverness to Kyle of Lochalsh stops at Strathcarron. No bus on to Coulags. Lochcarron Garage bus service 704 Inverness to Applecross (01520 722997) Wednesday and Saturday only (book in advance).
SPECIAL NOTES: Bothy is closed during the stalking season from 20th September to 20th October.

WALK 6 COIRE FIONNARAICH BOTHY & A CIRCUIT OF MAOL CHEAN-DEARG

His duties included the upkeep of the paths through to the head of the valley – all for the princely sum of 30 shillings per annum.

❸ Walking on from the bothy, the impressive mountains take centre stage, Fuar Tholl, and the striking ridge line of Sgorr Ruadh to the east, and the steep buttresses of Maol Chean dearg up ahead. Once past the curiously shaped Clach nan Con-fionn (a phallic-looking boulder said to have been used by the mythical warrior-giant Fionn to tether his hunting dogs), ignore the rocky path leading left up to the Bealach a' Choire Gharbh, (used as the descent route for this particular outing), and head on up the valley. After another half a mile you suddenly come upon Loch Coire Fionnaraich nestled behind a rocky lip. In this beautiful, restful spot you might glimpse dippers darting between the rocks and hear the familiar calls of meadow pipits and stonechats floating up from the heather. The trail skirts round the western shore of the loch and then begins the steep climb up to Bealach na Lice. The reward for your exertion is a fabulous view back down the glen and across to the remote peaks of Attadale.

❹ Just before the saddle, keep trending left, ignoring a stalkers' path that leads off across to Bealach Bàn, and quickly reach the pass. Here beneath the steep rock bands of Coire Liath, you catch the first glimpse of the islands of Loch an Eoin and the impressive summit pyramid of Beinn Damh beyond. After an easy descent to the loch side, continue round to the junction of paths at Cadh' an Sgadain. Turn left, leaving the main track as it snakes away north down to Glen Torridon, and press on to an impressive set of stepping

CLACH NAN CON-FIONN

COIRE FIONNARAICH BOTHY

SGORR RUADH & LOCH COIRE FIONNARAICH

WALK 6 COIRE FIONNARAICH BOTHY & A CIRCUIT OF MAOL CHEAN-DEARG

stones, which cross the burn linking Lochan Domhain to Loch an Eoin. Be aware that this could pose a serious challenge in times of spate. ❺ Hop across the boulders and start to contour round the western flanks of Maol Chean-dearg, to reach a remote corner of heather moorland where you may see a red deer but not another living soul. Revel in the intoxicating solitude, if only for a brief moment.

After a solid mile of walking, the path starts to arc round to the stunning Loch Coire an Ruadh-staic, set beneath the brooding sandstone buttresses of An Ruadh-stac and the thrust of quartzite that forms Maol Chean-dearg's southerly limb. On the exhilarating final climb up to the Bealach a' Choire Ghairbh you could almost be negotiating a pass in the Pyrenees. To the right, a towering cliff line sharpens to a point at the teardrop-shaped Loch a' Mhadaidh Ruadh (Loch of the Red Fox). At the loch, take the faint trail which heads left bearing north-east. It is easy to miss but don't be tempted to continue on the more distinct path up to Bealach an Ruadh-stac at 603m, which soon peters out. Keep to the contour and cross to the Bealach a' Choire Ghairb, slightly lower at 587m. ❻ From the saddle pick up the obvious stone chute path from the summit of Maol Chean-dearg down into glen, following the course of the Allt Mnatha Luadhadair. Descend slowly through the boulders, and within half an hour you are back on the stalkers' path that leads back to the bothy. Pause for a moment and drink in the glorious surroundings, before gathering yourself for the last couple of miles back to Coulags.

The first memorial plaque on a stone slab a few hundred yards south of the bothy commemorates a Breton walker, Michael Conon, whose final wish was to have his ashes scattered here. On the mantelpiece of the bothy's communal room is a framed letter penned in French Gothic font by his son Alan. Sadly, Alan died two years later and according to a moving inscription on the stone's second plaque, he has been 'reunited with his father in these peaceful hills forever'.

Notes: The walk requires some navigational skills especially in poor weather, and takes you through two passes, the Bealach na Lice 420m, and the Bealach 'Choire Ghairbh 587m. The first section from Coulags up to the Bealach na Lice follows the route of the Cape Wrath Trail, which continues north-east through the Bealach Bàn.

BEALACH NA LICE

AN RUADH-STAC

DIRECTIONS

❶ From the lay-by on N side of A890, just W of bridge at Coulags (NG 957 451), head up the farm track signposted to Glen Torridon. After 200 yards take a path L of a cattle grid, round the farm and turn L again, onto a wide access road which connects a new hydro scheme to the main road (this is currently not marked on the 1:50,000 map).
0.4km/0.25 miles

❷ Shortly take a path on R that heads up into the glen. After just over a mile of gentle climbing, pass the new dam, then a little further on cross the Fionn-abhainn via a footbridge (NG 951 472). Continue another half a mile to reach Coire Fionnaraich Bothy (NG 950 480).
2.8km/1.75 miles

❸ Stick to the obvious path winding into the upper reaches of the glen, ignoring a path L leading up to the Bealach a' Coire Gharbh and Maol Chean-dearg marked by a cairn (NG 948 490). (This is the descent route for this walk.) Continue past Loch Coire Fionnaraich up towards Bealach na Lice to a point where the path splits (NG 936 508).
3.3km/2 miles

❹ Take the L fork up to Bealach na Lice (420m) and down towards Loch an Eoin. Continue round the northern shore of Loch an Eoin, ignoring a turn R down to Torridon, to reach stepping stones that cross the outflow from Loch an Eoin to Lochan Domhain (NG 920 512).
2.2km/1.4 miles

❺ Once over the stream, contour round the western flank of Maol Chean-dearg and up to Loch Coire an Ruadh-Staic. Climb steeply up to a point close to Bealach an Ruadh-stac, 603m, then head L on a faint trail over to Bealach a' Choire Ghairbh 587m (NG 931 488). (If you reach the Bealach an Ruadh-stac you've gone too far S. Concentration is required here especially in misty conditions.)
4.2km/2.6 miles

❻ Here join the main path which heads from the summit of Maol Chean-dearg down into the glen. A final turn R leads back to the bothy and Coulags.
6.6km/4 miles

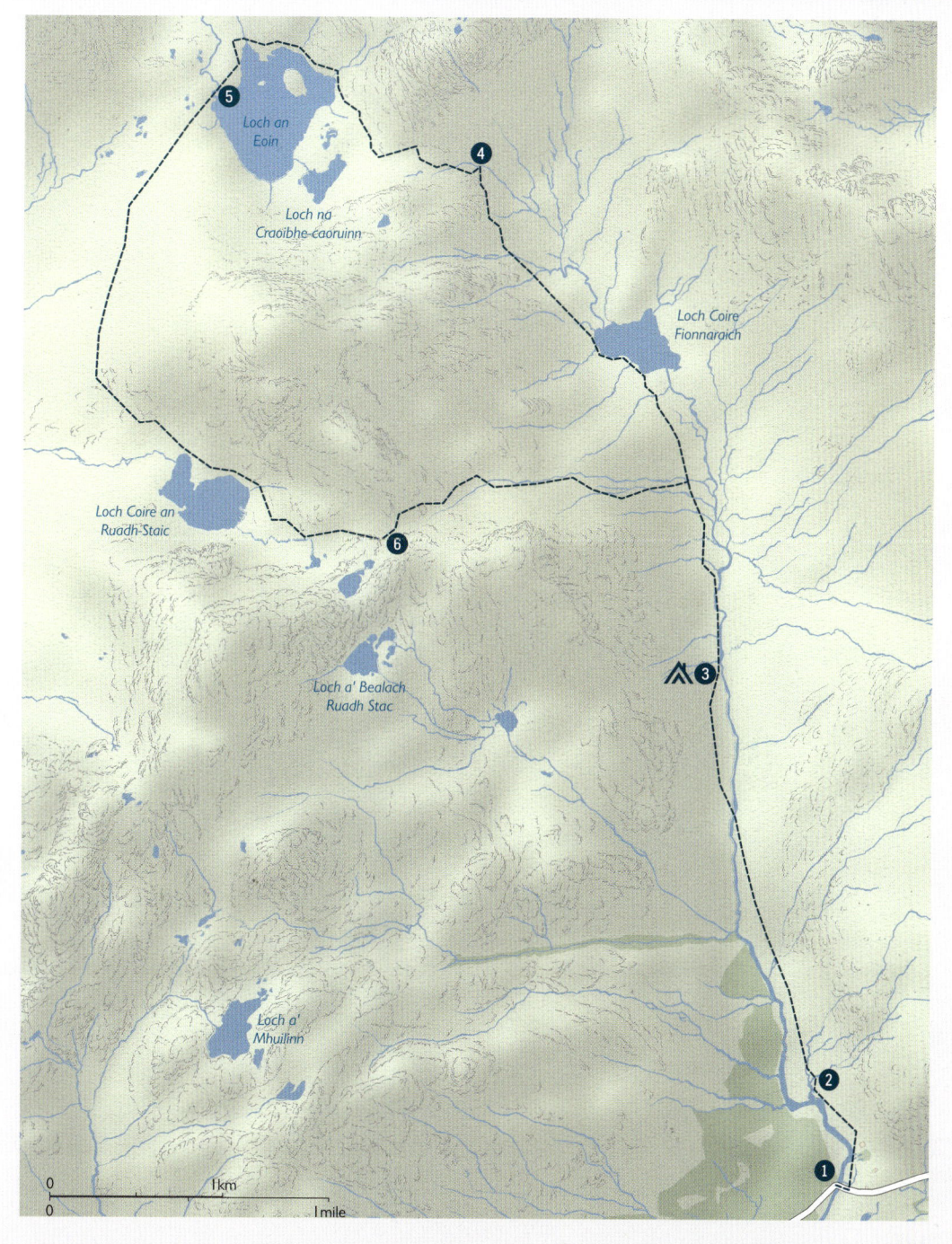

WALK 6 COIRE FIONNARAICH BOTHY & A CIRCUIT OF MAOL CHEAN-DEARG

LOOKING OUT TO DUN CAAN, RAASAY & LOCH TOSCAIG

WALK 7

UAGS BOTHY & THE APPLECROSS PENINSULA

A splendid walk across the remote southern coastal fringe of the Applecross Peninsula to Uags bothy, with fabulous views over to the Skye Cuillin and Raasay.

Blessed with the Gaelic name A' Chomraich, 'The Sanctuary', by St. Maelrubha, an Irish missionary in the 7th century AD, the Applecross Peninsula has a long-held reputation as a tranquil and isolated backwater. The last lonely outpost between Wester Ross and the Isle of Skye, its landward perimeter protected by a series of towering sandstone buttresses. Until the 1970s, the sole vehicular access through this natural barrier was via the hair-raising switchbacks of the Bealach Na Bà, one of the highest passes in the UK and often blocked by snow in the winter months. Crofting communities scattered along the coast were still only accessible by footpath or by boat well into the 20th century, and had a far closer connection to the sea than to the interior beyond the mountains.

Applecross has a rich recorded history and was settled by some of the very first Mesolithic hunter-gatherers in Scotland over 9000 years ago. The peninsula was also one of the earliest centres of Christianity on mainland Britain. The Mackenzie clan laid claim to the land in the mid-1600s, and it remained under their control until the mid-19th century. The family built an impressive tower house close to Applecross village, and the estate, which covers the majority of the peninsula, employed a significant number of local people. In 1975, when the new coast road from Shieldaig was completed, the Applecross Trust took over the management of the estate, with the emphasis on preserving the natural and cultural heritage of the peninsula.

INFORMATION

MAPS: LR 24 Raasay & Applecross, Explorer 428 Kyle of Lochalsh, Plockton & Applecross.
START/END GRID REF: NG 710 378. Please park at Toscaig Pier and not Upper Toscaig. The path begins just before the bridge over the River Toscaig (NG 714 386).
DISTANCE: 11km/7 miles (round trip).
TIME: 4–5 hours, including time spent at the bothy.
TOTAL ASCENT: 169m
HIGHEST POINT: 90m
NAVIGATION: Easy
TERRAIN: Easy. Well defined path all the way to the bothy.
DIFFICULTY: Easy
PUBLIC TRANSPORT: ScotRail train service from Inverness to Kyle of Lochalsh, stops at Strathcarron. Lochcarron Garage bus service 704 Inverness to Applecross village (01520 722997) Wednesday and Saturday only (book in advance). No bus on to Toscaig.
SPECIAL NOTES: The bothy is open all year round and owned by the Applecross Estate (01478 613489) or email admin@applecross.org.uk.

With more convenient year-round access, Applecross soon began to receive an increasing number of visitors. Its recent inclusion in the much-heralded North Coast 500, a circular tourist route akin to America's Route 66 and designed to boost the local economy, has attracted visitors from around the globe.

There is no escaping the magnetic draw of the Bealach Na Bà as you reach the shores of Loch Kishorn and stare up at Sgùrr a' Chaorachain and Meall Gorm, the steep cliffs that guard the entry into Applecross. Rising to 626m above sea level in little more than three miles, the single-track road is relentlessly steep, with gradients of over 20 per cent and tight hairpin bends that would not be out of place on a high Alpine pass. Once the saddle is reached, the full majesty of the peninsula reveals itself: the wild moorland is an enchanting patchwork of tiny lochans, and there are stunning views over the sea to Skye and the Inner Hebrides. Reaching the village, known locally as The Street, head south past the popular Applecross Inn, and down the coast, to the old pier at Toscaig, now the recommended parking point for the walk into Uags Bothy. ❶ Go back along the road to the junction for Upper Toscaig, and walk past a line of cottages to the turning area at the end of the tarmac where there is a signpost to Airigh-drishaig, an old stalkers' cottage on the southern coast, and to Uags.

This sleepy corner of the peninsula has an authentic air and you feel fortunate to be able to wander along a wild, unspoilt stretch of coastline with few fellow travellers. ❷ Once across a wooden footbridge, head past a ramshackle barn to a second signpost, barely 200 yards from the start of the track. The right fork leads to Airigh-drishaig, the left to Uags, following a muddy path through a farm gate and out onto the open moor. Although indistinct, the trail is far more obvious than it used to be. Wander through the rocky terrain left of a small lochan and down to an obvious circular area of pasture, the site of an old summer shieling. On a clear day the views across to the Skye Cuillin and back to the distinctive flat top of Dun Caan on Raasay are mesmerising, and even when the cloud obscures the horizon the craggy outline of the Crowlin Islands is enough to soothe the eye. ❸ Just before the shieling, ford the Allt Loch Meall nam Feadan, a potential obstacle after heavy rain, and look out for a small cairn marking the way ahead on the far side of the flat, grassy field. The path becomes much clearer as it continues on, leading up a small rise and then over the heather back down towards the shore.

OLD SUMMER SHIELING

UAGS BOTHY

WALK 7 UAGS BOTHY & THE APPLECROSS PENINSULA

UAGS BOTHY

The final approach to the bothy passes through some captivating pockets of woodland, containing rare Atlantic oak found only in isolated spots along the western seaboard of Scotland, Ireland, France and Spain. Soon Uags comes into sight, perched on a rocky promontory above the tideline of Caolas Mòr. A sturdy, old stone cottage, the two-storey shelter is one of a handful of dwellings in a small settlement that developed in a clearing above a small, sheltered bay. The community was finally abandoned in the 1930s. The Gaelic name na-h-Uamha means 'The Little Caves', and exploration along the shore reveals a number of gaps in the rocks, more readily visible from the sea. Occasionally porpoises are seen out in the bay, and the odd fishing boat heading to or from Kyle of Lochalsh. This really is a magical spot and well worth the effort of the walk in. Retrace your steps back to Toscaig at your leisure, and raise a glass in the Applecross Inn on your return.

DIRECTIONS

VIEW OVER TO SKYE

❶ From the pier (NG 710 378), walk back up to the junction for Upper Toscaig. Turn R, and follow the road to the last cottage, continuing on a path signposted to Uags and Airigh-drishaig.
1.5km/1 mile

❷ Immediately cross and the footbridge over the River Toscaig, and after less than 500 yards turn R where the path forks, signposted to Uags. Head up onto the open moor on an increasingly well-trodden path towards an old shieling (NG 718 368), passing a nameless lochan to the E.
2km/1.25 miles

❸ Just before the shieling ford the Allt Loch Meall nam Feadan, which could be an obstacle in times of spate. Walk past the shieling and up to a small cairn on the far side of the open grassland, where a more established path leads back out onto the moor. Continue on undulating ground down to the coast, passing through a small wooded area before the bothy comes into view (NG 723 351).
2km/1.25 miles

❹ Return to Toscaig following the same route.

81

VIEW NORTH-WEST DOWN GLEN LICHD

WALK 8

BEINN FHADA & CAMBAN BOTHY

Outstanding walk with fabulous views over to the ridges of Glen Shiel from the high plateau of Beinn Fhada, visiting the bothy at Camban and returning along the final section of the Affric Kintail Way.

Beinn Fhada holds a patient, parental gaze over the precocious peaks of the Five Sisters of Kintail, and the neighbouring 'brothers' of the North Glen Shiel Ridge, which skip light-footedly away to the east of Loch Duich. Seen from the depths of Glen Lichd, this imposing plateau appears plodding and ponderous compared to the spritely, eye-catching ridge line. However, its simple Gaelic description, 'long hill', belies a far more complex mountain with its own varied repertoire of differing moods. Above the tidal salt marsh of Strath Croe, the high ramparts of Sgùrr a' Choire Ghairbh rise athletically towards the sky, while to the north, an impressive sequence of sculpted coires guards the high plateau. And beyond the uniformly steep, overbearing slopes of Beinn Fhada's southern flanks, the eastern spur glides gracefully into the headwaters of Glen Affric.

Ever since I first ventured to Kintail as a student, I have kept this small pocket of the Western Highlands close to my heart. As a fledging member of the Edinburgh University Mountaineering Club, I went on my first Hogmanay meet to the club hut at Glenlicht House, and on a brooding New Year's morn wandered up to the MBA bothy at Camban. On discovering there was a whole network of mountain refuges spread across the most wild and inaccessible areas of the country, my interest was piqued and a lifelong fascination with these simple shelters was born.

INFORMATION

MAPS: LR 33 Loch Alsh, Glen Shiel & Loch Hourn, Explorer 414 Glen Shiel & Kintail Forest.
START/END GRID REF: NG 960 210. Parking area by the Mountain Rescue Post and NTS office at Morvich.
DISTANCE: 25.75km/16 miles
TIME: 8-10 hours
TOTAL ASCENT: 1234m
SUMMITS: Beinn Fhada (Munro), 1032m; Sgùrr a' Dubh Doire (Munro Top), 962m.
NAVIGATION: Challenging over the plateau to the summit in misty conditions.
TERRAIN: Straightforward. Track, well defined paths, faint trail, open hillside.
DIFFICULTY: Challenging.
PUBLIC TRANSPORT: Scottish Citylink bus from Glasgow and Fort William to Skye, stops at Shiel Bridge Service 915, 916.
SPECIAL NOTES: Bothy is open all year round, no restrictions. Do not cut live wood from the nearby fenced area of saplings.

WALK 8 BEINN FHADA & CAMBAN BOTHY

❶ Setting off from the makeshift car park by the NTS Ranger Station and Kintail Mountain Rescue Post at Morvich, make your way along the single-track road past the campsite, and out into the open glen. There is a fine view of the crags below Sgùrr a' Choire Ghairbh but the summit of Beinn Fhada (Anglicised to Ben Attow) remains obscured by the crest of Meall an Fhuarain Mhòir. Just before reaching the outdoor centre, a Scottish Rights of Way signpost describes three paths: south-east to Glen Affric by Gleann Lichd (the return route for this walk); north-east to Glen Elchaig by the Falls of Glomach; and the initial section of this walk, Glen Affric by Bealach an Sgàirne. A little further on, turn left over a vehicle bridge spanning the River Croe, and after another 100 yards, take a path right signposted to the Falls of Glomach and all other walking routes.

❷ Wander along the banks of the Abhainn Chonaig, through a fenced enclosure built by the NTS to encourage natural regrowth of native trees. Saplings of birch, beech and juniper are already firmly re-established, as well as flourishing ground cover of heather and bilberry. Emerging into an open field, the path splits, the left fork heading on to the Falls of Glomach. Instead, take the right turn following an old stalkers' path round into Gleann Chòinneachain. On the steep, north-facing hillside the young woodland makes a stark contrast with the mature conifer plantation on the other side of the valley, slowly being felled for timber. Continue up towards the Bealach an Sgàirne (known as the Gates of Affric), past a number of tempting rock pools, tantalisingly out of reach down a vertiginous slope.

Within another half a mile, you catch a first glimpse of the rock-shattered coires below the summit plateau, partially hidden by a steep ridge of acutely angled Moine schist. ❸ The path crosses a ford over the Allt a' Choire Chaoil (which could be an obstacle in times of spate), and then zigzags up to junction marked by a small cairn. Turn right, onto another fine stalkers' path (marked only on the 1:250,00-scale map), which plots a well-considered line up to the eastern end of Coire an Sgàirne. This climb is a delight, reminiscent of hiking to a high Alpine pass, and so much easier than the two ambitious ascents of the tortuous southern side of Beinn Fhada I made from Glenlicht House in my youth.

❹ At the top of the slope, the stalkers' path arcs round the coire rim, but quickly turn left onto a faint trail marked by another cairn. This crosses the wide expanse of the Plaide Mhòr and up to the rounded top of Beinn Fhada, where there is a trig pillar and stone shelter. The panorama from the summit is tremendous, and you can happily spend time working out the names of all the peaks on show. The distinctive outlines of The Saddle, Ladhar Bheinn and Beinn Sgritheall poke their heads up beyond the Five Sisters ridge, while out to the west the Skye Cuillin floats above the Inner Sound. Working round to the north, Beinn Bhàn, Torridon, Lurg Mhòr, and the Mullardoch hills all get ticked off, each recognition sparking memories of past ascents or inspiring plans for future visits.

❺ Reluctantly heading off the summit, follow a faint path down towards the Munro top of Sgùrr a' Dubh Doire, which contours round the

LOOKING UP TOWARDS COIRE AN SGÀIRNE

SUMMIT BEINN FHADA

VIEW DOWN TO GLEN AFFRIC

CAMBAN BOTHY

crest of Coire Toll a Mhdaidh. Once beyond the subsidiary peak, a beautiful view opens out to the meandering River Affric, with the twin lochs of Affric and Beinn a' Mheadhoin stretching away into the distance towards Cannich. Here the path becomes almost non-existent, but with perseverance, the red roof of Camban is soon spied in the wide valley of Fionngleann. On the far side of the valley, the watershed west to Loch Duich, and east to the Beauly Firth, is clearly defined by two streams, the Allt Cam-bàn and Allt a' Ghlas-choire, each making a sharp dog-leg left and right within 500 yards of each other. Below the unnamed top at 825m, strike down the open slope towards the bothy, keeping left of a small stream channel to a fenced enclosure, constructed as part of the NTS reforestation programme. Seek out a gate and pick your way down through the saplings to a second gate 300 yards below, and out to the path leading from Glen Affric to Loch Duich. Turn left and proceed to the bothy, which is close by.

6 After a welcome break at Camban, the return to Morvich follows the old drovers' road used to transport cattle from the west coast to the livestock markets of Perthshire in the 18th and early 19th centuries, now part of the Affric Kintail Way. Head over the watershed and back towards Gleann Lichd, the path curving back and forth above the Allt Granda. Eventually, the trail contours round the steep slopes of Meall an Uillt Ghrainnda, and the Allt Granda waterfall comes into view, cascading down a 50m cliff into a deep plunge pool. A mile further on, cross two footbridges and continue on to Glenlicht House. The bothy has recently been renovated inside and out, and is much more plush than I remember from my student days! **7** From here, a vehicle track heads down the sweeping glen and back to civilisation.

Notes: The walk described is the easiest way up to the summit plateau of Beinn Fhada. There is a recognised route through the crags leading up to Sgùrr a' Choire Ghairbh and along a narrow ridge to the top of Meall an Fhuarain Mhòir, which involves a short, slabby scramble. In misty conditions walking across the flat expanse of Plaide Mhòr to the summit trig pillar requires good navigational skills. Camban was one of the earliest renovations undertaken by the MBA and the project, which was led by the organisation's founder Bernard Heath, was a massive logistical exercise. This isolated cottage lies over 7 miles from any road.

ALLT GRANDA WATERFALL

DIRECTIONS

1 From the car park beside the Kintail Mountain Rescue Post at Morvich (NG 960 210) continue down the single-track road, past the campsite, and round to a Scottish Rights of Way signpost. Take the path to Glen Affric by Bealach an Sgàirne. A little further on, turn L over a vehicle bridge, ignore a turning R (which leads to the end of the metalled road), and after another 100 yards turn R along a path signposted to the Falls of Glomach/other routes.
1km/0.6 miles

2 After 200 yards pass through a gate into a fenced enclosure. Continue through woodland for three-quarters of a mile before heading back out into an open field, where the path splits (NG 981 222). Take the R-hand path, which leads into Gleann Chòinneachain. The trail climbs steadily up towards the Bealach an Sgàirne, to a ford over the Allt a' Choire Chaoil (NH 004 213).
4.4km/2.75 miles

3 The path then zigzags up steeply to junction marked by a small cairn. Turn R, onto the stalkers' path that climbs up to the E side of Coire an Sgàirne.
1.8km/1.1 miles

4 At the top of the slope (NH 011 202), the stalkers' path traverses round the coire rim, but after 200 yards bear L onto a faint trail marked by a cairn. Continue on this path, crossing the Plaide Mhòr and up to the summit of Beinn Fhada, where there is a trig pillar and stone shelter (NH 019 192).
1.4km/0.9 miles

5 Descend S then SE along a faint path round the top of Coire Toll a Mhdaidh to the Munro top of Sgùrr a' Dubh Doire. Continue on to an unnamed top at 825m, then drop to the 700m contour (NH 048 191). Here descend the open slope SE, towards Camban, L of a small stream channel to a fenced enclosure. Pass through a gate (NH 051 186), and down 300m to a second gate. Join a path leading from Glen Affric to

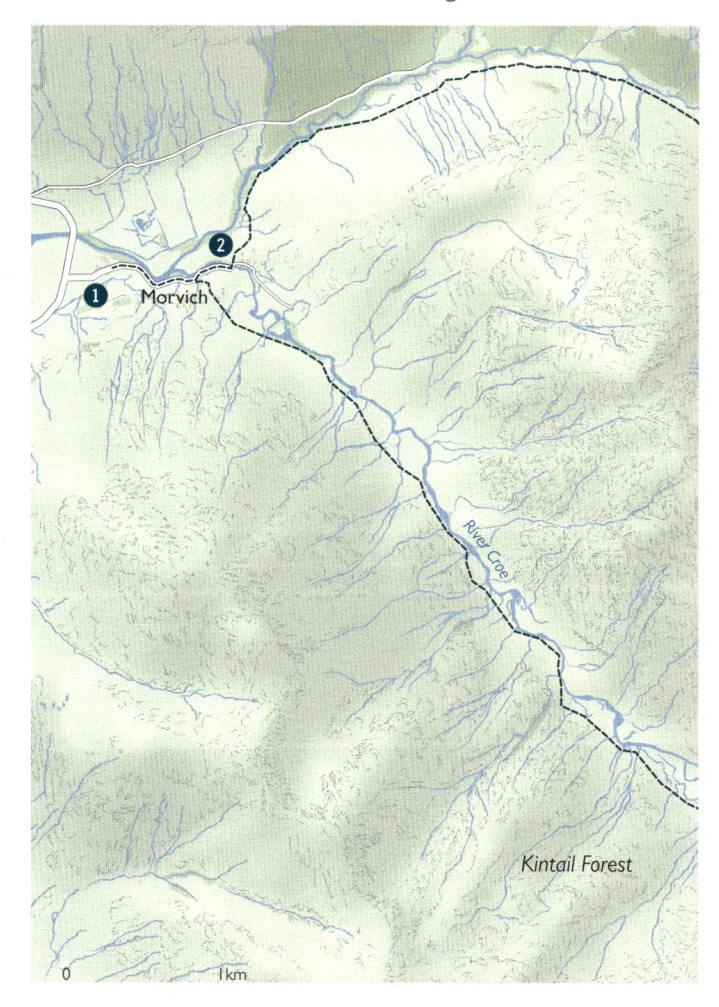

88

WALK 8 BEINN FHADA & CAMBAN BOTHY

Loch Duich, turning L to the bothy (NH 053 184).
4.8km/3 miles

6 Head W across the watershed and down to Gleann Lichd, following the route of the Affric Kintail Way. After 2.5 miles, pass the Allt Grannda waterfall, then descend another mile to a footbridge over the Allt Grannda. Soon after, cross a second bridge over the Allt an Làpain, and down to the locked bothy Glenlicht House (NH 006 173).
5.6km/3.5 miles

7 Continue down Gleann Lichd along a winding vehicle track to the metalled road, then turn L back to Morvich.
6.3km/4 miles

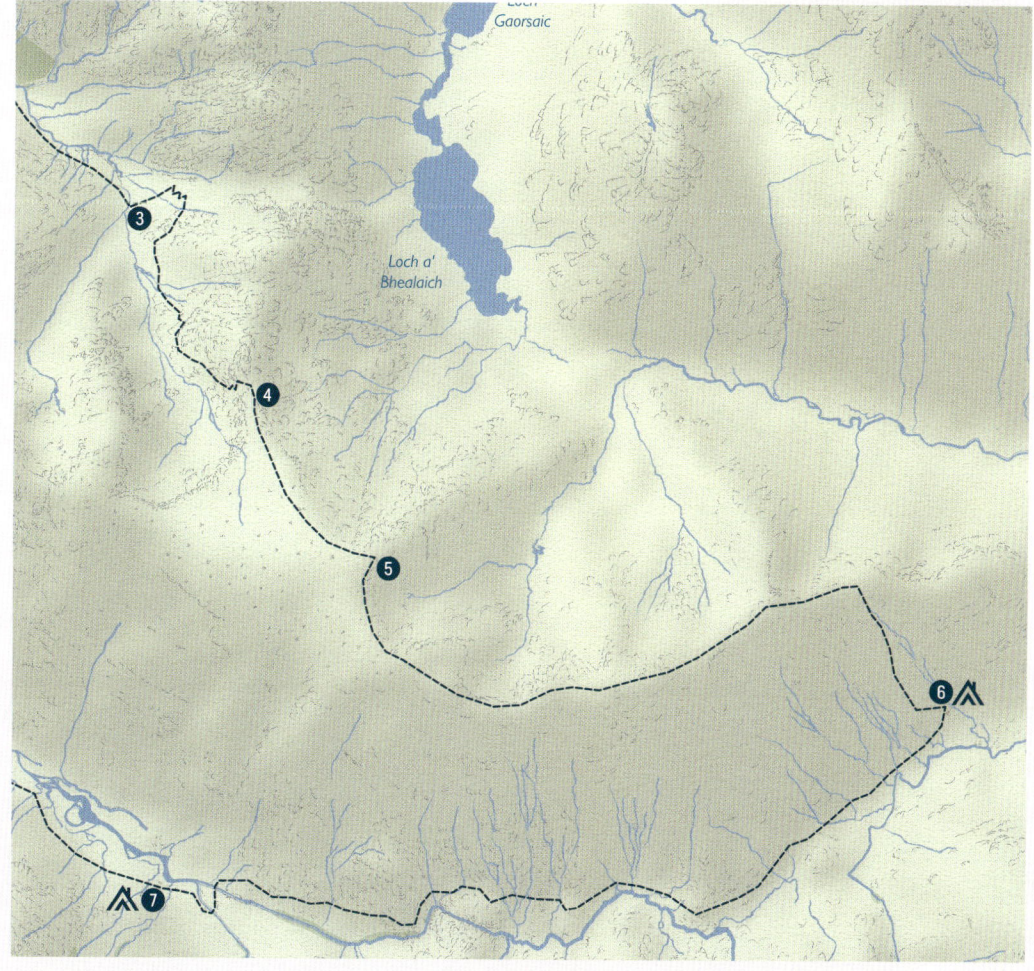

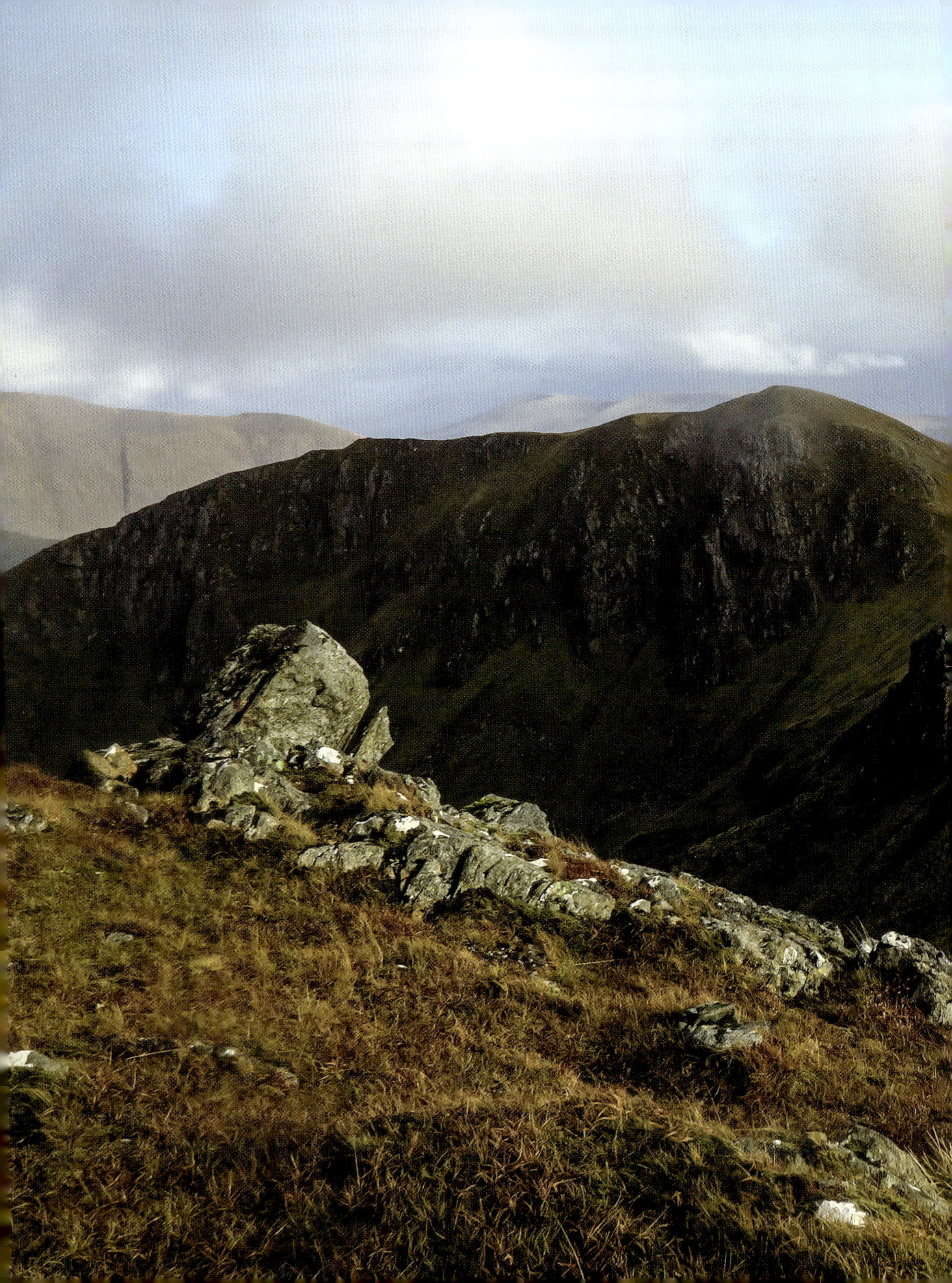

WESTERN HIGHLANDS

GLENFINNAN MONUMENT & LOCH SHIEL

WALK 9

KNOYDART & THE ROUGH BOUNDS VIA SOURLIES BOTHY

Two-day expedition through superb hiking country with an overnight stop at Sourlies. Use public transport to access this remote, rugged terrain and leave the car behind.

Renowned for its steep-sided peaks, deep lochs, and wild, inaccessible terrain, the Rough Bounds, Na Garbh Chriochan, boasts some of the finest mountain scenery in Scotland. And by a happy coincidence it also has the highest concentration of bothies in the country! There are several possible through routes linking these remote shelters, which are spread over a wide area from Loch Hourn in the north, to Loch Shiel in the south-east (including the Knoydart Peninsula, Loch Morar and Moidart). I have spent many contented hours plotting different itineraries across the region. For this car-free expedition you arrive at Inverie by ferry (from the train terminus at Mallaig), spend a night in Sourlies Bothy, then return on the West Highland Line towards Fort William from Glenfinnan.

Only accessible by boat or foot, the tiny village of Inverie, on the western shore of the Knoydart Peninsula, has a unique atmosphere. It has an island mentality, while still being strongly rooted to the interior. Ruled over by Clanranald and later the MacDonnells of Glengarry, Knoydart once supported a population of over a thousand in settlements dotted around the coast. However, during a particularly brutal episode of the Highland Clearances, many families were forced to emigrate and the dwindling population had to endure a succession of unsympathetic absentee landlords. The most infamous, Alan Ronald-Cairn (later Lord Brocket) purchased the estate in the early 1930s. After World War II, he came into conflict with a band of seven local men, including Army veterans, who had laid claim to

INFORMATION

MAPS: LR 40 Mallaig & Glenfinnan, Explorer 398 Loch Morar & Mallaig.
START GRID REF: NG 764 001, pier at Inverie.
END GRID REF: NM 906 808 Glenfinnan Visitor Centre car park.
DAY 1: Inverie to Sourlies 15km/9.25 miles
TIME: 5–6 hours
DAY 2: Sourlies to Glenfinnan 29km/18 miles
TIME: 9–11 hours
TOTAL ASCENT: Day 1, 700m
HIGHEST POINT: 550m
TOTAL ASCENT: Day 2, 1090m
HIGHEST POINT: 471m
NAVIGATION: Straightforward
TERRAIN: Straightforward. Tracks, defined paths, river crossings.
DIFFICULTY: Challenging.
PUBLIC TRANSPORT: ScotRail Glasgow Queen St. to Fort William and Mallaig. Citylink coach service 915/916 Glasgow to Fort William. Shiel Buses service 500 Fort William to Mallaig (01397 700 700). Ferry Mallaig to Inverie, regular daily service Western Isles Cruises (01687 463233).
SPECIAL NOTES: Both bothies are open throughout the year. Keep to main paths during the stalking season (September–October). Sourlies is popular so be prepared to camp.

WALK 9 KNOYDART & THE ROUGH BOUNDS VIA SOURLIES BOTHY

a small area of arable land around the village and further pasture on the hillside. These 'land raiders' were successfully prosecuted by Lord Brocket, but he sold the estate soon afterwards. In 1999, the local community and a consortium of interested parties (including the Highland Council and the John Muir Trust) mounted a successful buyout and established the Knoydart Foundation, whose aims are to promote the local economy and preserve the peninsula's natural environment.

Moving through the Rough Bounds, over the bealach from Loch Nevis into Glen Dessarry, evidence of the Clearances is clearly visible. Once the land was emptied of people, a huge sheep farm was established around Loch Arkaig and Glen Garry, with cottages for the shepherds constructed in the late-1800s. These include A' Chùil Bothy and two other properties, Kinbreack and Glenpean, which are also open shelters. They formed part of a small community centred at Strathan, an outpost at the head of the loch where the tiny school doubled up as a church. Over a century before, this was a stronghold of the Cameron clan, supporters of the Jacobite rebellion of 1745, gathering at Loch Shiel before the defining Battle of Culloden. After the calamitous defeat, government forces built a small barracks – Tigh nan Saighdearan, 'The Soldiers' House' – at Strathan to control this strategic through route to the west coast.

Even after numerous journeys over the years, I still get a thrill travelling up from Glasgow to Mallaig on the West Highland Line. The section from Fort William is a particular highlight, sweeping past Loch Eil, over the Glenfinnan Viaduct (where the ScotRail service actually slows to a halt so tourists can snap the fantastic view down Loch Shiel) and on to Arisaig and the Silver Sands of Morar, before arriving at the fishing port. From here, a small, local ferry traverses the choppy mouth of Loch Nevis towards the whitewashed cottages of Inverie, home to the Old Forge – the most remote hostelry in mainland Britain. Stepping off the boat, the pulse quickens as you prepare to put your plans into action and the full commitment of the expedition hits you.

❶ Leaving the day trippers behind, walk through the village past the tempting pub, ranger's office and a small cairn commemorating the Seven Men of Knoydart. Approaching Inverie House the tarmac ends, take the track signposted to Strathan and Kinlochhourn, curving up through the canopy of birch and pine. After a short ascent, contour round into Gleann an Dubh-Lochain following the northern bank of the Inverie River. Soon a monument to Lord Brocket comes into view, built on the top of a rocky knoll, Torr a' Bhalbhain. Just before the monument, it is possible to follow the track winding down to the Bailey Bridge, where a small path turns sharp left along the riverbank, heading towards Gleann Meadail. An easier option is to walk another 500 yards, where a second right turn leads to a vehicle bridge that joins the first path on the far side of the river. **❷** Approaching the turn you get your first real sense of the immense scale and remoteness of the terrain – a line of impassive, angular mountains guarding the routes through to Loch Hourn and Loch Nevis. To the north-east a sharp ridge line

TORR A' BHALBHAIN

VIEW FROM THE BEALACH TO SGURR NA CÌCHE

SOURLIES BOTHY

leads up to the dramatic pinnacle of Ladhar Bheinn, while Luinne Bheinn and Meall Buidhe loom in the wings.

Once across the bridge continue east through the pasture beneath the steep ridge line of Druim Righeanaich, wandering through pockets of birch woodland, before entering the narrowing gap below the dark crags of Tòrr an Tuirc. Cross the Allt Gleann Meadail by a wooden footbridge, and begin the slow ascent up to the high mountain pass between the peaks of Meall Buidhe and Meall Bhasiter. The final pull up to Màm Meadail is hard work but the views at the top are fantastic. The remote interior of the Rough Bounds is laid out in fabulous detail, overlooked by the unmistakable cone of Sgùrr an Cìche. ❸ Now zigzag steeply down to the River Carnach, heading for the ruins of the small township of Carnoch, perched above the meandering channel. Having reached the valley floor, take a track heading round to the pier at Camusrory, then, after a short distance, cross the fast-flowing water via a new (2019) footbridge, which replaced its precarious predecessor. ❹ Head along the riverbank a couple of hundred yards towards the shores of Loch Nevis, where a trail heads straight out across the bog. There is no clear path, and deep drainage channels to negotiate, so a better option is to follow the stream marked on the 1:25,000-scale map to the mudflats below Eilean Tioram. This may add 10 minutes, but you are much more likely to keep your feet dry.

Reaching the water's edge, pause to absorb this truly magical location where the imposing slopes of Bac Gobhar and Druim a' Ghoirtein drop to the depths of the loch and the salty tang of the kelp reminds you how close you are to the sea. At low tide it is possible to walk along the rocky shore, otherwise clamber over higher ground and down to Sourlies Bothy. This one-roomed shelter is deservedly popular, especially in summer, but it is easy to share your delight in reaching this breathtaking spot. There is an almost irresistible urge to start wandering along the shore, looking out for mussel beds among the sunken boulders bedecked in pretty pink sea thrift, or climb up the steep slopes above the bothy, where there is a fabulous view back down the loch towards Tarbert.

BRIDGE OVER THE ALLT COIRE NA CICHE

WALK 9 KNOYDART & THE ROUGH BOUNDS VIA SOURLIES BOTHY

5 If you are hoping to catch the evening train from Glenfinnan, you need to crack on in the morning. (Other itinerary options are discussed in the route summary). Head inland along the obvious path towards the ruins of Finiskaig, and on up the northern bank of the Finiskaig River to a footbridge over the Allt Coire na Ciche. **6** Once over the burn, zigzag steeply up through the bluffs, before the gradient relents beneath the crags of Druim nan Uadhag. Here the river snakes down from the beautiful twin pools of Lochan a' Mhàim through Màm na Cloich Àird (Pass of the High Rocks). Carefully ford the river (which could be a serious obstacle when in spate), and with some relief continue on past the two tranquil lochans, crossing a couple of submerged points on the path via strings of stepping stones. Soon the watershed is reached, where three adjacent cairns – known as the March Cairn – mark the boundary point of the old clan territories of Lochiel, Lovat and Glengarry.

7 Descend into Glen Dessarry and make for a large forestry plantation. Just before you reach it, ignore a path heading right into the depths of the conifers, and continue along the boundary fence, crossing the Allt Coire nan Uth via another footbridge. At the far edge of the plantation, A' Chùil Bothy comes into view, tucked away below a blanket of conifers on the far side of the glen. Take the faint trail to the right that follows the tree line down to the River Dessarry, over a wooden bridge and into the welcoming interior of the bothy. This is the perfect place for a breather and one last look back at the impressive ridge line stretching west from Sgùrr nan Coireachan towards the high summits of Knoydart.

8 Suitably rested, head up to the forestry track that contours clockwise into Glen Pean. After a couple of miles of steady going, the track splits. Ignore the left turn to Strathan and continue right. After a further half-mile keep a keen eye out a for a small path that descends through the gloom of densely packed trees to a bridge over the River Pean. It can be easily missed! **9** Once across the bridge, the territory opens up again, the striking peak of Streap (described in Walk 10) guarding the high pass of Gleann a' Chaorainn, a classic V-shaped notch on the skyline. There is a choice of paths on either side of the Allt a' Chaorainn, though only the one on the western side of the burn is marked on the map. If the water level is high, stick to the east bank and ford the stream further up the valley.

It is a long slog up to Bealach a' Chaorainn, but knowing this is the last obstacle before the downhill slalom into Glenfinnan helps maintain

A' CHÙIL BOTHY

LOCHAN A' MHÀIM

BEALACH AN LAGAIN DUIBH

WALK 9 KNOYDART & THE ROUGH BOUNDS VIA SOURLIES BOTHY

morale. The last section up to the high point of 471m is surprisingly steep, and is particularly tricky in waterlogged or icy conditions.

(10) The downhill path is much clearer, descending steeply to the footbridge over the Allt Coire a' Bheithe below Coire Thollaidh, and the hills of the Corryhully Horseshoe. Continue on, fording the Allt a' Choire Chàrnaig, before reaching Corryhully, the Electric Bothy, for a final pit stop. If you are apprehensive about missing the last train, this is an easy overnight alternative before heading on in the morning.

(11) A little further on, turn left onto the surfaced road and stride out for the last two miles. A few hundred yards before the main road, pass under the Glenfinnan Viaduct (better known these days as the Harry Potter Bridge). Turn right on the main road and after another half a mile Glenfinnan station comes into view. Returning on the train in high spirits, you feel a real sense of achievement.

Notes: Any trek across Knoydart and the Rough Bounds is a serious undertaking. Although there are few navigation issues, the journey requires a good level of fitness and high degree of self-sufficiency. From Sourlies Bothy it is possible to split the journey into a two-day adventure, stopping overnight at A' Chùil (just 5 miles), or heading round to Glenpean (10 miles), though from Glenpean you do have to double-back before heading up Gleann a' Chaorainn. The road end at Strathan, though a remote location, provides a potential exit point if the expedition has been compromised. The route from Sourlies to Glenfinnan follows the route of the Cape Wrath trail in reverse.

GLEANN A' CHAORAINN

DIRECTIONS

Day 1 Inverie to Sourlies

1 From the pier at Inverie walk through the village, turning L onto a track signposted to Strathan and Kinlochhourn by Inverie House. After a short ascent, contour round into Gleann an Dubh-Lochain. After a mile ignore a path to R just after passing a monument on Torr a' Bhalbhain and continue on to a second junction (NM 797 991).
4 km/2.5 miles

2 Here, where the main track heads on to Barrisdale, turn R following a track down to a vehicle bridge over the river, and continue E into Gleann Meadail on a well-established path. After just under a mile cross the Allt Gleann Meadail by a footbridge, and begin the slow ascent up to Màm Meadail 550m, the path rising steeply in the final approach to the saddle.
6.5km/4 miles

3 From the bealach zigzag steeply down to the River Carnach, heading for the ruins at Carnoch, and continuing on the track towards Camusrory for a short distance before turning L, crossing the river via a new footbridge (NM 866 965).
2.4km/1.5 miles

4 Now head along the riverbank for 200 yards and straight across the marsh to the shore of Loch Nevis, or follow the stream to the mudflats below Eilean Tioram. At low tide walk along the shore; otherwise take the L path over higher ground and down to Sourlies Bothy (NM 868 951).
2.1km/1.25 miles

Day 2 Sourlies to Glenfinnan

5 From Sourlies take the path towards the ruins of Finiskaig, and on up the N bank of the Finiskaig River, crossing the Allt Coire na Ciche via a footbridge (NM 879 945, not marked on the map).
1.3km/0.75 miles

6 Zigzag steeply up through rocky ground and ford the river (NM 890 945) beneath the crags of Druim nan Uadhag, which could be an obstacle in times of spate. Continue past Lochan a' Mhàim to the watershed at the Bealach an Lagain Duibh marked by cairns.
3.5 km/2.25 miles

7 Descend into Glen Dessarry towards a large forestry plantation. Just before it, ignore a path on R and continue along the boundary fence, crossing the Allt Coire nan Uth via a footbridge (NM 931 937). At the far edge of the plantation, follow a faint trail on R (not marked on the OS map), down to the River Dessarry over a wooden bridge and reach A' Chùil Bothy (NM 944 924).
5km/3.25 miles

DIRECTIONS

8 From the bothy, take the forestry track that continues round into Glen Pean. After just under two and a half miles, where the track splits, continue R and after another half a mile turn L down a small path through the plantation and cross the bridge over the River Pean (NM 969 907).
5km/3.25 miles

9 Now follow the path marked on the W side of the Allt a' Chaorainn, but if the water level is high, stick to the E bank and ford the stream further up the valley. Continue up to the Bealach a' Chaorainn: the last section is steep and can be challenging in poor conditions.
4.75km/3 miles

10 Descend steeply to the footbridge over the Allt Coire a' Bheithe before fording the Allt a' Choire Chàrnaig and heading on to Corryhully Bothy.
4km/2.5 miles

11 From the bothy, turn L onto the metalled road leading to the A830 by Glenfinnan Visitor Centre. The railway station is just over half a mile to the west along the main road.
5km/3 miles

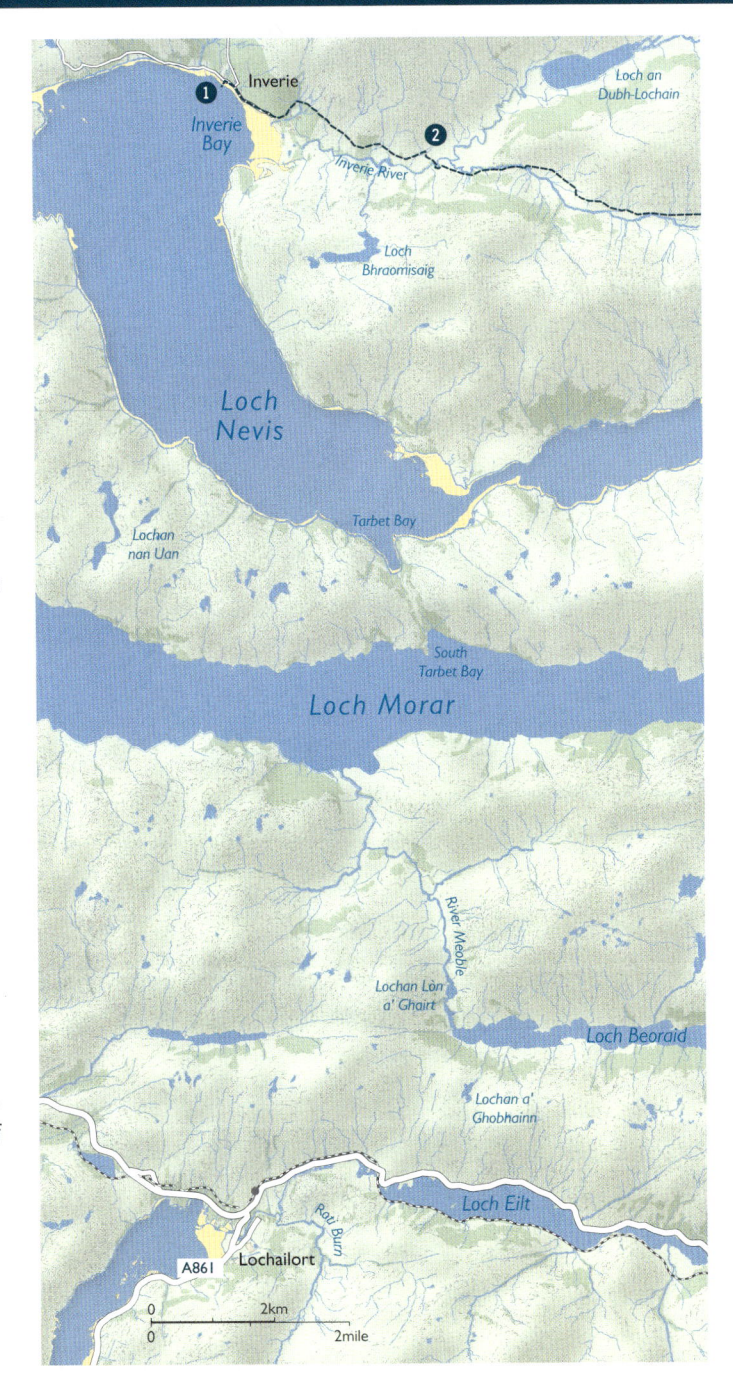

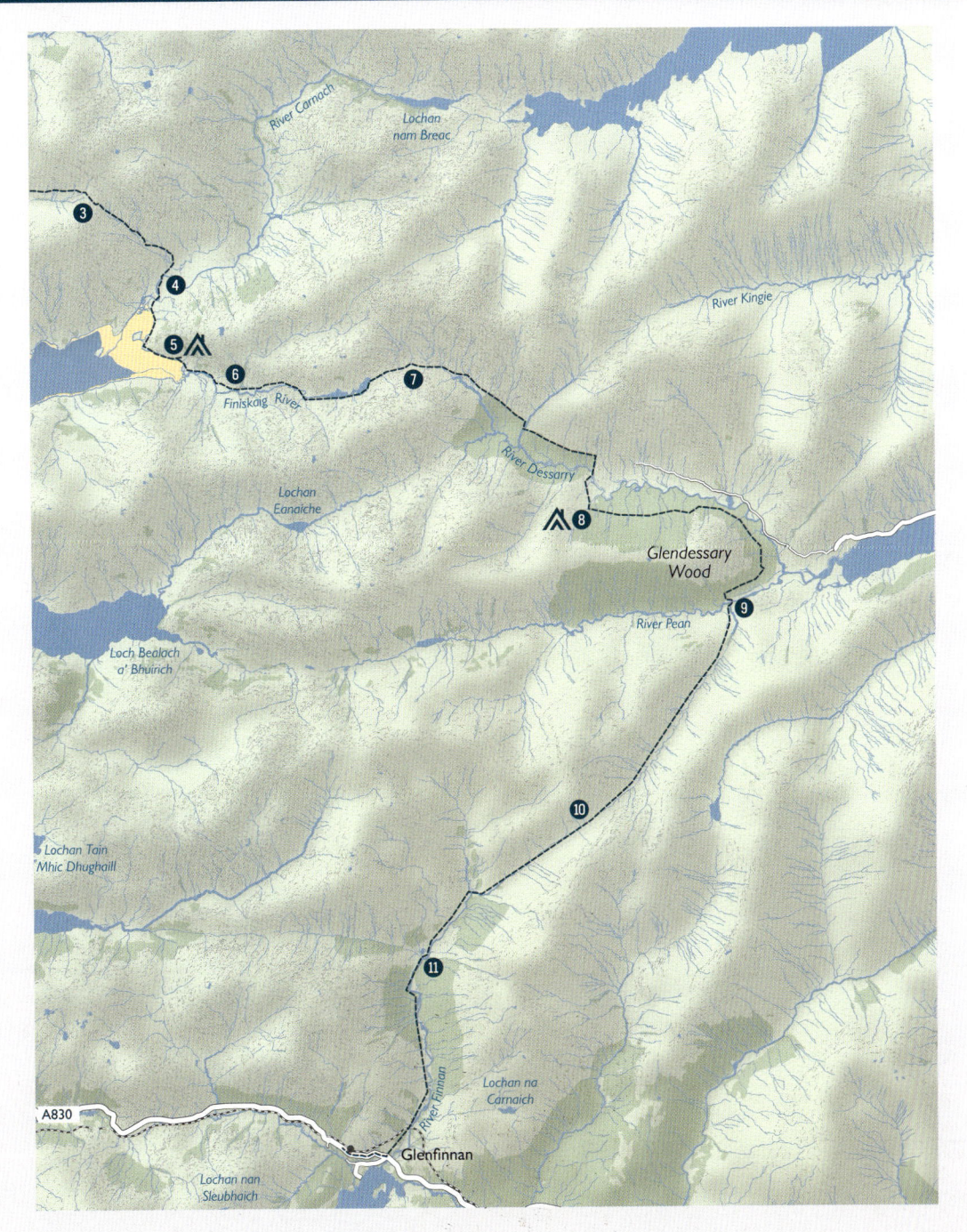

WALK 9 KNOYDART & THE ROUGH BOUNDS VIA SOURLIES BOTHY

103

RIDGE BETWEEN STOB COIRE NAN CEARC & STREAP

WALK 10

STREAP & GLEANN DUBH-LIGHE BOTHY

Tremendous mountain walk, via a peaceful valley and superior bothy, negotiating a testing ridge up to the pyramid peak of Streap, with views into the Rough Bounds and Knoydart.

Although to an Anglicised ear Streap sounds like an outlying fell in the Lake District, perhaps eulogised in a Wainwright guide, the name has Gaelic roots which are very apt: climb, scale, mount with difficulty; strife or struggle. Through a quirk of fate, the height of this rugged, undulating mountain north of the Road to the Isles falls just below the magic number of 3000 feet, classifying it as a Corbett rather than a Munro. Consequently, despite being a classic walk, the round of Streap, and its neighbouring tops, is far less frequently climbed than the nearby summits of Sgùrr Thuilm and Sgùrr nan Coireachan, combined to form the equally impressive 'Corryhully Horseshoe'. With no path to speak of once you leave the safety of the glen, except along the vertiginous ridge leading up to the summit, this is a tough, but thoroughly rewarding walk. It is reminiscent of a previous age before the allure of Scotland's high mountains caught the popular imagination, and hillsides became conspicuously embellished by wide tracks and unnecessary cairns. *Streap-aidh an duine glioc*, the wise man shall scale.

Gleann Dubh-lighe is only a couple of miles down the road from the magnetic attraction of Glenfinnan, but is a world away from the tourist crush. Instead of cars and coaches shoehorned into every available parking space, as the Flying Scotsman chugs across the 'Harry Potter' viaduct in the summer months, look for a small layby tucked away behind a screen of birch trees, a few hundred yards east of a far more prosaic railway overpass.

INFORMATION

MAPS: LR 40 Mallaig & Glenfinnan, Explorer 398 Loch Morar & Mallaig.
START/END GRID REF: NM 931 799. Small lay-by (easy to miss; marked by 2 grey bollards) at Drochaid Sgainnir off the A830 'Road to the Isles'.
DISTANCE: 17.5km/11 miles
TIME: 6–8 hours
ASCENT: 1197m
SUMMITS: Meall an Uillt Chaoil, 844m; Stob Coire nan Cearc, 887m; Streap (Corbett), 909m; Streap Comhlaidh, 898m.
NAVIGATION: Straightforward.
TERRAIN: Straightforward/challenging. Track, faint trails, open hillside, river crossing.
DIFFICULTY: Straightforward/challenging.
PUBLIC TRANSPORT: ScotRail West Highland Line Glasgow Queen St. to Mallaig stops at Glenfinnan. Citylink coach service 915/916 Glasgow to Fort William. Daily bus from Fort William to Mallaig stops at Glenfinnan (Shiel Buses 01397 700700) Service 500, then 2-mile walk on A830 from Glenfinnan to start of track.
SPECIAL NOTES: Bothy open all year. Contact Fassfern Estate during stalking season (01397 722217 or 01397 772288) regarding access.

WALK 10 STREAP & GLEANN DUBH-LIGHE BOTHY

There is some confusion about the translation of Gleann Dubh-lighe, which could mean 'black doctor' or simply 'black river', but no mistaking the sinister undertones of Drochaid Sgainnir, Bridge of Shame or Scandal, a mere stone's throw from the start of the walk. ❶ The track to the bothy poses no problems, gently winding its way up the quiet, secluded glen through a dense canopy of conifers. The trail remains close to the fast-flowing river and it is a pleasure to listen to the sound of the water tumbling over a series of waterfalls into deep pools. After a short, steeper section, turn sharply right where the track forks, heading down across the river via a sturdy wooden bridge and the bothy comes quickly into view. It was lovingly reconstructed by the MBA, with the help of the Fassfern Estate, the original bothy having accidentally burnt down in 2012 when a faulty gas cylinder was ignited by a candle flame.

❷ After a quick stop in its comfy interior, continue on up the valley, Streap and its satellite Streap Comhlaidh coming into view just around the next bend. The conifers soon thin out, replaced by birch and ash, and after another half a mile you reach a high deer fence. Beyond is the open hillside. Once through a kissing gate, continue on to a footbridge over the river, close to the ruins of an old farmstead and shieling.

Surprisingly this bridge is not marked on the 1:50,000 or 1:25,000-scale maps of the area. ❸ Now the whole ridge is clearly visible, and a decision needs to be made about which slope to tackle to attain the rocky skyline. The most conservative approach is to follow the course of the deep cut Allt Coire an Tuim where birch trees grow in the gully shadows, and continue round to the Bealach a' Chait over the sodden coire basin. Alternatively, stick closely to the left-hand bank of the Allt Caol, and climb the steep, grassy ridge to the top of Meall an Uillt Chaoil. Although unforgiving, most of the rock obstacles can be avoided. A braver and quicker option is to ascend the tightly packed contours leading up to Bealach Coire nan Cearc, scrambling through the odd outcrop of slippery schist and quartzite.

GLEANN DUBH-LIGHE BOTHY

STREAP & STREAP COMHLAIDH

WALK 10 STREAP & GLEANN DUBH-LIGHE BOTHY

extraordinary views north and west to the remote terrain of the Rough Bounds and Knoydart. And on a clear day Ben Nevis and the Mamores are just visible on the south-eastern horizon.

❻ Stepping carefully off Streap's airy perch, a reasonably recognisable path drops down a slender ridge towards Streap Comhlaidh. On the far side of the narrow bealach, a tempting trail cuts across the slope to avoid the short, steep ascent to this secondary summit peak. If you head to this second top, quickly cross to a grassy triangular high point before starting the long, slow descent to the valley floor. Rejoin the other path before it peters out as the ground steepens. ❼ Aim for the track that leads up to the watershed of Gleann Camgharaidh, crossing a couple of streams incised into the slope. With some relief wander down the boggy track to the final obstacle of the day, crossing the Allt Coire Chùirn as it tumbles down towards the Dubh Lighe. When in spate this could be tricky, though it is possible to jump across the channel at its narrowest point. From here head back to the footbridge and descend to the bothy, turning one final time to marvel at what you have accomplished in one day.

❹ A broad ridge leads from the summit of Meall an Uillt Chaoil, narrowing as it approaches Stob Coire nan Cearc. Follow a faint trail through a series of bluffs and pay attention, especially in misty conditions, to avoid backtracking, as off-route the rocky obstacles steepen unexpectedly. The path becomes more defined once you clamber up to the top of Stob Coire nan Cearc, where the pyramid summit of Streap rears up into view. The final grassy arête is exhilarating, and less intimidating than it looks. Take a well-earned break by Streap's summit cairn, enjoying the

Notes: This is a more strenuous day out than you might assume from an examination of the OS map because of the rough nature of the terrain, and the lack of an obvious path leading up and along the ridge. Also, after heavy rain, Allt Coire nan Chùirn can flood and may be an obstacle. If in any doubt, check the water level before you head up the hill: the crossing point is 5 minutes out of your way, beyond the footbridge.

GLEANN DUBH-LIGHE

ALLT COIRE NAN CHÙIRN

WALK 10 STREAP & GLEANN DUBH-LIGHE BOTHY

DIRECTIONS

① From the small parking area (NM 931 799) squeeze through a tight kissing gate, and take the wide forestry track which heads N through an extensive forestry plantation, towards Gleann Dubh-lighe Bothy. After just under 1.5 miles of gentle climbing, take a sharp R turn where the track splits, down to a vehicle bridge over the river. The bothy quickly comes into view as the trees begin to thin out (NM 944 820).
2.8km/1.75 miles

② Continue along the track, which contours above the river, through woodland to a gate in the boundary fence. Head out into the open glen to a footbridge over the river (NM 948 838) by the ruins of an old farmstead.
2km/1.25 miles

③ Cross to the far bank, and quickly take to the open hillside, plotting a course to either: A) Bealach a' Chait, and up to the summit of Meall an Uillt Chaoil. B) Directly to the summit of Meall an Uillt Chaoil via the steep E ridge or C) up to the Bealach Coire nan Cearc, scrambling through rocky outcrops.
1.8km/1 mile

WALK 10 STREAP & GLEANN DUBH-LIGHE BOTHY

4 Follow a faint trail down the broad ridge from the summit of Meall an Uillt Chaoil to the Bealach Coire nan Cearc, and up the next top Stob Coire nan Cearc (NM 937 852).
1.2km/0.75 miles

5 Drop down to the next saddle, then ascend the sharp ridge onto the summit of Streap (NM 947 864).
1.6km/1 mile

6 Now head down the E ridge of Streap to the next bealeach and either climb steeply through the boulders to the summit of Streap Comhlaidh and down to its second top (859m), or traverse across the slope on an obvious path.
1km/0.6 miles

7 Descend to the floor of the glen, picking a route down the open hillside, making for the track heading up towards Lochan a' Chomhlain, crossing small streams.
1.2km/0.75 miles

8 Follow the track down to a ford over the Allt Coire Chùirn (NM 949 843). Once across, continue to footbridge, and on to the bothy.
3.3km/2 miles.

9 Return to the roadside, retracing your steps along the forestry track.
2.8km/1.75 miles

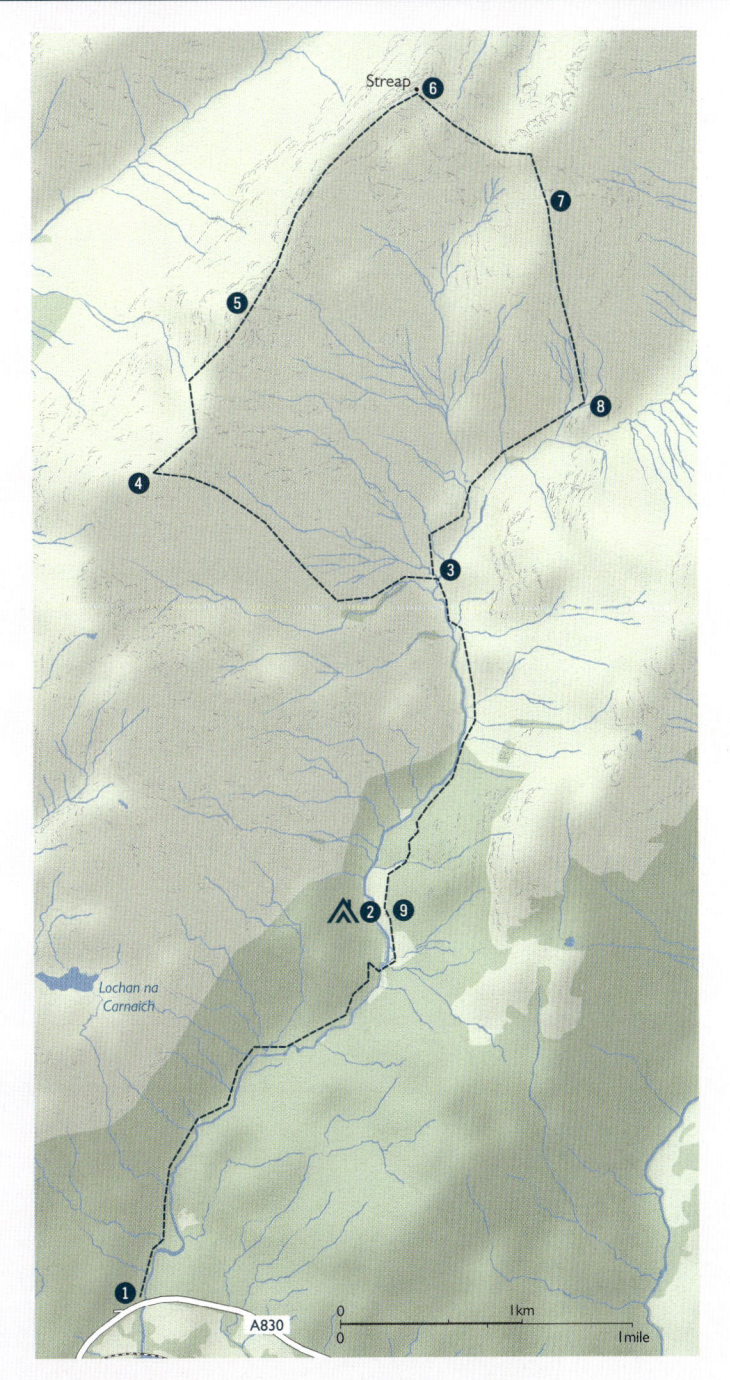

LOOKING OUT ACROSS THE BAY BELOW PEANMEANACH

WALK 11

PEANMEANACH BOTHY & THE ARDNISH PENINSULA

A fabulous outing through Ardnish, a rugged promontory tousled of moorland heath, intimate bays and low tumbling cliffs to Peanmeanach, a ruined beachside settlement with a magical bothy.

The quiet, unassuming peninsula of Ardnish is easily overlooked among the star attractions on the 'Road to the Isles', yet walking through this remote landscape of intricately folded Lewisian gneiss is a real joy with wonderful views at every turn. Looking out over the peaceful Sound of Arisaig, Peanmeanach sits above a lovely, crescent-shaped bay and for many bothy enthusiasts, it is a familiar and beloved refuge. Marriage proposals have been uttered within its walls, and memories of first childhood footsteps across the threshold retold across the generations.

Evidence of habitation in the bay stretches back to the Iron Age: two vitrified hill forts dated to 800 BC were unearthed on Eilean nan Gobhair (Goat Island) out in the tidal flow beyond the shingle shore. A satellite photograph showed the faint outline of the slipway of an old Viking 'naust', a wooden boathouse constructed above the high-water mark, and the bothy's name indicates an early Norse system of land division. Pean derives from *peighinn* meaning 'pennyland': 20 of these, each with a farm, made up an 'ounce land', an acreage capable of producing an ounce of silver in rent. 'Meanach' simply means 'middle'. One of a row of stone-built, thatched black houses, the bothy was part of a small township that grew up after the Highland Clearances, when sheep were moved onto productive land and tenants forcibly evicted to marginal coastal areas. During the mid-19th century, over 80 people lived in the vicinity of

INFORMATION

MAPS: LR 40 Mallaig & Glenfinnan, Explorer 398 Loch Morar & Mallaig.
START/END GRID REF: NM 742 835. Lay-by at Polnish on the A830.
DISTANCE: 11km/7 miles round trip (13.5km/8.5 miles for extension to Singing Sands).
TIME: 4–5 hour round trip (allow all day if exploring the coast).
TOTAL ASCENT: 187m
HIGH POINT: 151m
NAVIGATION: Easy
TERRAIN: Easy. Well defined path, faint trail to Singing Sands, river crossing.
DIFFICULTY: Straightforward. Although an easy walk in fair conditions, it is trickier in deteriorating weather.
PUBLIC TRANSPORT: ScotRail West Highland Line Glasgow Queen St. to Mallaig, nearest stop Lochailort 2.5 miles. Shiel Buses service 500 Fort William to Mallaig stops on request 01397 700700).
SPECIAL NOTES: The bothy is open throughout the year. Access is restricted during stag-stalking, 15 August to 20 October and during the hind cull from 21 October to 15 February. Please comply with notices posted in the vicinity when out walking.

Peanmeanach, and the bothy functioned as the post office for the scattered communities around the Sound of Arisaig. When the railway cut off the peninsula in 1901, the community began to decline and the last remaining family, the MacQueen's, moved out during World War II.

The path to Peanmeanach, constructed at the turn of the last century, was maintained by two road builders who were partly paid by the remaining crofters. ❶ Beginning at a lay-by on the widened A830 Fort William to Mallaig Road, head along a gravel path signposted to Peanmeanach, which curves steeply downhill for a short section before crossing a small concrete bridge over the Western Highlands Railway line. If you are lucky you may catch a glimpse of 'The Jacobite', a steam train that travels back and forth from Fort William to Mallaig twice a day in the summer months, its smoky plume extending like a white scarf round the coast. ❷ Once across a wooden plank spanning a small stream, the route ascends through stands of birch trees, following a stone staircase up the rocky flanks of Cruach Doir' an Raoigh. Although arduous, a fabulous view soon extends out over the clear waters of Loch Nan Uamh ('Loch of the Caves') and out to the Inner Hebridean islands of Eigg and Muck. Bonnie Prince Charlie landed here as he mustered his forces for the Battle of Culloden in 1745, and also left from the same spot after the Jacobite Uprising was crushed, fleeing to exile in France. Finally the terrain eases, the path contouring through rocky bluffs and tough moorland grasses before skirting the shallow basin of Loch Doire a' Ghearrain. ❸ After crossing the outflow stream via a set of stepping stones, the path gently meanders down through an enchanting wooded hollow of birch and rare Atlantic oak, the canopy sculpted into an angled roof by the prevailing westerly winds. Emerging onto a flat marshland of tall reeds, the bothy comes into sight, the boggy terrain to the coast negotiated by an arrow-straight line of sunken flat stones. You cannot help but smile as you reach the bothy door and gaze out across the sound to the distant outline of Ardnamurchan. Beyond the small, sandy beach, mussel beds are exposed at low tide and wading birds busy themselves looking for shellfish and shrimps in the muddy shallows. A sense of peace soon descends in this serene location, an unspoilt stretch of coast to explore and cherish.

PEANMEANACH BOTHY

WALK 11 PEANMEANACH BOTHY & THE ARDNISH PENINSULA

❹ If you have a couple of hours to spare before heading back to Polnish, it's worth considering a wander along the coast to an enchanting beach known locally as Singing Sands, which is only fully revealed at low tide. Like its well-known neighbour Camas an Lighe (further south in Kentra Bay on the edge of Ardnamurchan), the grains of sand here have unique properties – completely round, of a precise diameter, and with a particular level of humidity – that generate a low-frequency sound when you skip across the surface. From the bothy head west, quickly crossing the Allt Loch Doire' a' Ghearrain before picking up a faint trail to the ruin of Glasnacardoch. Here the path peters out, so continue on open ground to the coast, over the rocky foreshore to the sands ❺.

PEANMEANACH BAY

116

DIRECTIONS

1 From the lay-by on the A830 at Polnish (NM 742 835) head down a path to the railway line, passing over the tracks by a concrete bridge. Quickly cross a stream via a footbridge and start the steep ascent towards Loch Doire a' Ghearrain.
0.4km/0.25 miles

2 After just over a mile the gradient eases and the path passes a high point of 151m, before skirting the edge of the loch.
2.8km/1.75 miles

3 Descend towards the coast, crossing the Allt Loch Doire a' Ghearrain (NM 715 819) via stepping stones before entering mixed woodland. Emerge close to the coast, crossing a flat area of waterlogged reeds on a muddy path to the grassy shore and reach the bothy (NM 712 805).
2.8km/1.75 miles

4 Head W from the bothy, quickly fording Allt Loch Doire' a' Ghearrain, and follow the faint trail to Glasnacardoch. Continue over open ground to Singing Sands (NM 700 806).
1.2km/0.75 miles

5 Return to the bothy and back to the road.
6.75km/4.25 miles

OTTER FOOTPRINTS ON SINGING SANDS

LOCH NAN UAMH

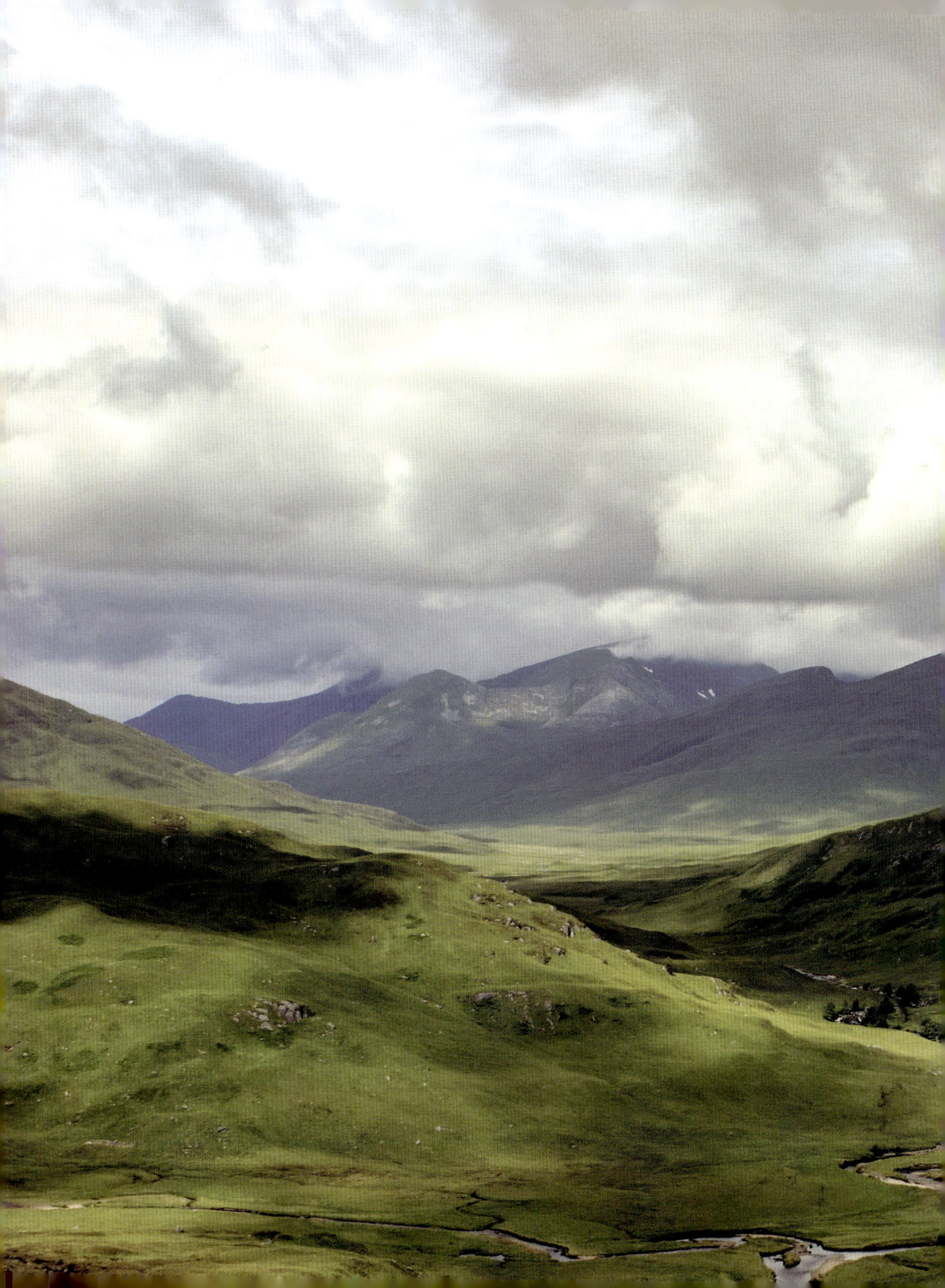

CENTRAL HIGHLANDS

STAOINEAG BOTHY

WALK 12

OVERNIGHT AT STAOINEAG BOTHY

Revitalising expedition from the spectacular stop at Corrour station to the sweeping glen of the Abhainn Rath and on to Staoineag for the quintessential bothy experience.

Over the years Staoineag has been a steadfast friend, a place I have returned to again and again. Tucked beneath steep crags on the banks of the meandering Abhainn Rath (a remote valley north of Rannoch Moor, and east of Glen Nevis), the bothy makes a perfect place to go off-grid, and forget day-to-day preoccupations. The easiest approach to the bothy is via Corrour station, the only railway stop in the UK not accessible by car. Alighting from the train you are plunged straight into the wilderness, without having to strain every sinew to get there. This saves an extra 10-mile trek from the road end at Rannoch station (and an even longer trek from Spean Bridge). And, although the walk-in from Corrour still provides a healthy challenge, it is manageable in all weathers. The reward is overnight accommodation in a stunning location, with plenty of space, two well-used fireplaces, and a reliable wood supply along the banks of the river. Because it is accessible without the need of a car, the bothy encourages a wide cross-section of visitors, beyond the stereotyped outdoor enthusiast, and this firmly enriches the experience.

As you watch your West Highland Line train disappear from view, the sense of isolation is palpable. Famously used as a location in Danny Boyle's culture-defining film *Trainspotting*, the station was originally built as a tourist destination in the late Victorian era. Guests staying at the exclusive lodge at the far end of Loch Ossian were taken by carriage down to the lochside, before boarding a paddle steamer for the final part of

INFORMATION

MAPS: LR 41 Ben Nevis–Fort William & Glen Coe, Explorer 485 Rannoch Moor & Ben Alder.
START/END GRID REF: NN 356 664 Corrour railway station.
DISTANCE: 17km/10.5 miles
TIME: 2.5–3 hours (round trip 6 hours).
TOTAL ASCENT: 100m
HIGHEST POINT: 410m
NAVIGATION: Easy
TERRAIN: Easy. Track and well defined path all the way to the bothy.
DIFFICULTY: Straightforward. Bothy in a remote location.
PUBLIC TRANSPORT: ScotRail West Highland Line from Glasgow Queen St. to Fort William, stops at Corrour station.
SPECIAL NOTES: Bothy is open throughout the year, but hill access may be restricted during stag-stalking from 15 August to 20 October, and the hind cull from 21 October to 15 February. Contact the Killiechonate and Mamores Estate (01855 831337) for information.

WALK 12 OVERNIGHT AT STAOINEAG BOTHY

LOCH TREIG

the journey. The derelict waiting room has since been converted into an SYHA hostel, providing useful fall-back accommodation if you are caught out by bad weather. There is also an enticing café and restaurant in the station house (open in the summer season), and even an Airbnb in the signal box. But don't be lulled into complacency. Once you set off beyond the psychological comfort blanket of the railway line, a creeping awareness of how far you are from civilisation begins to concentrate the mind.

❶ From the opposite side of the level crossing at the northern end of the platform, turn right parallel to the railway tracks and walk along to the bridge over the fast-flowing Allt Lùib Ruairidh, where a new access road descends to Loch Treig. Once a boggy morass with free-floating wooden planks over areas of waterlogged peat, this stretch now has a well-maintained path with footbridges across the streams. **❷** The wide track down to Loch Treig was bulldozed through for the construction of a small hydroelectric power facility, completed in the autumn of 2015. This is dwarfed by the Loch Treig dam, built in the late-1920s as part of an impressive scheme to provide electricity for an aluminium smelter in Fort William. At the time, the 15-mile section from Loch Treig to the plant was the longest water-carrying tunnel in the world. The track continues along the southern shore of Loch Treig to the abandoned lodge at Creaguaineach – all that remains of a small township submerged when the dam was completed.

❸ Just before the lodge, leave the main track, turning left onto a rough path running close to the Abhainn Rath's southern bank. There is a signpost here, but because the route is not a Scottish Right of Way, there isn't a reassuring arrow pointing the way. The directions described are north to Spean Bridge, and back in the direction you have come from and onto Rannoch. (The Right of Way to Glen Nevis is on the far bank of the river.) Although there is still a fair way to go, the very committed might want to gather some kindling from beneath the Scots pines nestled around the lodge. A closer supply is consistently found on the wide meander just over half a mile further on, washed downstream after the river has been in spate. Once you have navigated this curving bend, the path climbs through enchanting birch groves, before following the fence line up past tumbling rapids and onto the flats that open up just before bothy. Finally Staoineag is in sight, standing impervious to the elements on a rocky prow above the river.

ABHAINN RATH

STEPPING STONES BELOW STAOINEAG BOTHY

WALK 12 OVERNIGHT AT STAOINEAG BOTHY

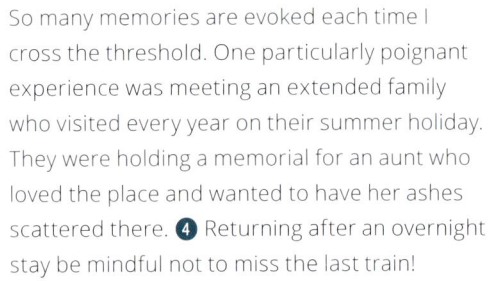

So many memories are evoked each time I cross the threshold. One particularly poignant experience was meeting an extended family who visited every year on their summer holiday. They were holding a memorial for an aunt who loved the place and wanted to have her ashes scattered there. ❹ Returning after an overnight stay be mindful not to miss the last train!

Notes: A typical itinerary would be to arrive on the morning train from Glasgow (or earlier on the sleeper from Euston), and return the following evening after 6pm. One particularly adventurous possibility is to take the evening train in the depths of winter, arriving after 9pm in the pitch-dark, perhaps with a hint of snow on the breeze (at 1339ft the halt is the highest station in Britain). The area is well served by bothies with short distances between them, creating various multi-day walking options. Stepping stones outside the bothy may be submerged after rain.

DIRECTIONS

① From the station (NN 356 664) head NW, parallel to the railway line, along a path signposted to Spean Bridge to a footbridge over the Allt Lùib Ruairidh (NN 342 681).
2.3km/1.5 miles

② Pick up a wide, unmetalled road leading down to a hydroelectric scheme on the short S side of Loch Treig. Continue on round the loch until you see Creaguaineach Lodge (NN 309 689). Just before the bridge over the Abhainn Rath ignore the new signpost and take the small path to the L that follows the S side of the river.
4km/2.5 miles

③ Cross a carpet of coarse heather and after 500 yards walk up under a close canopy of silver birch high above a wide meander. Ford the Allt Cam nan Aighean (NN 303 679 and normally passable even in spate), and continue past some impressive rapids, onto the flats just before the bothy. Although it is easy to navigate in daylight, the path around the long meander can be tricky in the dark. Look out for a line of old iron estate fence posts that lead W parallel to the riverbank.
2.1km/1.25 miles

④ Retrace the route back to Corrour station.

NOTES: There are stepping stones across the Abhainn Rath, very close to the bothy. From here a trip to Meanach Bothy is a straightforward 3-mile journey but be careful when the river is in spate. If in any doubt, go back down to the bridge at Creaguaineach Lodge, cross there and access the bothy via the river's N bank.

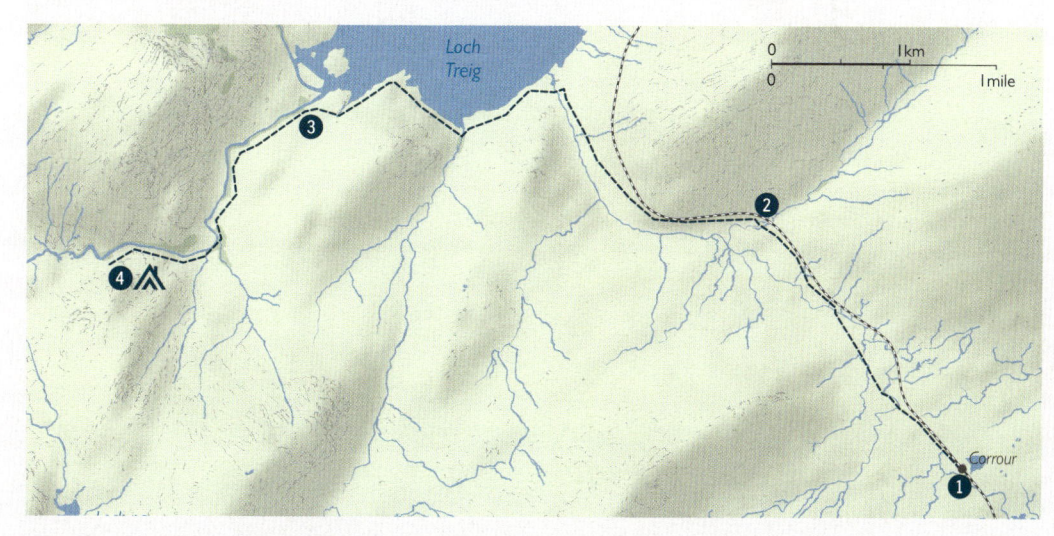

BEN ALDER COTTAGE

WALK 13

A BEN ALDER CROSSING FROM RANNOCH TO CORROUR STATION

Classic two-day expedition through the vast, upland moors in the heart of the Central Highlands, staying overnight in atmospheric Ben Alder Cottage.

Since the 1920s, stravaigers and mountain walkers have sought solitude in the empty quarter of the sprawling Grampian Mountains bounded by the West Highland Railway line, and the highway over the Drumochter Pass from Blair Atholl to Aviemore. Dominated by the guiding presence of the Ben Alder plateau, and the long, muscular arm of Loch Ericht, this remote region is notable for the absence of public roads, houses or people. Nestled above a semicircular, loch-side bay in the mountain's shadow lies Ben Alder Cottage, also known as McCook's Cottage. The bothy has long had a reputation for being haunted, though this never seems to have impacted on its popularity! Numerous stories of seeing or hearing a ghost have been embellished over the years, even by such luminaries as W.H. Murray who related a tale of the mysterious scraping of hobnail boots outside the cottage in his seminal book, *Undiscovered Scotland*.

I can still vividly remember flicking through a newly acquired copy of *Classic Walks*, and seeing a picture of Ben Alder Cottage for the first time. A slightly off-colour photo of Hamish Brown returning to the cottage fully laden with firewood evoked a real sense of adventure and self-sufficiency, and inspired me to make the journey. The walk in to the bothy is fairly testing: my first attempt did not end well and I was forced to beat a hasty retreat after becoming disorientated in the conifer plantation beneath Sròn na h-Oissin. The experience is reminiscent of an account in *Mountain Days and Bothy Nights* concerning an overly optimistic

INFORMATION

MAPS: LR 42 Glen Garry & Loch Rannoch, Explorer 485 Rannoch Moor & Ben Alder.
START GRID REF: NN 506 577. Car park at Tigh an Uillt by Bridge of Gaur on the B846, 6 miles E of Rannoch station.
END GRID REF: NN 356 664 Corrour railway station.
DISTANCE: 30km/18.5 miles
DAY 1: 13.5km/8.5 miles
TIME: 4–5 hours
DAY 2: 16.5km/10 miles
TIME: 5–6 hours
TOTAL ASCENT: 750m
HIGHEST POINT: 662m
NAVIGATION: Easy.
TERRAIN: Challenging. Track, well defined path and open moor.
DIFFICULTY: Challenging.
PUBLIC TRANSPORT: ScotRail West Highland Line Glasgow Queen St. to Fort William stops at Rannoch and Corrour stations. Dial-a-Bus service from Rannoch station to the start of the walk: book 24 hours in advance (01882 632418).
SPECIAL NOTES: Open all year with unrestricted access. During deer control (mid-Aug–Feb 15th) stick to paths where possible and use prominent ridges to access the hilltops. Contact Ben Alder Estate (01540 672000) for information.

group from Glasgow who had hoped for 'a quick and easy dander across the moor', but ended up getting stuck in a snowdrift. Narrowly avoiding hypothermia, they only just made it to the cottage.

Apart from the sad loss of the postbus service, little has changed since the eloquent description penned by Richard Gilbert in 1982, entitled '*A Ben Alder Crossing*'. If you are arriving by train, the first challenge that confronts you is the six-mile journey from Rannoch station to the sawmill close to Bridge of Gaur, where the recommended walk in begins. The possibility of hitching a ride from someone meeting the train hangs in the air, or if you are more organised there is now a bookable minibus. ❶ Heading up the wide forestry track through the fresh-scented spruce, you soon leave the first complex of plantations. A real sense of anticipation builds as you take to the open moor and get a first glimpse of the granite-capped Ben Alder plateau far in the distance. This view becomes even more impressive when you reach the southern shore of Loch Ericht, where your gaze is drawn straight down the loch towards Dalwhinnie, over 15 miles away.

❸ Once you commit to crossing the vehicle bridge over the Cam Chriochan and stride out up the lochside, you become keenly aware of how remote this territory is. As the massif of Ben Alder slowly looms larger, civilisation seems increasingly far away. The track weaves its way between the water's edge and the boundary fence of another conifer plantation, before abruptly stopping just over two miles from Alder Bay. A faint path continues on, winding its way through the trees above the shoreline, then you climb up the rocky knoll of An Grianan through a stand of larches. Finally the bothy comes into view, a cheering sight after a solid few hours walking with a fully laden rucksack.

The cottage was originally named after Joseph McCook, a deerstalker and forester who resided here with his family for over 40 years. After he retired to Newtonmore just before World War I, increasing numbers of walkers, fishermen and poachers took refuge in the empty building, though for a time it was also used as a bunk house for navvies constructing the Loch Ericht dam. Rumours about the bothy being haunted began to circulate during this period, including the blatant untruth that McCook had hanged himself from the rafters. These stories were concocted by the head stalker Finlay McIntosh and his novelist friend Ian Macpherson in an attempt to frighten away unwanted visitors. Others accounts have reinforced the idea of a ghostly presence in the bothy, and the night-time creaks can certainly evoke irrational fears in the exhausted, lone walker. Another less sinister story attached to the bothy concerns Bonnie

LOCH ERICHT

BEN ALDER COTTAGE

Prince Charlie. In a jumble of rocks a little way up the hillside, a hideout called Cluny's Cage was allegedly where the prince sought refuge for a time after the Battle of Culloden.

Be sure to start out early for the journey on to Corrour station so you do not miss the evening train. In Gilbert's account in *Classic Walks*, he tackles the mountain plateau before dropping down to the Uisge Labhair, but this is a serious undertaking when encumbered with a heavy pack. ❹ The low-level option follows the old stalkers' track up to the Bealach Cumhann, the path contouring beneath Sgairneach Mhòr, before ascending up to the saddle. As you climb, take in the fine view of the Alder Burn meandering down to the loch with Ben Lawers and the Perthshire hills just visible on the horizon. Once through the gap, the trail continues round to the steep pass of the Bealach Dubh, beneath the imposing bulk of Ben Alder. ❺ Instead of continuing on this route, veer off and descend steeply to the Uisge Labhair through an obstacle course of moraines, peat hags and heather. Cross to the far bank of the river, then follow an obvious trail that eventually leads down to a footbridge close to Corrour shooting lodge. If the river is in spate, you may have to wander quite a way upstream before finding a safe place to wade through the channel. ❻ There are a number of fording points to negotiate (these are marked on the 1:25,000 map; the most significant being the Allt Feith a' Mheallain), before you reach the rounded boulders near the confluence of the Uisge Labhair and the River Ossian, as it cascades north towards Glen Spean.

❼ After the intensity of traversing the wild terrain from the bothy, the walk down to the beautiful, tree-lined Loch Ossian is far more relaxing and straightforward. From the footbridge you can choose between tracks leading down and round the northern or southern sides of the loch. They are of similar distance and meet up just beyond the low, corrugated buildings of the Loch Ossian Youth Hostel, hidden within a stand of copper-coloured birch trees. ❽ On the final mile to the station, your focus is firmly on the café, hoping it will be open with enough time for tea and cake before the train rumbles into view. Conspicuous among passengers dressed for the high street in your crumpled outdoor kit, it can feel as if you have been parachuted in from a different realm! Yet any embarrassment is easily offset by an enormous sense of satisfaction as you head home.

Notes: The route assumes you make your own way to the start point at Bridge of Gaur by bus or lift from Rannoch station, if you arrive by train. Walking the whole way to Ben Alder Cottage from the station involves a challenging trek through to the end of Loch Ericht via Lochan Sròn Smeur and Lochan Loin nan Donnlaich, before picking up the track running up the western shore of the loch.

BEALACH CUMHANN

LOCH OSSIAN

DIRECTIONS

Day 1 Bridge of Gaur to Ben Alder Cottage

1 From the car park by the sawmill at Bridge of Gaur, head up the track, through a forestry plantation and out onto the moor. At the corner of the next plantation (NN 488 588), either continue along the track through the conifers, or follow a path along the boundary fence to join the original track further towards Loch Ericht.
5.5km/3.5 miles

2 Continue down to the S end of the loch, passing a locked estate building, then cross a vehicle bridge over the Cam Chriochan (NN 481 609), before heading up the western shoreline.
3.5km/2.25 miles

3 When the track stops abruptly (NN 491 654), continue on an obvious trail along the shore, cutting inland before the rocky promontory, An Grianan. A little further on cross the Alder Burn via the footbridge and you soon reach the bothy (NN 498 680), after fording the stream outside it.
4.5km/2.75 miles

Day 2 Ben Alder Cottage to Corrour Station

4 Head up the stalkers' path up to the Bealach Cumhann, 655m.
5km/3 miles

5 Leave the trail as it contours round to Bealach Dubh, descending steeply across open ground to the Uisge Labhair.
0.75km/0.5 miles

6 Cross the river (in spate you may have to head upstream to find safe passage) and follow an obvious trail down the N bank to a footbridge (NN 417 701). There are a number of fords to negotiate marked on 1: 25,000 map, the most significant being the Allt Feith a' Mheallain (NN 429 704), ¾ of a mile before the bridge.
4.7km/3 miles

7 Once back across to the S side of the Uisge Labhair, take the path L down to Corrour shooting lodge and continue round the S side of Loch Ossian, to a junction leading off to the Loch Ossian Youth Hostel.
5.7km/3.5 miles

8 From here it is an easy mile to Corrour station.
1.6km/1 mile

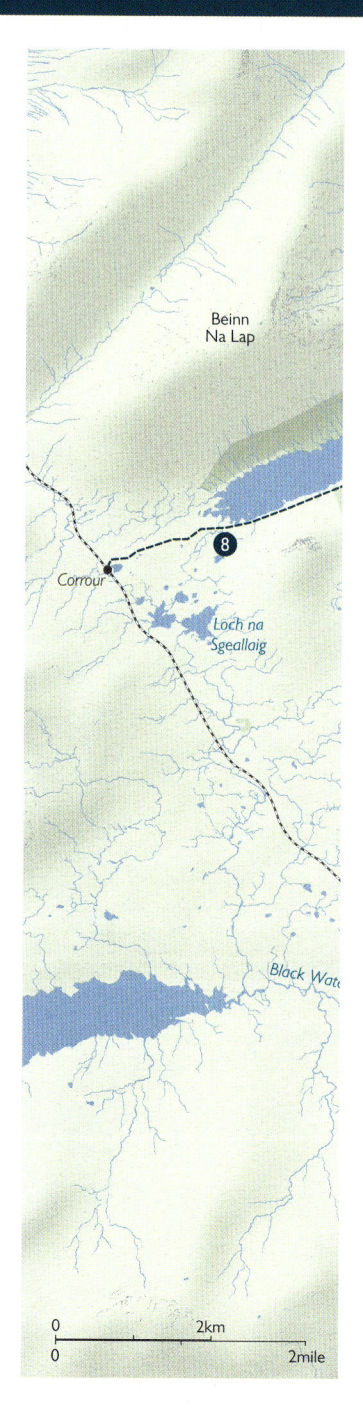

WALK 13 A BEN ALDER CROSSING FROM RANNOCH TO CORROUR STATION

133

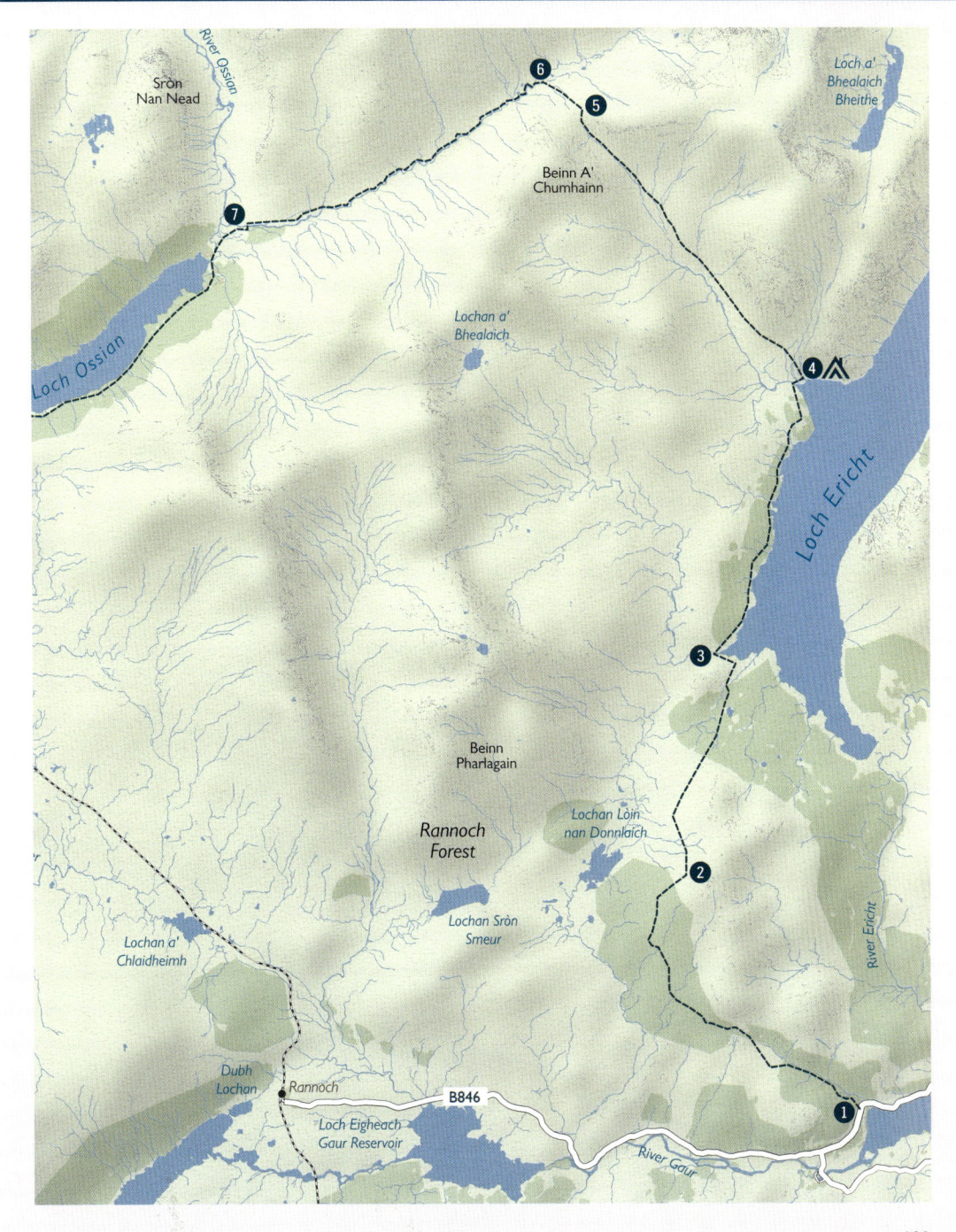

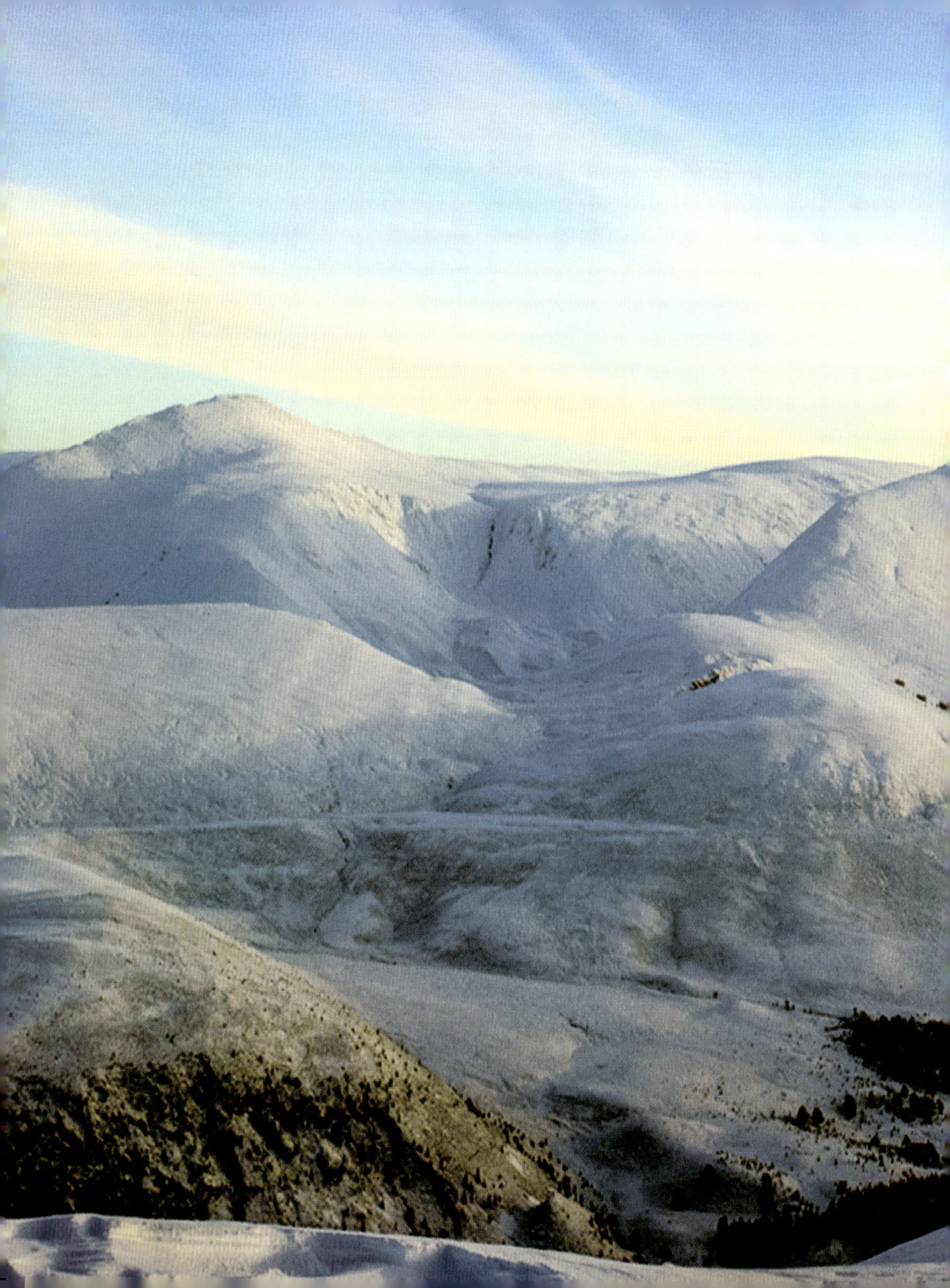

EASTERN HIGHLANDS

BEGINNING THE CLIMB OF MEALL A BHUACHAILLE FROM RYVOAN

WALK 14

MEALL A' BHUACHAILLE & RYVOAN BOTHY

Classic circular walk in the Cairngorms National Park, through the beautiful Scots pines of the Queen's Forest to Ryvoan Bothy, followed by panoramic views from the summit of Meall a' Bhuachaille.

Overlooking the tranquil waters of Loch Morlich in the Glenmore Forest Park, Meall a' Bhuachaille (Shepherd's Hill), is the highest point of a line of three carefully rounded triangular peaks which stand apart from the main Cairngorm plateau, close to the outdoor Mecca of Aviemore. With well-managed paths and simple navigation, the route provides a perfect introduction to the exceptional beauty and raw energy of the high montane habitat that is a unique feature of this vast National Park – the largest protected area in the whole of the UK.

The walk starts at the road end just beyond the national outdoor training centre at Glenmore Lodge. ❶ Follow the blue and orange waymarks along a wide gravel track, which traces the route of the old Thieves Road over from Nethy Bridge, once used by raiders smuggling cattle south to Perthshire. Within minutes of leaving the hubbub of Glenmore, and the traffic zipping up and down the Cairngorm ski road, you will find sanctuary among the venerable old Scots pines leading up into the narrow confines of the Ryvoan Pass. The dense trees soon thin out, revealing the impressive pyramid of Creag Loisgte, above the banks of the fast-flowing Allt na Fèithe Duibhe. Regrowth of the natural tree line has been encouraged on its steep eastern slopes, the heartening sight of new saplings visible all the way to the skyline.

INFORMATION

MAPS: LR 36 Grantown & Aviemore, Explorer OL57 Cairn Gorm & Aviemore.
START/END GRID REF: NH 989 095. Small parking area just beyond Glenmore Lodge. Pay-and-display car park by Glenmore Visitor Centre NH 977 097.
DISTANCE: 9km/5.5 miles
TIME: 3.5–4.5 hours
ASCENT: 570m
SUMMITS: Meall a' Bhuachaille (Corbett), 810m
NAVIGATION: Easy.
TERRAIN: Easy. Track and well defined paths.
DIFFICULTY: Easy.
PUBLIC TRANSPORT: ScotRail service from Glasgow/Edinburgh–Perth–Inverness and Scottish Citylink Coach Service M90/M91 Glasgow/Edinburgh–Perth–Inverness stop at Aviemore. Stagecoach Highlands service 31 Aviemore to Cairngorm Ski Centre.
SPECIAL NOTES: Open throughout the year. The bothy sits in an RSPB nature reserve so please abide by restrictions during nesting time.

137

WALK 14 MEALL A' BHUACHAILLE & RYVOAN BOTHY

RYVOAN BOTHY

Ryvoan Pass was carved into a deep, V shaped groove by glacial meltwater at the end the last ice age, isolating Meall a' Bhuachaille from the rest of the Cairngorm massif. As you approach its narrowest point, you reach An Lochan Uaine (Little Green Lochan), an enchanting teardrop lake set below the precipitous granite scree of Creag nan Gall. The genuinely startling turquoise tint of the water is said to be the handiwork of the fairies who wash their clothes in the crystal-clear pool. The scientific explanation of how the lake was formed is far more prosaic: a huge block of ice buried by the retreating glacier eventually melted to leave a kettle-shaped depression that subsequently filled with rainwater. ❷ The lake is a short detour down some steps from the main track, and it is well worth stopping for a moment's contemplation before continuing on to the head of the pass. When the track forks take the left-hand path signposted to Nethy Bridge, and within five hundred yards you reach Ryvoan (Ruighe a Bhothain, Sheil of the Bothy), one of the Eastern Highlands' most popular open shelters. A former croft vacated in the late-1800s, the bothy is now consolidated within a single room, with a steeply pitched roof, designed to prevent snow building up in the long winter months.

❸ Leaving the comfort of the bothy, climb the well-engineered stone steps that zigzag up the eastern flank of Meall a' Bhuachaille; the strength-sapping gradient finally relents at the 700m contour. Taking a breather, look north over the soothing, green expanse of Abernethy Forest stretching away to the wide floodplain of Strathspey. While on the far side of the pass,

AN LOCHAN UAINE

ABERNETHY FOREST

WALK 14 MEALL A' BHUACHAILLE & RYVOAN BOTHY

NORTHERN CORRIES

LOCH MORLICH

your gaze naturally follows the curving ridge line of Màm Suim and Sròn a' Cha-no that leads on to the summit of Cairn Gorm, and the Northern Corries. The top of Meall a' Bhuachaille is soon within reach, a crude stone shelter built into the large summit cairn which offers protection from the harsh, prevailing westerly winds. In favourable weather, the water of Loch Morlich twinkles far below in the sunlight, its shores enveloped by a blanket of spruce that covers the lower slopes of the plateau across to Rothiemurchus. ❹ Follow the obvious path off the mountain down to the bealach above Coire Chondlaich, where the trail carries on along the ridge line to Creagan Gorm and Craiggowrie. Instead, take the path that heads left down towards Glenmore and eventually enters the forest, then follow a small burn down towards the visitors centre. As the track splits take the right fork down to the roadside, where you'll find a welcoming café. ❺ The return to Glenmore Lodge is a 10-minute walk along the single-track road past the reindeer centre. An accessible route and a fine day out.

DIRECTIONS

1 From the car park just beyond Glenmore Lodge (NH 989 905), take the track R heading NE to An Lochan Uaine.
1.6km/1 mile

2 Continue up to Ryvoan Pass where the track forks (NJ 003 111). Take the L branch signposted to Nethy Bridge. The bothy is soon within sight (NJ 006 115).
1.2km/0.75 miles

3 From the bothy, make a steep ascent on the path that zigzags up the eastern flank of Meall a' Bhuachaille (NH 991 115). The gradient eases on the approach to the summit cairn.
2km/1.25 miles

4 Descend W to the bealach at 624m, then take the path on L that drops back down to Glenmore. Enter a forestry plantation, and follow the W bank of the Allt Coire Chondlaich. Where the track splits take the R fork and reach the Glenmore Visitor Centre.
2.8km/1.75 miles

5 If returning to the car park, turn L along a track, then quickly L again up the single-track road signposted to Glenmore Lodge.
1.5km/1 mile

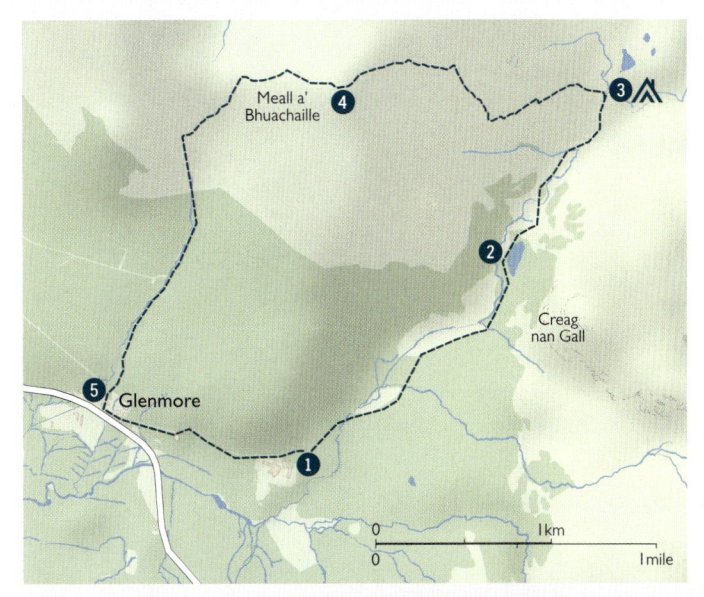

HUTCHISON MEMORIAL HUT & CREAGAN A' CHOIRE ETCHACHAN

WALK 15

BEN MACDUI VISITING BOB SCOTT'S BOTHY & HUTCHISON MEMORIAL HUT

Exceptional mountain walk through long, atmospheric glens and beautiful pine woods to the subarctic summit of Ben Macdui, the highest point of the Cairngorm plateau, from the Linn of Dee.

INFORMATION

MAPS: LR 36 Grantown & Aviemore/43 Braemar & Blair Atholl, Explorer OL57 Cairn Gorm & Aviemore, OL58 Braemar, Tomintoul & Glen Avon.
START/END GRID REF: NO 063 898. National Trust car park at Linn of Dee, pay-and-display (members free).
DISTANCE: 32km/20 miles
TIME: 10-12 hours. 7-9 hours from Bob Scott's Bothy.
TOTAL ASCENT: 1440m
SUMMITS: Ben Macdui (Munro), 1309m; Stob Coire Sputan Dearg (Munro Top), 1249m; Sròn Riach (Munro Top), 1113m.
NAVIGATION: Challenging on summit in misty conditions. Avoid steep cliffs on descent.
TERRAIN: Straightforward/challenging. Track and well defined paths, faint trail to summit.
DIFFICULTY: Challenging
PUBLIC TRANSPORT: Stagecoach Bluebird service 201/203 Aberdeen to Braemar. At present no bus service from Braemar on to the Linn of Dee.
SPECIAL NOTES: Mar Lodge Estate National Nature Reserve allows wild camping (no campfires). Dogs on leads. Bothies open all year round.

Hidden behind the huge granite ramparts of Am Monadh Ruadh (The Red Mountains), at the heart of vast wilderness stretching from Strathspey to Deeside, stands the domed peak of Ben Macdui, Britain's second-highest mountain after Ben Nevis. Simply translated as 'Hill of Macduff', after the Earls of Fife who once held sway here, the summit was held in great esteem by locals as the highest in the land. When, in 1847, the Ordnance Survey established that Ben Nevis was taller, they were aghast and mounted an ambitious campaign to build a giant cairn on the hilltop. Fortunately, this faltered for lack of funds.

Although generally benign in midsummer, the high plateau of Ben Macdui has a fearsome reputation in the winter season, which can begin as early as September and can last through until May. Exposed to the elemental forces of wind and ice, and often cloaked in seemingly impenetrable cloud, this can be a wild, unforgiving place as well as an eerie environment that challenges the senses. In mist or towards nightfall, you can understand why the enduring legend of Am Fear Liath Mòr (the Big Grey Man) has persisted over the years. Haunting the top of the mountain, the spectre is said to induce unease and even panic. The myth entered popular folklore in the mid-1920s, when esteemed academic and mountaineer, Norman Collie, admitted to having staggered blindly off the summit 30 years previously. He recounted hearing an eerie 'crunch, crunch' sound behind

WALK 15 BEN MACDUI VISITING BOB SCOTT'S BOTHY & HUTCHISON MEMORIAL HUT

LUIBEG BURN

him, though he could see nothing in the mist. Collie was also a renowned practical joker, but over the years many other strange tales came to light and were collated in Scottish historian Affleck Gray's fascinating study, *The Big Grey Man of Ben MacDhui*.

Any ascent of Ben Macdui can feel daunting, but the experience of traversing the desolate, rock-shattered plateau leaves you wide-eyed and exhilarated. The consistent high altitude across the Cairngorms massif is the closest the UK comes to experiencing the Arctic, and, although on first inspection the terrain appears barren, dwarf pines and flattened branches of juniper and willow creep across the wind-blasted ground. In summer, shy dotterel and more extrovert snow buntings (often seen looking for lunch crumbs at the summit cairn) are welcome visitors. The northerly ascent from the ski centre at Cairngorm Mountain Resort, up over Cairn Gorm and across the plateau, is the most straightforward route up the mountain. Approaching from Deeside to the south is far longer, but the opportunity to experience more of the Cairngorms' majestic scenery is not to be missed. The irresistible combination of mighty rivers, sweeping glens, high lochans and Caledonian Forest draws visitors back time and again.

Leaving Braemar and travelling up the winding, single-track road to towards the Linn of Dee, the braided, spruce-lined river valley opens up invitingly. In the distance, the Cairngorm plateau seems like a thin, grey pencil line above the softer, shaded purples of the outlying hills. ❶ From the National Trust car park take the well-trodden path signposted to Glen Lui through the woods, and along a section of boardwalk, turning left onto the main track heading into the interior. As you continue towards Derry Lodge, the high summits begin to feel a little closer, though Ben Macdui will remain out of sight until well into the walk. ❷ Turn left again after the bridge over Lui Water and after a couple of easy miles, the old lodge appears in the distance, surrounded by the first pockets of venerable Scots pines. Sadly the building remains shuttered and rather forlorn, recent plans to turn it into a hostel yet to come to fruition. Before the lodge, down by the riverbank and hidden by a heather-topped terrace, lies Bob Scott's Bothy, the club hut of a loyal, independent band of outdoor folk and a great base camp if you want to split the walk into two days.

From the lodge, wander down past the Mountain Rescue Post to the confluence of Luibeg Burn and Derry Burn, where handsome swathes of mature Scots pines hug the lower slopes of Derry Cairngorm and Sgòr Dubh.

❸ Cross the metal footbridge over the Derry Burn, and take the path signposted to Coylumbridge and Aviemore via the Lairig Ghru. It continues through the last pockets of pines

BOB SCOTT'S BOTHY

CAIRN TOUL & THE DEVIL'S POINT

VIEW NORTH-EAST OVER LOCH ETCHACHAN

WALK 15 BEN MACDUI VISITING BOB SCOTT'S BOTHY & HUTCHISON MEMORIAL HUT

SRÒN RIACH RIDGE

into Gleann Laoigh Bheag, to the mysteriously named Robbers' Copse (Preas nam Meirleach).

4 Approaching the Luibeg Bridge, leave the main path and take a smaller trail which contours below Carn Crom, and leads into the upper reaches of the glen, where the curving ridge line of Sròn Riach soon comes into view. Carefully ford the stream that tumbles down from Coire Sputan Dearg and ascend the ridge, quickly gaining height. From the rocky summit of Sròn Riach, the commanding bulk of Ben Macdui finally reveals itself, while further to the west, the spectacular sculpted coires of Cairn Toul dwarf its lowly neighbour The Devil's Point.

5 The most direct route to the summit plateau is a scramble up the steep boulder field close to the rim of Coire Sputan Dearg and on to Stob Coire Sputan Dearg, where there is a fine view below to Lochan Uaine. Alternatively, follow a faint path contouring left round to Caochan na Cothaiche, and tackle the steep, grassy slope leading up to the spring of the Tailor Burn (Allt Clach nan Taillear). Once on the plateau from either route, locate the path leading up from Loch Etchachan that heads west up to the Sappers' Bothy (marked as a ruin on the 1:25,000 map). The shelter was built for the surveyors who took measurements back in the 1840s to establish the mountain's height. In misty conditions, or with snow lying on the ground, it is best to take a bearing because, unlike the path across from Cairn Gorm, there are no cairns to guide you. With some relief, finally reach the summit where there is a large cairn, trig pillar and viewfinder. If the weather has been kind, a glorious tableau is revealed around you above the edge of the wide plateau rim: Cairn Toul and the remote coires of Braeriach to the west, round to Cairn Gorm, and east through waves of undulating granite hills to Ben Rinnes and Aberdeenshire. And hopefully there will be no encounter with the Big Grey Man!

6 The return leg begins by backtracking down the path towards Creagan a' Choire Etchachan, skirting the northern rim of Coire Sputan Dearg, and down to Loch Etchachan. In low visibility it is easy to lose your way and trend north into the Garbh Uisge Mòr on the east side of Càrn Etchachan where there is a precipitous dead end above the sheer-sided Shelter Stone Crag. Look out for the edge of Coire Sputan Dearg as

WALK 15 BEN MACDUI VISITING BOB SCOTT'S BOTHY & HUTCHISON MEMORIAL HUT

it suddenly appears (the teetering scree at the mouth of Narrow Gully is particularly treacherous), only relaxing when you reach the loch – the highest of its size in the UK. Here a wide scree path continues down into Coire Etchachan, where the Hutchison Memorial Hut provides a welcome refuge. Previously a glacially cold endurance challenge through the winter months, the bothy now boasts insulation and a stove; it feels more like a sauna than a fridge once a fire is lit. ❼ After a brief refreshment stop, head down to the bridge over the Coire Etchachan Burn before joining the path which descends from the Fords of Avon. The final obstacle heading into the heart of Glen Derry is crossing the powerful Glas Allt Mor, which could be a problem in times of spate. Once across, continue down the wide floodplain, passing two plantations of Scots pines, and finally reaching the mature forest. A path down across to the west bank of the river takes a more circuitous route back, but the bridge spanning the burn has been out of action since 2018 so it is best avoided. The main track contours above the valley floor before dropping back down to the outpost at Derry Lodge, and finally, exhausted yet elated by the expedition, you arrive back at Linn of Dee.

Notes: This is a demanding route, in one of Britain's most hostile environments. Deteriorating weather conditions can be seriously compromising on the summit plateau where expert navigational skills are essential. Ben Macdui is surrounded by very steep ground to the west and to the east the vertical cliffs of Coire Sputan Dearg need to be avoided on the descent. In winter, blizzards, white-outs and gale force winds can make the summit very hazardous. Bob Scott's Bothy is a classic staging post for Cairngorm expeditions, if you want to split the walk into two days. An alternative unofficial campsite can be found by the Derry Burn (NO 041 935), beyond the Derry Lodge.

STOB COIRE ETCHACHAN

GLEN DERRY

DIRECTIONS

1 From the Linn of Dee car park take the forest path signposted to Glen Lui, which cuts across to the unmetalled access road to the Mountain Rescue Post at Derry Lodge. Turn L onto the track, heading N to a vehicle bridge over Lui Water.
1.9km/1.25 miles

2 Cross the bridge, turn L and continue on to Derry Lodge. Just before the Caledonian pines surrounding the lodge, a path leads R down to Bob Scott's Bothy (NO 042 932).
3.2km/2 miles

3 From Derry Lodge take the footbridge over the Derry Burn and turn L onto a path signposted to Coylumbridge and Aviemore via the Lairig Ghru. Quickly join a track from the ford below the cottage at Luibeg and head on up Gleann Laoigh Bheag. Leave the main path (NO 019 938), turning R immediately before a forestry plantation, following the course of the Luibeg Burn.
2.8km/1.75 miles

4 Contour above the Luibeg Bridge into the upper reaches of the glen, fording the burn (NO 011 957), before ascending the curving S ridge of Sròn Riach to a small summit cairn at 1113m.
4.8km/3 miles

5 From the cairn, either scramble up the steep boulder field to Stob Coire Sputan Dearg, or follow vague path contouring L round to Caochan na Cothaiche, and up the steep slope to the spring of the Allt Clach nan Taillear. Once on the plateau from either route, locate the path leading up from Loch Etchachan and onto the summit of Ben Macdui.
2.1km/1.25 miles

6 Take the path back towards Creagan a' Choire Etchachan, avoiding N rim of Coire Sputan Dearg, and down to Loch Etchachan. Continue down into Coire Etchachan, to Hutchison Memorial Hut (NO 023 998).
4.4km/2.75 miles

7 Make your way down to the bridge over Coire Etchachan Burn before joining the path coming down from the Fords of Avon. Ford the Glas Allt Mor (NO 036 987) (which could be an obstacle in times of spate) and continue through Glen Derry back to Derry Lodge.
7.6km/4.75 miles

8 Retrace your steps to Linn of Dee.
5km/3.25 miles

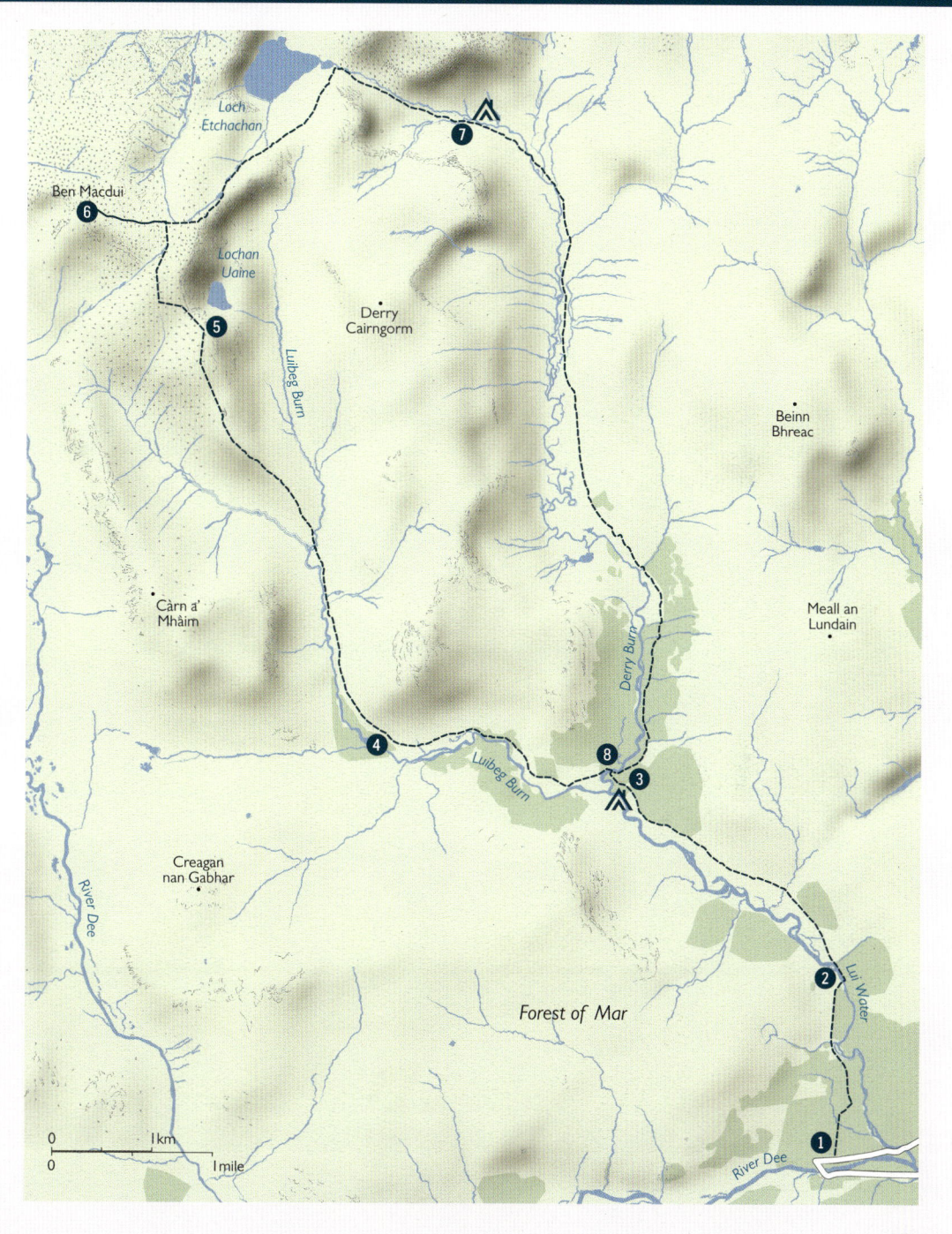

WALK 15 BEN MACDUI VISITING BOB SCOTT'S BOTHY & HUTCHISON MEMORIAL HUT

JOCK'S ROAD & THE ALLT AN LOCH

WALK 16

CALLATER STABLES & LOCH KANDER

An easy-paced walk in the Cairngorms National Park, through Glen Callater to tiny, jewel-like Loch Kander at the head of the valley, with a bothy stop at the halfway point.

The Callater beat of the Invercauld Estate cuts a deep, decisive line through the high plateau of Lochnagar and the Glenshee hills, south of the attractive Highland village of Braemar. With its busy river, elongated loch, and surprisingly wild interior, Glen Callater rises to a finale of dark, precipitous crags and an impressive coire containing a tranquil, deep-set lochan. Once a busy thoroughfare used by drovers herding sheep over the pass to the seasonal markets of Glen Clova, this unobtrusive glen was also the scene of a bitter dispute over land access in the late-19th century, which resulted in legislation re-enforcing Scotland's proud tradition of the right to roam.

❶ The signpost at Auchallater simply states 'Public Path to Clova', giving little indication of the significance of 'Jock's Road', which links Glen Clunie with Glen Doll. The Jock in question was reputed to be John Winters, a vociferous campaigner for the Scottish Rights of Way Society. He gave evidence in the Court of Session in Edinburgh against Duncan Macpherson, who bought the Invercauld Estate in 1885 and barred access to the land. Macpherson lost the case, which went to the House of Lords and was so expensive that both he and the Society were declared bankrupt. The judgement led to the passing of the Scottish Rights of Way Act in 1894, the most important piece of legislation for walkers until the 2003 Land Reform Act further clarified public rights of access.

INFORMATION

MAPS: LR 43 Braemar & Blair Atholl, Explorer OL52 Glen Shee & Braemar.
START/END GRID REF: NO 156 883. Car park at Auchallater farm on the A93, 2.5 miles S of Braemar.
DISTANCE: 19km/12 miles
TIME: 6-8 hours
TOTAL ASCENT: 490m
NAVIGATION: Easy.
TERRAIN: Straightforward. Track, well defined path, faint trail. One stream crossing, potentially boggy path up to Loch Kander.
DIFFICULTY: Straightforward.
PUBLIC TRANSPORT: No bus service directly to the start of the walk. Stagecoach Bluebird service 201 from Aberdeen to Braemar. Stagecoach bus service 71 Blairgowrie to the Spittal of Glenshee.
SPECIAL NOTES: Bothy is open all year round, no restrictions. No stove or fireplace.

WALK 16 CALLATER STABLES & LOCH KANDER

❷ Walking up the glen above the cascading river, the signs of estate management are much in evidence, continuing traditions that have been upheld over the generations. In the spring, the annual muirburn (controlled burning) leaves a distinctive patchwork of ground cover of differing heights across the mountainside. By clearing small areas of old, woody heather, fresh new growth can emerge along with a flush of plants such as bilberry or blueberry. These are a key food source for red grouse, deer, and mountain hares, as well as the resident population of golden plover, ptarmigan and curlews. Reaching Lochcallater Lodge, there is a paddock set aside for Highland garrons, the sturdy ponies used to transport deer carcasses off the hill during the stalking season. Once they were housed in the stables but this is now a well-maintained bothy. Look inside and you'll see floorboards covering the old cobblestones, while skylights in the roof lighten the gloomy interior.

Now a little local knowledge comes into play. ❸ Instead of carrying on round the east side of the loch along the route of Jock's Road, take the estate track that undulates above the shore on the western side. Pike and trout can often be seen darting in the shallows as you head towards the flats beyond the loch, where a pony path (not marked on the map) continues upstream. Taking this track avoids a precarious wade through the Allt an Loch on the approach to Coire Loch Kander, which is difficult to cross when the water is running high. Beyond the loch the atmosphere of the glen changes and the landscape begins to feel much more remote as you pass below the steep, boulder-strewn slopes of Creag an-Fhir-shaighe (Rocks of the Arrow Maker). ❹ The path hugs the edge of the narrowing floodplain beneath an obvious lateral moraine, crossing one small stream before reaching two straining posts used to tie up the garrons during the stalking season. Proceed up an ATV track which continues over the steepening ground, before petering out as the Allt Loch Kander comes into view. ❺ Look out for a large triangular boulder just before the stream, which marks the start of the meandering path leading up to the coire basin.

As you climb, you begin to appreciate the scale of the scene, set off by an impressive waterfall, Eas Allt Briste-amhaich, which plunges down the edge of the north-facing cliffs, mischievously referred to as Breakneck Falls. Once over the coire lip, Loch Kander is finally revealed – a calming presence below the imposing buttresses of mineral-rich mica schist that tower above the water's edge. In the summer months the slopes are filled with sedges, the crags with hardy alpine plants. In winter, snow patches linger in the shadows and the lochan itself is often frozen into a solid sheet of ice. It is possible to clamber up the lower rocks beyond the loch to gain a superior vantage point, before the slow descent back down to the flats, the bothy and Auchallater.

Notes: A shorter alternative to the walk to Loch Kander is to traverse round Loch Callater from the bothy. However, this involves fording the river at the head of the loch, which could be difficult in times of spate. Distance: 13km/8 miles, 4–5 hours, 200m of ascent.

EAS ALLT BRISTE-AMHAICH

LOCH KANDER

WALK 16 CALLATER STABLES & LOCH KANDER

LOCHCALLATER LODGE & CALLATER STABLES

LOCH CALLATER

DIRECTIONS

1 From the car park at Auchallater Farm, take the track signposted to Clova, through a locked gate and up into Glen Callater. Continue on this winding path above the Callater Burn to a vehicle bridge (NO 163 862).
2.5km/1.5 miles

2 Once across the bridge continue along track, ignoring the path heading R back over the river towards Bealach Buidhe, and after another mile reach Lochcallater Lodge and the bothy (NO 178 845).
2.75km/1.75 miles

3 Head down from the lodge to a bridge over the burn by the outflow of Loch Callater and proceed round the SW side to the end of the loch, ignoring a track on R leading up onto the shoulder of Carn an Tuirc.
1.7km/1 mile

4 Follow a faint path across the floodplain of Allt na Loch, crossing a small stream after half a mile (NO 192 827). Continue on to Allt Loch Kander.
1.2km/0.75 miles

5 From a distinctive triangular boulder just before the stream, head up a faint path to Coire Loch Kander and the loch.
1.2km/0.75 miles

6 Return by the same route.

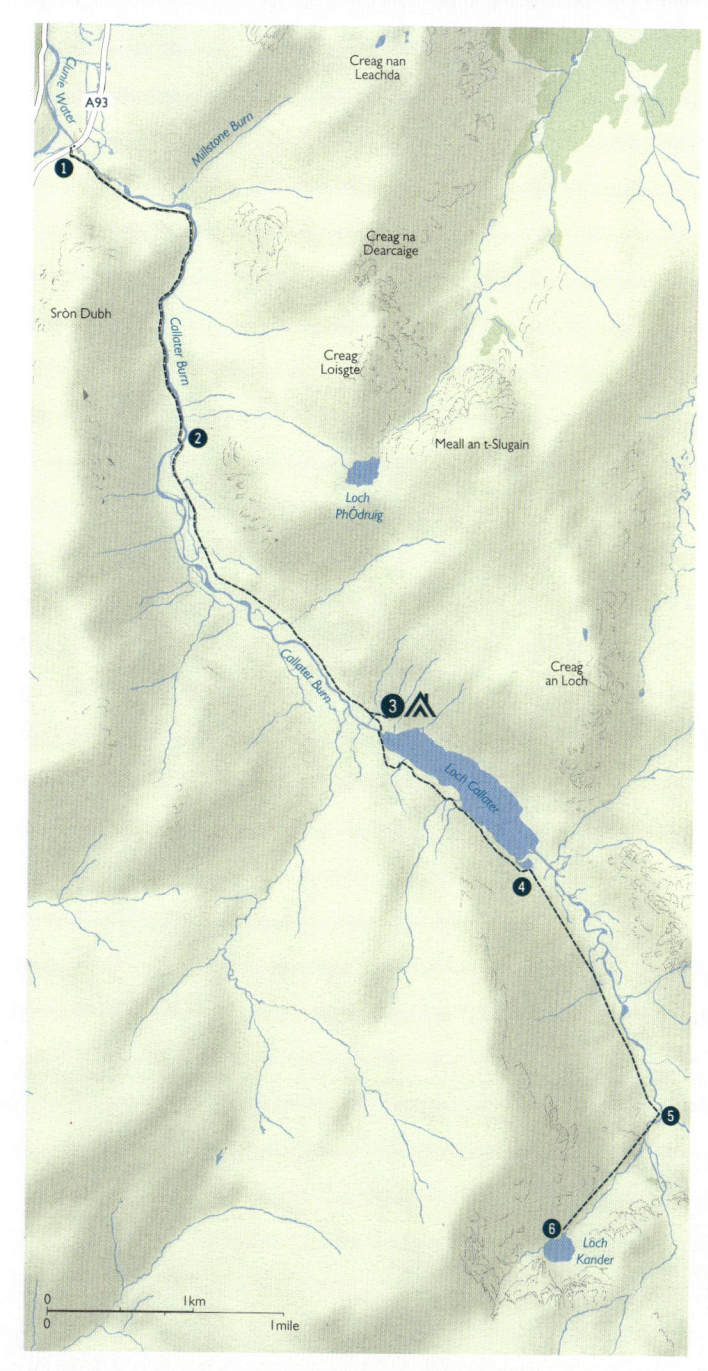

157

SUMMIT OF LOCHNAGAR, CAC CARN BEAG

WALK 17

LOCHNAGAR FROM BALMORAL & GELDER SHIEL STABLES

An adventurous round of Lochnagar's awe-inspiring north-east corrie from Gelder Shiel Stables, with grandstand views of the impressive crags towering over the shadowy loch which gives the mountain its name.

Rising nobly above Royal Deeside, on the edge of the sprawling Mounth Plateau, Lochnagar is one of the most celebrated and popular hills in the Cairngorms National Park. The mountain is the focal point of the southern quarter of this vast, protected region, its most prominent feature a huge amphitheatre of fractured granite buttresses that inspired Lord Byron's rousing poem of 1807, *Lachin Y Gair*. The last line exclaims: 'Oh for the crags that are wild and majestic! The steep frowning glories of the dark Loch na Garr.'

The main face of this crescent-shaped, glaciated coire has a northerly aspect, and consequently remains in near shadow for most of the year. Its deep-set gullies often hold snow well into early summer. Since the early days of Scottish mountaineering, the vertiginous crags have attracted a succession of pioneer climbers, from Harold Raeburn in the 1890s, to the prolific and charismatic Tom Patey, a stalwart Aberdonian, who made a number of first ascents here in the 1950s. These routes remain true tests of mountaineering nerve and skill, especially in harsh winter conditions, which can occur at very short notice. Patey satirised Byron's text, referencing his own Himalayan expeditions in a jovial song: 'Masherbrum, Gasherbrum, Distegal Sar, They're very good training for Dark Lochnagar.'

Lochnagar derives from the Gaelic Lochan na Gaire (Loch of the Noisy Sound) a description of the tranquil lochan found at the base of the mighty cliffs. The plateau itself is also known as

INFORMATION

MAPS: LR 44 Ballater, Glen Clova & surrounding area, Explorer OL53 Lochnagar, Glen Muick & Glen Clova.
START/END GRID REF: NO 265 941. Parking E of road junction at Easter Balmoral.
DISTANCE: 21km/13 miles
TIME: 6–8 hours
TOTAL ASCENT: 1089m
SUMMITS: Lochnagar/Cac Carn Beag (Munro) 1115m; Cac Carn Mòr 1150m.
NAVIGATION: Straightforward.
TERRAIN: Straightforward. Track, well defined paths, faint trails.
DIFFICULTY: Straightforward in summer conditions; potentially challenging expedition in winter.
PUBLIC TRANSPORT: Stagecoach Bluebird service 201 from Aberdeen to Braemar stops at Crathie.
SPECIAL NOTES: Bothy is open throughout the year. Contact the Balmoral Estate (01339 742534) before planning a trip between 1st September and 20th October.

WALK 17 LOCHNAGAR FROM BALMORAL & GELDER SHIEL STABLES

Beinn Chiochan (Hill of the Breasts), a reference to the twin peaks that guard the mountain's eastern flanks, Meikle Pap and Little Pap. How the lochan's name came to denote the mountain remains a mystery, but it was already the convention when Byron penned his famous lines. A number of routes lead up to the summit, including a long approach from Glen Callater, and a meandering walk through the stately old pines of Ballochbuie Forest and out onto the open hillside, with the option of tackling the 'Stuic', a sporting scramble up the narrow arête above Loch nan Eun. The most well-trodden and unimaginative route heads in from Glen Muick up a straightforward track and onto the eastern slope of Meikle Pap, but the best way to experience the full splendour of the lochan and those fearsome crags is to approach from the north at Crathie, close to Balmoral Castle. From here, follow the climbers' path beyond Gelder Shiel Stables straight into the coire basin before heading up onto the main plateau.

Bypassing the throngs of curious sightseers and watchful security personnel outside the perimeter railings of the royal residence, continue round the South Deeside road to what is effectively the tradesmen's entrance at Easter Balmoral. Most of the traffic heading this way is destined for the Royal Lochnagar whisky distillery a little further up the glen, but do not get distracted. ❶ Head up by the delightful estate cottages, with their well-kept allotments, and past the last security checkpoint. Once through a wooden gate, enter into the Dubh-chlais (Dark Furrow), a steep-sided, tree-lined gap, before turning left as the track forks, quickly reaching the open moor. Immediately the sleek curves of Lochnagar draw your attention, the high crags in deep shadow above the wide, sculpted bowl of the coire. On either side of the rim, the sharpened points of Meikle Pap and the summit tor Cac Carn Beag are a watchful presence. After a mile or so of gentle walking, the track forks again, the main path climbing arrow-straight towards the gap between Conachcraig and the plateau. Instead, take the right turn, which dips down towards the Gelder Burn before heading up left to Gelder Shiel, the lodge and adjacent bothy sheltering within an exposed stand of Caledonian pines.

Many wistful reminiscences have been transcribed about this rather anonymous-looking refuge, housed in the old stables adjacent to the more venerable lodge. Once renowned as a cold, uncomfortable doss, the bothy has recently had a much-appreciated facelift, and the standard of accommodation is more in keeping with its royal association. It is remarkable that an open bothy still lies within potential earshot of any royal asides, but there is tight security when any party arrives from Balmoral. ❸ Set off across the Gelder Burn and up onto the undulating heather-clad moraines that sweep down from the Corrie of Lochnagar. The track stops abruptly at a grouse butt, but continue on the faint but persistent climbers' path that plots a steady course up towards the loch, contouring round the lower slopes of Creag Liath, before steepening in the final approach. Off-piste, away from the crowds, you become accustomed to

GELDER SHIEL LODGE & STABLES

VIEW NORTH DOWN GLEN GELDER TO BALMORAL

SUMMIT VIEW NORTH-WEST TO THE CAIRNGORM PLATEAU

the startled cries of black grouse, as they shoot skywards from the undergrowth, and the sight of mountain hares scurrying between the jumble of boulders piled up before the coire lip. Suddenly the dark, curving lochan appears, and above it the imposing crags. The sheer scale of the cliffs is difficult to comprehend unless there are climbers on the rock face. An enticing checklist of classic routes stands on parade, framed between Douglas-Gibson Gully on the left and the deep, cavernous Black Spout on the right, including the dizzying Eagle Ridge, Parallel Gullies A and B, the Tough-Brown Face, and Raeburn's Gully.

With the appropriate level of experience, the summit can be attained via the tottering scree shoot of the Black Spout or the boulder-strewn ridge of the Sneck o' Lochnagar, west of the main face. ❹ For the average walker, though, it is far easier to take a line from the outflow of the Lochnagar Burn up to the bealach south of Meikle Pap, scrambling over supersized granite blocks before ascending the steep, grassy slope. Looking back, there are spectacular views of the coire, which quickly feels a world away. ❺ Now follow the well-worn trail leading up from Glen Muick and continue on towards Cuidhe Cròm, before traversing round the edge of the cliffs to the small tor at Cac Carn Mòr, a granite pimple topped with a regulation cairn. In misty conditions it could easily be mistaken for the actual summit, Cac Carn Beag, a far larger protrusion 500 yards to the north, complete with trig pillar and an old, weathered viewfinder. Confusingly mor (big) and beag (small) are the wrong way round in terms of both height

and size. On a clear day, a splendid panorama unfolds: Ben Macdui and the heart of the Cairngorm plateau are steadfast in the north-west, while the huge whaleback of Beinn a'Bhùird and the distinctive tors of Ben Avon dominate the skyline above Deeside. Looking south there are no higher points between the Mounth and the English border, so you might be surprised to spot the Pentland Hills beyond Edinburgh and even make out the Cheviots on the horizon in the most advantageous conditions.

❻ To complete the circular walk back to Gelder Shiel, descend steeply north-west on a faint trail, carefully avoiding the wet slabs sliding away unnervingly due north of the summit. Quickly reach the bealach below Meall Coire na Saobhaidhe, and continue down the course of the Allt Coire na Saobhaidhe before seeking out the climbers' path back towards the grouse butts at the end of vehicle track. Take a last, lingering look back at the coire, content with the day's exertions, before retracing your route to Gelder Shiel and on to Easter Balmoral.

Notes: Before setting out on an ascent of Lochnagar, be mindful of the forecast. The weather conditions on the plateau can quickly deteriorate, making navigation particularly difficult, especially in winter conditions.

WALK 17 LOCHNAGAR FROM BALMORAL & GELDER SHIEL STABLES

THE CORRIE OF LOCHNAGAR

DIRECTIONS

❶ From the lay-by at Easter Balmoral, head L past estate cottages to a security checkpoint. Go through a gate into a forestry plantation, and after 500 yards, turn L where the track splits (NO 256 935).
1.2km/0.75 miles

❷ Reach the open moor and continue over gently rising ground to a second junction. The main track heads on towards Conachcraig, but instead turn R down to the Gelder Burn, then L up to the bothy (NO 258 900).
4km/2.5 miles

❸ From the bothy cross the Gelder Burn via a footbridge, and follow a track leading up towards the Lochnagar plateau

WALK 17 LOCHNAGAR FROM BALMORAL & GELDER SHIEL STABLES

until it terminates. Continue on a faint trail that contours round the lower slopes of Creag Liath before steadily rising up to the coire lip.
4km/2.5 miles

❹ Cross the outflow of Lochnagar and clamber over huge granite boulders before ascending the steep, open slopes to the bealach below Meikle Pap.
0.8km/0.5 miles

❺ Pick up the obvious well-made path from Glen Muick, which traverses round the top of the coire wall to the small granite tor, Cac Carn Mòr (NO 246 857). This could be mistaken for the top in misty conditions. In winter the cairns that line the route are often snow-covered and a substantial cornice overhangs the cliffs. Be wary of walking too close to the edge. After another 500 yards reach the true summit of Lochnagar, Cac Carn Beag (NO 244 861).
2.4km/1.5 miles

❻ Now descend steeply NW on a faint trail, avoiding wet slabs due N of the summit, to the bealach below Meall Coire na Saobhaidhe. Follow the Allt Coire na Saobhaidhe to pick up the climbers' path back to the vehicle track heading down to the bothy.
3.5km/2.25 miles

❼ Return to Easter Balmoral.
5.2km/3.25 miles

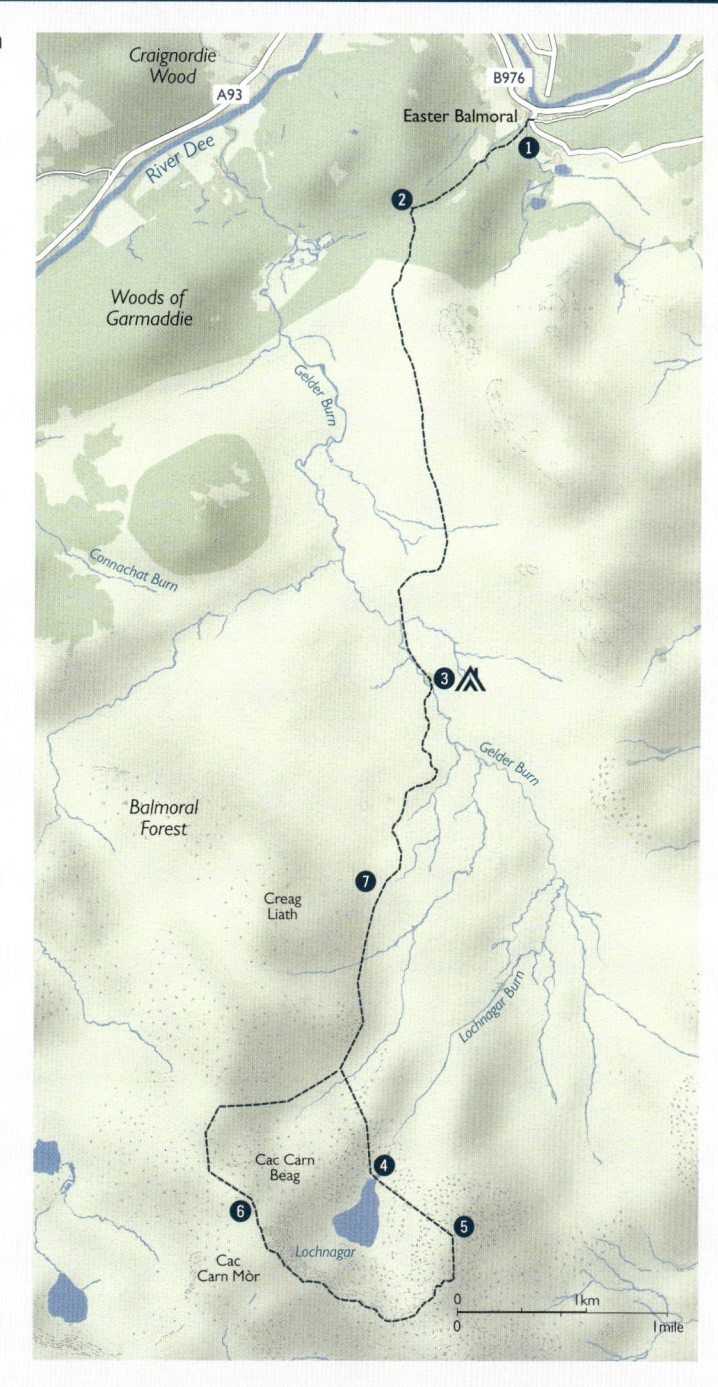

ALLT SCHEICHEACHAN BOTHY & BEINN DEARG

WALK 18

BEINN DEARG & ALLT SCHEICHEACHAN BOTHY

A rewarding ascent of Beinn Dearg, an outlying Munro on the southern boundary of the Cairngorms National Park above Blair Atholl, via the old stables at Allt Scheicheachan.

High above the gleaming fairy tale turrets of Blair Castle, and east of the dramatic, V-shaped fault line of Glen Tilt, stands the gently domed peak of Beinn Dearg (Red Hill), named after the distinctive pink granite boulders that adorn its upper slopes. Reached by an ancient byway leading onto the rarely visited Minigaig Pass, this quiet, understated peak offers a worthy challenge to the dedicated hillwalker. (A second Munro, also named Beinn Dearg, is found north of the Ullapool Road in Wester Ross.) The route follows a long, winding ascent through the Forest of Atholl to the edge of a wild expanse of unpopulated upland moor, stretching north to the distant mountain tops of Glen Feshie and the Cairngorms plateau.

Leaving behind the hum of traffic trundling through Glen Garry on the A9, head through Blair Atholl, turning right in the village centre and take the single-track road signposted to Menzie, Glen Fender and the Glen Tilt car park, which is located just beyond Old Bridge of Tilt. ❶ Heading off from the car park, turn left along the last stretch of metalled road, skirting the boundary wall of the extensive parkland surrounding Blair Castle. Tantalisingly, the sculpture gardens, follies and artificial lake in the castle grounds are just out of view. Continue straight on at the crossroads at Old Blair, following the waymarked trail of black arrows into the tightly knit woodland that hugs the banks of the Banvie Burn. Wander gently up through the dense canopy of larch and pine, keeping a lookout for the red squirrels who have regained a foothold here after years of decline. Ignore

INFORMATION

MAPS: LR Map 43 Braemar to Blair Atholl, Explorer OL51 Atholl Glen Tilt, Beinn Dearg & Carn nan Gabhar.
START/END GRID REF: NN 874 662. Glen Tilt car park.
DISTANCE: 29km/18 miles
TIME: 9–11 hours
TOTAL ASCENT: 1377m
SUMMITS: Beinn Dearg (Munro), 1008m
NAVIGATION: Straightforward
TERRAIN: Straightforward. Tracks and well defined path.
DIFFICULTY: Challenging.
PUBLIC TRANSPORT: ScotRail service from Glasgow/Edinburgh–Perth–Inverness and Scottish Citylink coach service M90/M91 Glasgow/Edinburgh–Perth–Inverness stops at Blair Atholl.
SPECIAL NOTES: Bothy is open throughout the year. Stalking between August and 20th October (excluding Sundays). For details phone the Atholl Estate on 01796 481740 or 01796 481355 or email pf@atholl-estates.co.uk. Information is also displayed on the noticeboard at Glen Tilt car park.

WALK 18 BEINN DEARG & ALLT SCHEICHEACHAN BOTHY

LADY MARCH CAIRN

ALLT SCHEICHEACHAN BOTHY

ALLT AN T-SEAPAIL

two tracks heading down to the burn, each signposted with a black waymarker, and continue on to a gate in the deer fence that marks the boundary of the Whim Plantation, and out onto the open hillside.

❷ Steadily ascend towards the Allt an t-Seapail, passing an ornate cairn dedicated to Lady March, marking the spot where she and a party from Blair Castle, including the 7th Duke of Atholl, enjoyed a picnic in the mid-19th century. The group built a small cairn to commemorate their day, and slowly added to the pile on successive visits. The formal pillar was built at a later date. Persevere through the heather-clad slopes, past numerous grouse butts, to a high point of 514m before dropping down to the bothy at Allt Scheicheachan. The small, one-room refuge is a fine objective in itself but makes an excellent refreshment stop if spirits are flagging. Here the ancient droving road heads on through Glen Bruar and crosses the Minigaig Pass. This was once the main route north to Badenoch and Strathspey before General Wade plotted his Military Road through Drumochter in the 1720s, after the first Jacobite uprising.

❸ After a brief break, take the stony track up the Allt Scheicheachan, crossing a ford immediately after the bothy, which could be an obstacle in times of spate. The riverbanks soon steepen alarmingly, and at a second ford, take the path leading up to Beinn Dearg which climbs sharply left, zigzagging across the shoulder of Meall Dubh nan Dearcag, before reaching a wide, rolling plateau. After a short section across the saturated peatbog, the final approach to the

BEINN DEARG

CARN LIATH & THE PERTHSHIRE HILLS

WALK 18 BEINN DEARG & ALLT SCHEICHEACHAN BOTHY

GLEN TILT

summit traverses a broad boulder-strewn ridge, up to a trig pillar and wind shelter. Looking north beyond the spring waters of the Tarf Water to the bleak territory beyond, you can truly appreciate the scale and remoteness of this wild, unforgiving land. Nothing but distant, seldom climbed hills are in view, before the grey outline of the high Cairngorms appears on the horizon.

❹ Backtracking south, head down to the Allt Scheicheachan, but instead of retracing your steps back to the bothy, cross the burn and take the track heading towards the Allt Slanaidh, overlooked by the sedate slopes of Beinn a' Chait. Descending towards Glen Tilt, a fine view opens up north-east towards Carn a' Chlamain and east, beyond the deep-set valley, to the prominent summit of Carn Liath. ❺ Cross a ford through the Allt Slanaidh, which could be another obstacle when in spate, and pass a locked shooting hut that once functioned as a rough-and-ready bothy. ❻ After another mile or so you reach a conifer plantation before confronting a security fence enclosing a military firing range at Croft Crombie. ❼ Skirt along the boundary then contour round into Blairuachdar Wood, ignoring a path heading down towards Cumhann-leum Bridge. The track turns sharply left then right before leaving the forest, and then follows a charming, tree-lined lane past the farm at Blairuachdar to return to the crossroads at Old Blair. Turn left onto the short stretch of tarmac back to the car park, and your journey's end after a long, satisfying day.

Notes: The noticeboard at the Glen Tilt car park displays stalking information and notices about times of firing at the rifle range at Croft Crombie (NN 8769) close to the end of the walk. If there is live firing, return to the car park via the bothy rather than heading over the bealach and down the Allt Slanaidh.

DIRECTIONS

1 From Glen Tilt car park (NN 874 662) turn L along the last section of metalled road to the crossroads at Old Blair. Continue straight on through a forestry plantation above the Banvie Burn, temporarily following a waymarked trail of black arrows. Ignore two turnings L that drop down to the stream and exit the plantation by a gate in the boundary fence (NN 854 678).
2.6km/1.5 miles

2 Head on up onto the open moor, the track quickly climbing away from Glen Banvie, up to the source of the Allt an t-Seapail, passing an ornate cairn. Once over the low bealach 514m, between Meall Dubh and Meall Tionail, descend to Allt Scheicheachan Bothy (NN 835 737).
6.8km/4.25 miles

3 Take the track running alongside the Allt Scheicheachan, crossing a ford immediately after the bothy. At a second ford (NN 849 749), head straight on, then L climbing steeply up a zigzag path across the shoulder of Meall Dubh nan Dearcag. (The track on R that crosses the burn is the descent route for this walk.) Continue over boggy ground and up via the summit ridge to the top of Beinn Dearg (NN 853 778).
5.5km/3.5 miles

4 Go back down the path to the ford over the Allt Scheicheachan.
3.6km/2.25 miles

5 Once across head up to the watershed of the Allt Slanaidh and down into the glen, then cross the burn (NN 867 719), which could be an obstacle when in spate.
4km/2.5 miles

6 Continue down to the forestry plantation at Ruigh-loisgte Wood and on to the boundary fence of the rifle range at Croft Crombie.
2.4km/1.5 miles

7 The track then runs alongside the security fence before contouring round into Blairuachdar Wood. Ignoring a path heading L down towards Cumhann-leum Bridge, descend towards Old Blair, the track turning sharp L then R before leaving the forest, then passing the farm before reaching the crossroads. Turn L and return to the car park.
4.2km/2.5 miles

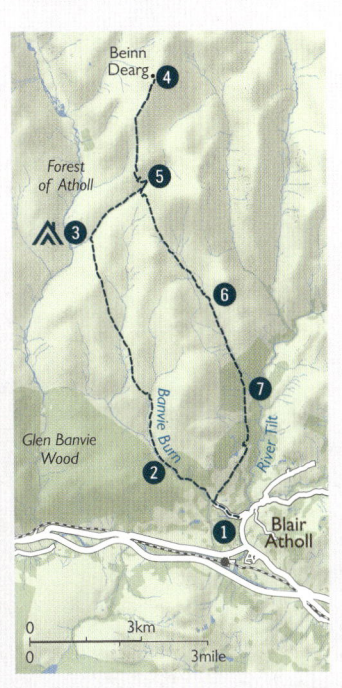

171

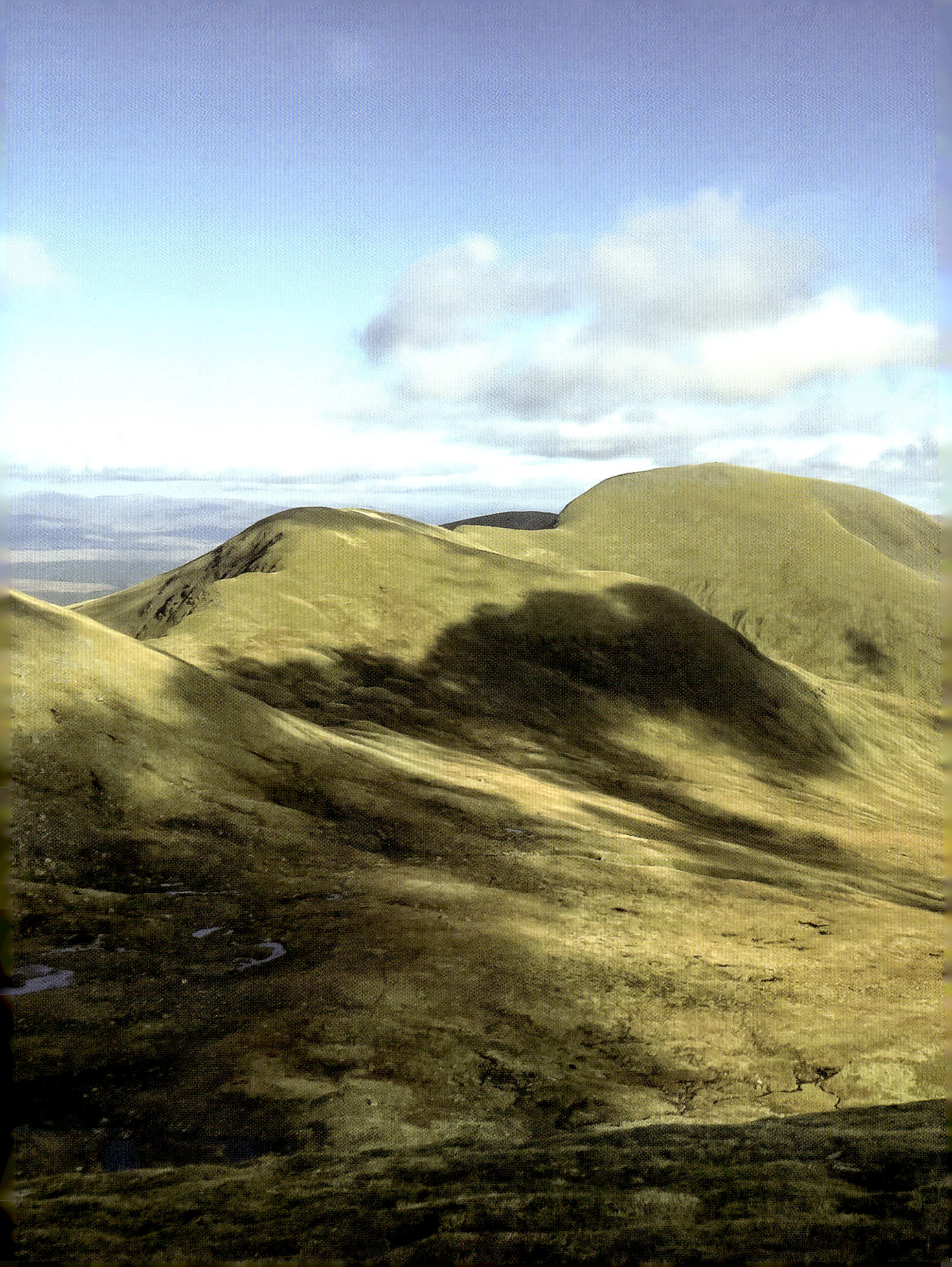

SOUTH WEST HIGHLANDS

LOOKING ACROSS TO THE BLACK MOUNT FROM COIRE ACHALADAIR

WALK 19

BEINN A'CHREACHAIN & BEINN ACHALADAIR VIA GORTON BOTHY

Challenging mountain walk along the spine of the Bridge of Orchy hills above the awesome expanse of Rannoch Moor, via the welcome outpost of Gorton Bothy.

I never tire of the views that open up above Tyndrum, heading north on the Glencoe road. First the striking volcanic cone of Beinn Dòrain, its steep inclines corrugated by deep runnels streaming down into Allt Kinglass, then the deceptively close bealach above Allt Coire an Dòthaidh, as you slow through Bridge of Orchy. Finally, having negotiated the tight hairpin bend up on to the Black Mount, there is a fine vista looking back across Loch Tulla. At the viewpoint on the A82 just before the road heads over Rannoch Moor, the shadowy, north-facing slopes of Beinn an Dòthaidh, Beinn Achaladair and Beinn a'Chreachain are seen at their best advantage, stretching away into a lost netherworld, the thin, black ribbon of the West Highland Railway line winding tightly along their lower flanks.

The Bridge of Orchy hills are a collective of five Munros, the four major summits: Beinn Dorain, Beinn an Dòthaidh, Beinn Achaladair and Beinn a'Chreachain, linked by a long, winding ridge. Viewed light-heartedly as a rock band, Beinn Dòrain would be the lead singer, showy and loud, while Beinn a'Chreachain – the highest point in the range – the quietly superior lead guitar. Beinn Achaladair, might be the drummer, kicking out the beats, and Beinn an Dòthaidh, the ever-reliable bass, holding the ensemble together. The fifth peak, Beinn Mhanach, shuns the limelight, much like a session musician with an occasional solo. Completing the entire ridge line is an ambitious undertaking. Each major summit is over 1000m in height, and ascents are typically split into two separate expeditions. The less demanding

INFORMATION

MAPS: LR 55 Glen Orchy & Loch Etive, Explorer 377 (Gorton is just off the map).
START/END GRID REF: NN 314 438. Large car park on track signed to Achallader Farm off A82 Glasgow to Fort William, 3 miles N of Bridge of Orchy.
DISTANCE: 25.5km/15.5 miles
TIME: 8–10 hours
TOTAL ASCENT: 1300m
SUMMITS: Beinn a'Chreachain (Munro), 1081m; Meall Buidhe (Munro Top), 978m; Beinn Achaladair (Munro), 1038m; South Top 1002m
NAVIGATION: Straightforward
TERRAIN: Straightforward. Track, well defined path, open hillside.
DIFFICULTY: Challenging
PUBLIC TRANSPORT: ScotRail West Highland Line from Glasgow Queen St. to Fort William, stops at Bridge of Orchy. Citylink coach service 915/916 Glasgow–Fort William, stops on request at the turn-off to Achallader Farm.
SPECIAL NOTES: Please check with the Black Mount Estate (01838 400 255) before going onto the hills during periods of deer control, 12th August to 15th February.

WALK 19 BEINN A'CHREACHAIN & BEINN ACHALADAIR VIA GORTON BOTHY

walk involves doubling back over Beinn Dorain and Beinn an Dòthaidh from Bridge of Orchy Hotel. The stiffer proposition is to tackle the two outlying peaks, Beinn Achaladair and Beinn a'Chreachain, from Achallader Farm. Gorton Bothy is a useful stopping point, before the ascent to the ridge.

❶ The hum of speeding traffic quickly recedes as you march along the wide gravel track towards Achallader Farm from the car park (now sited a short distance from the road, rather than in the old courtyard). This is an ancient drovers' road through the floodplain of the Water of Tulla, a route frequented by cattle rustlers, clansmen and Hanoverian troops over the course of its long history. Ignore a signpost directing you up the hill towards Coire Achaladair (used as the descent route for this particular outing), and walk on to the farm, guarded by the ruins of a 16th-century tower house. Once a stronghold of the fearsome Black Duncan – Sir Duncan Campell of Glen Orchy – the fortress suffered repeated attacks during clan wars and was partially demolished during the Jacobite uprising of 1689. Three years later, rebel leaders were summoned to the castle to sign the Treaty of Achallader and proclaim allegiance to King William III, but John Maclain, Chief of the MacDonalds of Glencoe, failed to sign before the deadline of 1 January 1692. Just over a month later, government forces used the delay as an excuse to attack his clan, an atrocity now known as the Glencoe Massacre. Shot holes in the surviving walls are the only visible reminders of the carnage.

From the farm, head down a neat, turf-capped drystone dyke to the ford of the Allt Coire Achaladair, the one significant obstacle on the route to the bothy. In spate this could be a risky proposition, though it is possible to follow a sheep trail upstream to a new concrete bridge (it serves a small hydroelectric scheme further up the glen), returning on the far bank. ❷ Continue through the pasture down to the stony bank side, ignoring a second ford left through the channel to the farm at Barravourich. After another half a mile, finally cross to the river's northern bank via a rather dilapidated vehicle bridge. ❸ Climb slowly up through the sandy remnants of kame terraces and lumpy moraines deposited by a huge glacier that retreated over Rannoch Moor at the end of the last ice age. Across on the far bank, the wonderful old Scots pines of Crannach Wood hug the hillside on the lower slopes of Beinn a'Chreachain, recently fenced off to encourage new growth. Eventually the bothy comes within sight, just off the main path. The former farmstead is a respectable, if spartan, refuge and was occupied as recently as the 1950s.

❹ Suitably refuelled after a well-earned pit stop, return to the main track, crossing back over the river on a wooden footbridge, before passing under the railway line – a constant companion along the walk up the glen. Briefly follow a muddy ATV track under a line of pylons, and up the side of the fenced plantation by Bad na Gualainn. Now pick a line up the steep, grassy slope: sticking to the increasingly obvious ridge to the left is the easiest gradient. Once height is gained, a breathtaking vista of Rannoch

LOCH TULLA

GORTON BOTHY

RANNOCH MOOR

LOCHAN A'CHREACHAIN

WALK 19 BEINN A'CHREACHAIN & BEINN ACHALADAIR VIA GORTON BOTHY

Moor opens up to the horizon with a ring of mountains visible on its far boundary. The Black Mount, Glencoe, and on a clear day Ben Nevis and the Mamores, float above the vast, dappled carpet of heather, peatbog, boulders and ribbon lochs. Approaching the unnamed top at 894m, the beautiful Lochan a'Chreachain is revealed, nestling beneath the vertical cliffs of the coire wall. From this high point, a faint path leads on to the distinctive summit cairn of Beinn a' Chreachain (Hill of the Clam Shell), a pyramid of shiny mica schist and quartzite.

❻ The distance to over to Beinn Achaladair looks rather daunting, but the ground is quickly covered. Descend steeply down the rocky scree and take the obvious path across to the grassy slopes of Meall Buidhe, before dropping to the Bealach an Aoghlain. **❼** The ridge up to the long, flat top of Beinn Achaladair is quite steep and eroded, especially in its lower section, but the path is obvious and very little scrambling is involved to gain the upper slopes. Confusingly there are two distinctive summit cairns, and the high point at 1038m is a small pile of stones somewhere in between. The stunning view is certainly worth all the exertion – Stob Ghabhar and the sequence of craggy peaks undulate towards the horizon, providing a fine backdrop above the serene, tabular shape of Loch Tulla. And further to the west, the distinctive beacons of Ben Starav and Ben Cruachan draw the eye towards Oban and the distant sea. **❽** Although it is possible to throw caution to the winds and head straight down the western slope of Beinn Achaladair to the valley below, you would be well advised to take the obvious path round to the bealach above Coire Daingean, where a small cairn marks the descent into Coire Achaladair.

❾ Ford the Allt Coire Achaladair with care below a cascading waterfall, at the confluence of two feeder tributaries (this could be an obstacle when in spate), then continue down the western bank of the burn, following a muddy path towards Achallader Farm. Then cross a fine, old iron bridge which arcs over the railway line and soon after, take the diverted path on the left, which skirts round the farm and back to the car park.

Notes: The route can be completed either clockwise or anticlockwise, depending on preference. Going in a clockwise direction, if the weather deteriorates there is an escape route down from the east of Coire a' Chreachain into Crannach Wood and over the railway bridge, before following the muddy southern riverbank to the track back to Achallader Farm just after the vehicle bridge (NN 338 453). The bridge marked on the map at NN 353 468 by Dun Aigheannach at the edge of the wood is in a perilous state, and a crossing should not be attempted.

SUMMIT BEINN A' CHREACHAIN

179

DIRECTIONS

1 From the car park, head along the wide track towards Achallader Farm, ignoring a path R signposted 'Footpath to hill', which is the return route for this walk. Once past the farm continue down a drystone dyke to a ford over the Allt Coire Achaladair. If it is impassable, follow a sheep trail upstream to a new concrete bridge (NN 323 440), returning on the far bank.
1.6km/1 mile

2 Once across the stream continue along the track to a bridge over the Water of Tulla (NN 338 453), ignoring a track L that fords the river and leads on to Barravourich.
1.6km/1 mile

3 Follow the track as it winds its way up the glen to Gorton Bothy, which is set just off the path (NN 375 481).
5km/3 miles

4 From the bothy rejoin the track, crossing back over to the N bank of the river via a footbridge. Go through a tunnel under the railway line, and a little further on pass under power lines, before starting the ascent of Beinn a' Chreachain. There is no path up the steep slope, so pick a line up to the ridge to the high point of 894m above Coire Dubh Mòr.
3.7km/2.25 miles

5 Now follow a faint but increasing obvious path that leads up to the summit of Beinn a' Chreachain.
1.6km/1 mile

6 Descend steeply down rocky scree, and take the obvious path across to the grassy slopes of Meall Buidhe, before dropping to the Bealach an Aoghlain.
2.4km/1.5 miles

7 Climb the steep ridge up to the flat top of Beinn Achaladair. There are two summit cairns, but the high point 1038m, is marked by a small pile of stones somewhere in-between.
0.8km/0.5 miles

8 Now take the obvious path across to the S top of Beinn Achaladair and on to the bealach above Coire Daingean, where a small cairn marks the descent into Coire Achaladair.
3.2km/2 miles

9 Head down the path to the Allt Coire Achaladair, crossing at the confluence of two tributaries and continue down the W bank on the path towards Achallader Farm. Cross the railway line via a footbridge, divert L to skirt round the farm and return to the car park.
5km/3.25 miles

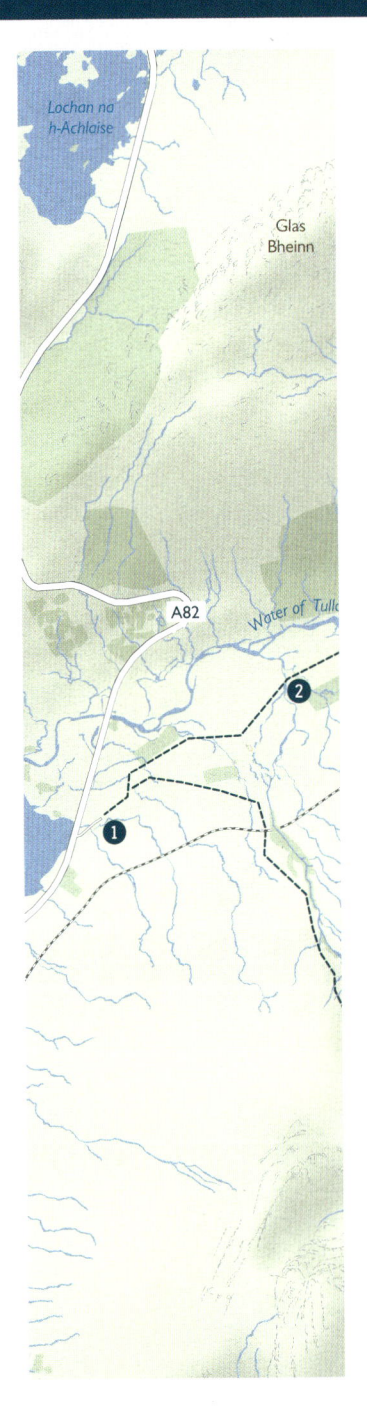

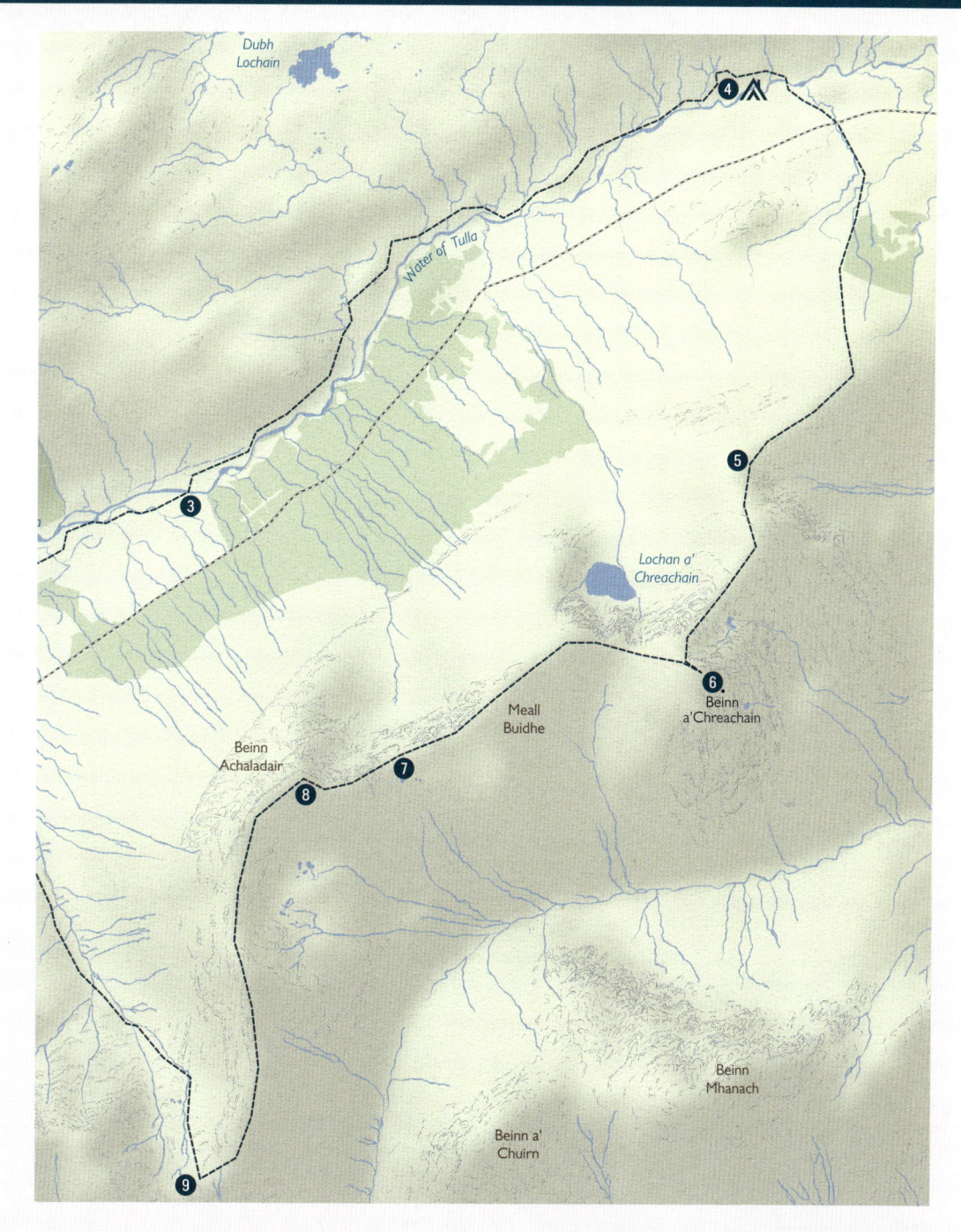

WALK 19 BEINN A'CHREACHAIN & BEINN ACHALADAIR VIA GORTON BOTHY

Dubh Lochain

Water of Tulla

Lochan a' Chreachain

Meall Buidhe

Beinn Achaladair

Beinn a'Chreachain

Beinn a' Chuirn

Beinn Mhanach

181

LOCH AWE FROM ABOVE KILNEUAIR

WALK 20

KILNEUAIR BY LOCH AWE TO CARRON BOTHY

A meditative journey through solitary upland moor between Loch Awe and Loch Fyne following in the footsteps of early Christian missionaries, drovers and traders.

Encompassing the wide expanse of mountains, moorland, and maritime coast between the greater Glasgow metropolis and Oban, Argyll and Bute is a beguiling mix of craggy hills, deep lochs, a long, winding shoreline, and spectacular islands. It is also regarded as one of the richest prehistoric landscapes in the country. Scanning the OS maps of Knapdale and Mid Argyll, a whole host of ancient sites are revealed, centred around the incredible Neolithic monuments in Kilmartin Glen and the nearby hill fort of Dunadd. The fort was a focal point of the Kingdom of Dál Riada, where early Scottish kings were anointed. Burial cairns, standing stones, and Bronze Age cup and ring inscriptions abound, along with a handful of enigmatic crannogs dotted along the shores of Loch Awe.

The walk in to Carron Bothy from Loch Awe follows an old drove road, which crosses the heather-clad moorland over to Loch Fyne. Soon after leaving the road, you'll come across a ruined medieval chapel, hidden amongst the bracken behind a copse of birch and Sitka spruce. Kilneuair, the 'Church of the Yews', is a remarkable find. Dedicated to St Columba, there is historical evidence to suggest that it might be the site of 'Cella Diuni', one of Iona's earliest satellites, built by St Diuni, a disciple of the early missionary. Inside the propped-up walls are the remains of a weathered table tomb, trefoil (three-ringed) arch and a sandstone slab with a faint, five-toed imprint referred to as the 'Devil's Hand'. Outside, an ornate stone enclosure protects a holy well, and within the nearby burial ground there are two ancient grave slabs believed to be of Norman origin.

INFORMATION

MAPS: LR 55 Lochgilphead & Loch Awe, Explorer sheet 360 Loch Awe & Inveraray.
START/END GRID REF: NM 884 037. Small improvised parking spot at Kilneuair by a track leading to Finchairn on the B840.
DISTANCE: 17km/10.5 miles' round trip.
TIME: 5–6 hours
TOTAL ASCENT: Inward 442m, Return 285m.
HIGH POINT: 360m
NAVIGATION: Easy
TERRAIN: Easy. Track all the way to the bothy.
DIFFICULTY: Straightforward
PUBLIC TRANSPORT: None.
SPECIAL NOTES: Bothy is open throughout the year. Stag-stalking takes place between 20 September and 20 October to the south and west of the bothy. The Ederline Estate discourages dogs, especially during the lambing season.

WALK 20 KILNEUAIR BY LOCH AWE TO CARRON BOTHY

'CHURCH OF THE YEWS'

1 Once you've explored Kilneuair and returned to the track, you begin the long, meandering ascent onto the high upland moor. At the junction immediately by the church, the main track leads east towards Finchairn, while the neglected old drove road – often waterlogged and hard to make out – heads south, straight up the hill, to a crossroads half a mile away. The pragmatic option is to continue on the Finchairn track, turning sharp right at the next junction, which leads back up to the crossroads. **2** Now take the upgraded track south-east through the Bealach Ruadh (Red Pass) to Loch Gainmheach, which is dammed at its southern end as part of a hydroelectric scheme. At a new concrete bridge spanning the outflow from Loch nan Cèard Mòr, the improved gravel section ends and the old drove road returns to its original stony surface.
3 Climb up through the Bealach Gaoithe (Pass of the Winds), to a swathe of rocky crags, heather and blanket bog patterned with beautifully sculptured hill lochs. After a mile traversing this timeless landscape, descend towards the River Add, skirting the boundary fence of a conifer plantation and down towards the bothy. The peaceful one-room refuge is guarded by two trees, a sycamore and a Sitka spruce.

Here the old drove road meets another ancient byway originating at Kilmichael Glassary, close to Dunadd, and the Mòine Mhòr (Great Moss) the sea-bound floodplain of the River Add. A beautifully constructed old stone bridge a few hundred yards from the bothy is the only sign that this lonely glen was a once well-travelled route. Along with cattle, and later sheep, charcoal

LOCH GAINMHEACH

CARRON BOTHY

WALK 20 KILNEUAIR BY LOCH AWE TO CARRON BOTHY

CRANNOG ON LOCH AWE

from the woodland by Loch Awe was also transported through this wild terrain and carried by packhorse down to the iron smelter in Furnace, built in 1755. Today, large tracts of forestry plantation cover the valley and an array of wind turbines stretch down to Lochgilphead. Despite these intrusions, this is a strangely peaceful spot as the many glowing entries in the bothy book attest. With one more pause for thought, return over to Kilneuair and Loch Awe.

LOOKING DOWN TO THE RIVER ADD

DIRECTIONS

1 From the roadside at Kilneuair head up to track towards Finchairn for 200 yards, before turning R, onto a boggy path that leads up to a crossroads (NM 893 032). (Alternatively continue on the track, turning sharp R at a junction, then on up to the crossroads.)
1.2km/0.75 miles

2 Take a wide track SE from the crossroads, gently ascending to the Bealach Ruadh and round towards Loch Gainmheach. Ignore a new track L (not marked on the map), and continue to a vehicle bridge at the head of the loch, where the access road ends.
3.2km/2 miles

3 Continue up a rough track that zigzags steeply to the Bealach Gaoithe and across the open moor, passing three small lochans before descending by the boundary fence of a recent forestry plantation to the bothy (NR 944 996).
4km/2.5 miles

4 Return by the same route to the shore of Loch Awe.
8.5km/5.25 miles

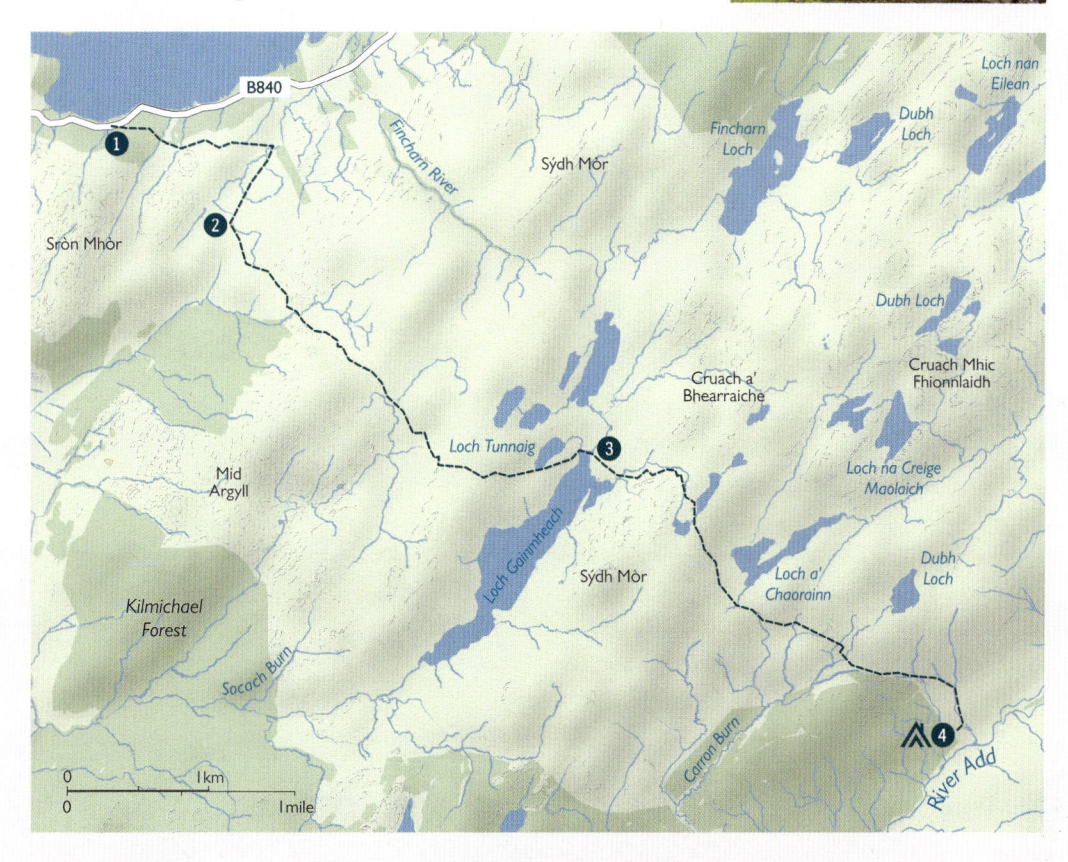

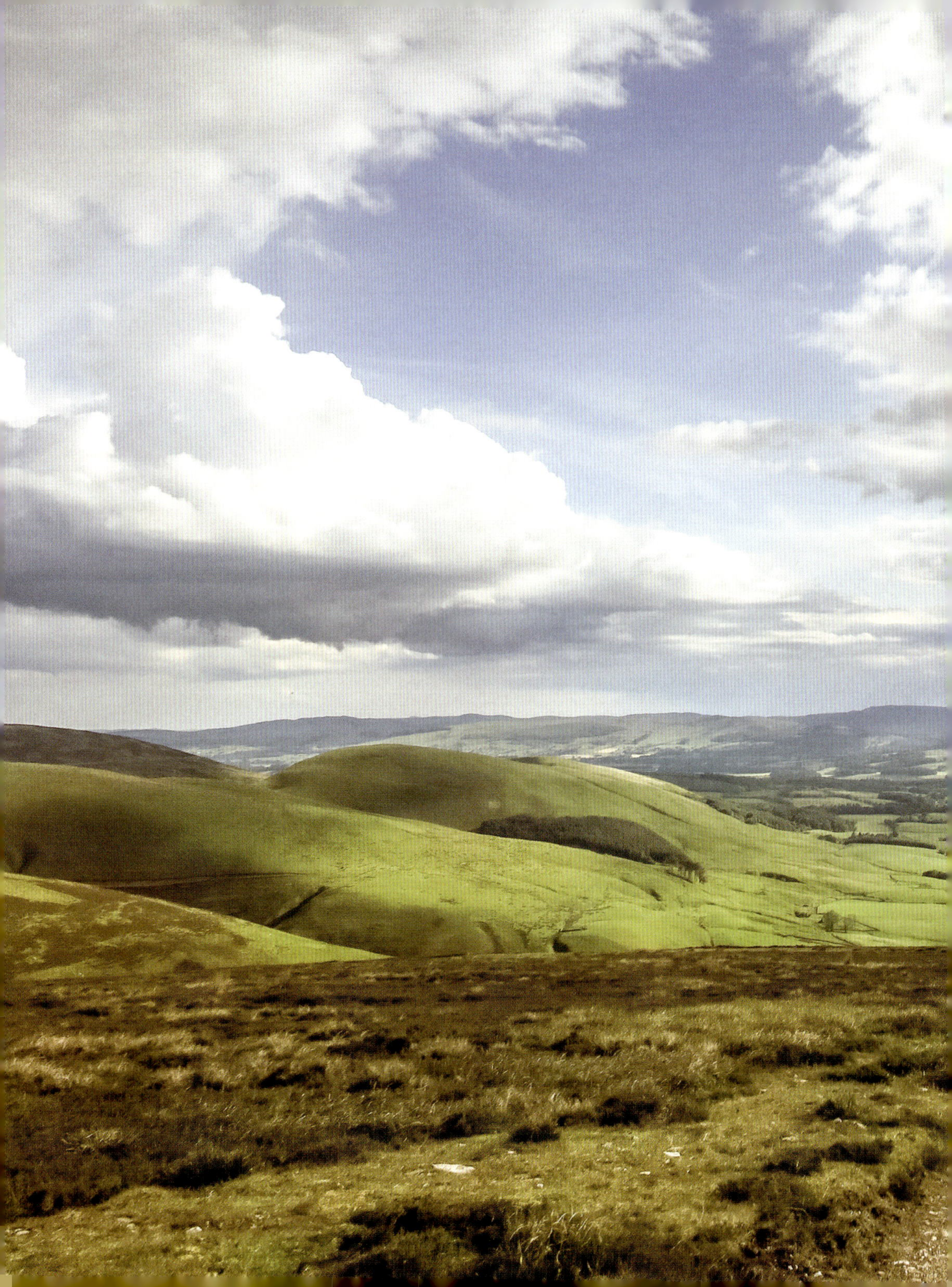

SOUTHERN SCOTLAND

MOORBROCK HILL FROM THE SLOPES OF BENINNER

WALK 21

CLENNOCH BOTHY & CAIRNSMORE OF CARSPHAIRN

A day's circular walk in old Dumfriesshire, climbing up to the outstanding viewpoint at Cairnsmore of Carsphairn, before seeking out the tiny hideaway bothy at Clennoch.

INFORMATION

MAPS: LR 77 Dalmellington & New Galloway, Explorer 320 Castle Douglas, Loch Ken & New Galloway.
START/END GRID REF: NX 637 948. Parking on roadside verge by Craigengillan.
DISTANCE: 18km/11 miles
TIME: 6–7 hours
TOTAL ASCENT: 890m
SUMMITS: Cairnsmore of Carsphairn (Corbett), 797m; Beninner (Donald Top), 710m.
NAVIGATION: Straightforward
TERRAIN: Straightforward. Track, well defined path, open hillside.
DIFFICULTY: Straightforward
PUBLIC TRANSPORT: None
SPECIAL NOTES: Bothy is open all year round, no restrictions. No fireplace or stove.

In a forgotten corner of South West Scotland steeped in local folklore and pock-marked with evidence of Neolithic and medieval settlements, you'll find the Glenkens, the largest valley in Galloway. Rising above the floodplain stands the whaleback ridge of Cairnsmore of Carsphairn, the highest summit of three hills named Cairnsmore in the region, celebrated in an old Galloway rhyme: 'There's Cairnsmore of Fleet, and Cairnsmore o' Dee, and Cairnsmore of Carsphairn, the highest o' the three.' It commands a fine view of the Rhinns of Kells, Merrick, and the Firth of Clyde, with the promise of the Arran peaks and Kintyre away to the north-west horizon on a clear day.

Driving west from the artists' enclave of Moniaive, the B road to the parish of Carsphairn climbs up and over into the catchment of the Water of Ken, traversing an isolated and timeless stretch of rolling upland moor where the past seems to be very connected to the present. On a rocky promontory above the river, close to Smittons Bridge (and the narrow lane that leads up to the start of the walk at Craigengillan), lie the ruins of the fort on Stroanfreggan Craig. This is one of a number of Iron Age cairns and burial chambers dotted along the floodplain, and charcoal dug from its foundations has been carbon-dated to 7000 BC. A more recent archaeological find was a collection of over 2000 coins unearthed in the fields close to the track heading towards Moorbrock Hill. The hoard included Scottish pennies dating from the time of Robert the Bruce and the English kings, Edward I and II. Some of the best examples are now on display in the National Museum of Scotland.

WALK 21 CLENNOCH BOTHY & CAIRNSMORE OF CARSPHAIRN

❶ Starting from the cottage at Craigengillan, stride out along the forestry track running parallel with the Polifferie Burn. After just under a mile, go through a metal farm gate as the main track curves away to the left. ❷ Cross the Poldores Burn by way of the old bridge – itself a relic from an earlier age – then follow the overgrown path leading off up to the estate houses at Moorbrock to a new gravel access road. Once through the complex of cottages, ford the Poltie Burn, and then turn sharply left, climbing a track through a patchwork of conifers running parallel to the stream. Above the plantation boundary, the track turns 90 degrees left, contouring round the base of Green Hill, before heading along to a forestry watchtower, where the slopes of Beninner come into view.

❸ Head down the first forestry firebreak to the Poldores Burn, cross a stone dyke, then the stream, and take to the open hillside. Straight up the slope there is a line of weakness in the broken granite fringe protecting the upper slopes (at the shallowest point in the crags) but if you don't fancy a bit of scrambling, traverse left of the steep ground before ascending the brow of the hill. ❹ From Beninner's summit cairn, descend west-north-west to the Nick of the Lochans, over a stile in the sheep fence, and on to Cairnsmore of Carsphairn. A faint path leads up onto the whaleback ridge, the majestic view opening up as you approach the crest. To the west, the familiar pyramid shape of Ailsa Craig can be seen in the Firth of Clyde, while further south the knotted peaks of the Galloway Hills stretch away into the distance. Boulders are strewn across the plateau, and built up into a windbreak around the OS trig pillar marking the summit. According to local legend, the Devil was so upset that a church had been built in Carsphairn that he hurled rocks from the top of the hill in an attempt to destroy it.

❺ After a gentle descent to Currie Rig, the slope steepens to the valley below, where Clennoch Bothy is just a small dot beneath the snaking line of wind turbines on Dugland and Windy Standard. Crossing the Bow Burn (which could be an obstacle in times of spate), you head through a fenced area of birch and willow saplings to the bothy. Once part of one of the

CAIRNSMORE OF CARSPHAIRN

BENINNER

MOORBROCK HILL & GREEN HILL

WALK 21 CLENNOCH BOTHY & CAIRNSMORE OF CARSPHAIRN

most remote sheep farms in Southern Scotland, the homestead was finally vacated before World War II then rebuilt as a single-roomed shelter by the MBA in the mid-1970s. ❻ From here, a flat, wide forestry track leads south past Moorbrock Hill, then retrace your steps back to Craigengillan.

Notes: Although access to the lower slopes of Beninner and Cairnsmore of Carsphairn is via wide, easy forestry tracks with simple orientation, be prepared to negotiate a stone dyke and sheep fences, cross two streams and navigate over rough, open hillside to climb to the summits. The route can be extended to include Moorbrock Hill (650m), another Donald tick, but it adds another hour and 250m of ascent to the trip. Please ask permission to park by the cottage at Craigengillan and be aware that there have been reports of damage to parked cars clipped by fast-moving trucks transporting timber. A gated estate track 500m to the north has a 'no parking' sign by the entrance.

LOOKING DOWN TO CLENNOCH

CLENNOCH BOTH

DIRECTIONS

1 From the cottage at Craigengillan (NX 637 948), follow the track N parallel to the Polifferie Burn before crossing the stream via an old bridge where the main track swings away to L.
1.5km/1 mile

2 Head along an overgrown path for 500 yards to a new access road to Moorbrock. Once through the cottages, ford the Poltie Burn, and turn sharp L following the track as it contours round Green Hill.
2.5km/1.5 miles

3 At a forestry watchtower (NX 617 970), descend the first firebreak to the Poldores Burn, cross and gain the open hillside. Either ascend Beninner via an obvious break in the rocky outcrops that protect the summit, or traverse L, avoiding the crags and climb up to the summit along a broad ridge (NX 606 972).
2.5km/1.5 miles

4 Descend WNW to the Nick of the Lochans, and up the whaleback ridge to the trig pillar on Cairnsmore of Carsphairn (NX 594 980).
1.5km/1 mile,

5 Drop down N to Currie Rig, cross the Bow Burn, then walk through the fenced area to Clennoch Bothy close by (NS 603 002).
1.5km/1 mile

6 From the bothy, return via a forestry track heading S past Moorbrock Hill to rejoin the walk-in route below Green Hill back to Craigengillan.
8km/5 miles

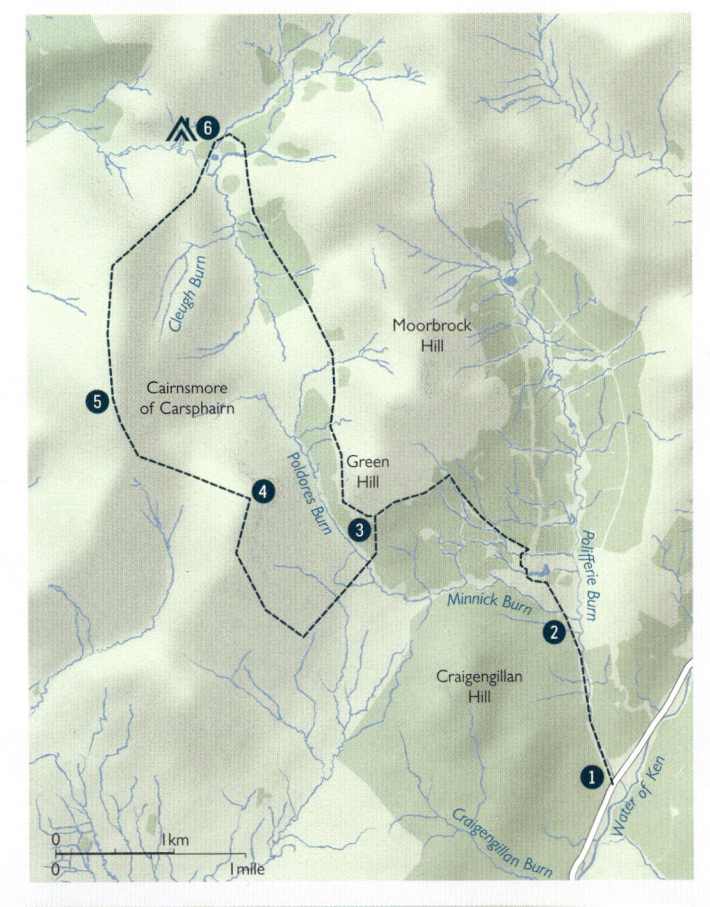

195

VIEW DOWN TO LITTLE SCAW'D LAW

WALK 22

KETTLETON BYRE & SCAW'D LAW

A circular ramble through the rolling fells above Nithsdale in the southern Lowther Hills via the pocket-sized bothy of Kettleton Byre.

Straddling the old county boundary between Lanarkshire and Dumfriesshire, the Lowther Hills cover a compact area of high upland heath. Powerful glacial meltwaters moulded the landscape into a collection of attractive, rounded peaks, hummocks and hollows, as well as steep-sided, quiet glens of understated charm. Set above the fertile floodplains of Annandale and Nithsdale, this is classic Borders sheep country and grouse moor, and a strategic natural barrier traversed by ancient byways and drove roads.

Tucked away in the shadow of the hills, the sleepy hamlet of Durisdeer once marked the start of a Roman road – the Well or Wald Path – that connected the Solway Firth and Clydesdale. The outline of protective ramparts and ditches of a fortlet built during the occupation are clearly seen on the route of the road, just over a mile from the last terrace of cottages. The imposing parish church also has an intriguing history. Built during the 1720s on the site of a medieval chapel, it is the kirk for the country seat of Drumlanrig Castle, owned by the Dukes of Queensberry and Buccleuch who rank among the largest landowners in the UK. The east wing of the church contains a remarkable marble mausoleum to the Queensberry ancestors.

The walk begins by the cemetery just outside Durisdeer, where there is a small lay-by, though the best place to park is by the old war memorial next to the village green. ❶ Head back down the hill, turn left up a track following the boundary wall of the cemetery to a roofless, stone-built barn, and continue onto the sheepfolds by the Hapland Burn, passing through a locked

INFORMATION

MAPS: LR Map 78 Nithsdale & Annandale, Explorer 321 Nithsdale & Dumfries.
START/END GRID REF: NS 894 037. Parking in the village square, Durisdeer.
DISTANCE: 12km/7.5 miles
TIME: 3.5–4.5 hours
TOTAL ASCENT: 590m
SUMMITS: Scaw'd Law (Donald), 663m; Little Scaw'd Law, 594m; Glenleith Fell (Donald Top), 612m – a quick detour from the route.
NAVIGATION: Easy
TERRAIN: Easy. Track and well defined path, boggy in places.
DIFFICULTY: Easy
PUBLIC TRANSPORT: Stagecoach West Scotland Service 102 from Edinburgh to Dumfries, stops at Durisdeer.
SPECIAL NOTES: Bothy is located within the boundary of a hill farm. Nearby pens may be in use, particularly in the lambing season April–mid-May. Keep dogs under close control at all times. Buccleuch Estate ask for your co-operation during shooting season (mid August–November, excluding Sundays). Please call the head keeper (07771 886949) the day before you go to check if there is shooting arranged for the following day.

metal gate. ❷ Ignore the track rising steeply to the left on to Blackgrain Shoulder, and instead continue into the deep notch of Glenaggart. Buzzards, ravens and red kites – all natural scavengers – are often seen circling above, particularly after a shooting party has finished for the day. This path is marked as a droving road on the original 6-inch OS map of the area dated 1882, connecting the old farm at Kettletonhead to another sheep station at Mitchellslacks by the banks of Capel Water 5 miles further to the south-east. There are a number of new access tracks leading left and right off the main track up through the glen but the main track is obvious to follow. After a slow, steady ascent past the appropriately named Sleepy Cleuch, the track levels out by a metal gate, and just beyond it the bothy comes into view. This little refuge is held in great affection, and over many visits I've happily read bothy book entries from excited kids, Duke of Edinburgh Award groups and other first-timers.

❸ Although there is a faint, steep ATV trail heading directly up on to Glenleith Fell from the bothy, it is far easier to continue round to Blackhill Moss and Kettleton Farm (now a locked shooting lodge), before ascending to higher ground. Ignore a turning right leading down to Kettleton Reservoir, and after another few hundred yards, take a track left, which cuts across the steep slope of Glenleith Fell at a more forgiving angle. As the contours relent, tack to the right, skirting round the unremarkable high point of 612m, and descend to the track running between Blackgrain Shoulder and Wedder Law. The abrupt drop to the east is one of a number of deeply incised meltwater channels cutting through the friable sandstone of the region.

❹ At the T-junction, turn left towards Scaw'd Law through a farm gate by Smuring Hags, to a point where the track begins to dip down back towards Glenaggart. Here an unmarked path ascends right (not marked on the 1:25,000 map) to reach an old drystone dyke running along the county boundary. Turn left onto a faint path running parallel to the dyke, up to the summit of Scaw'd Law – an unflattering Scots term for a speckled, scabby or patchy hill. The top is barely distinguishable from the gentle undulating moor (and not even marked by a cairn), but it is an ideal spot to take in the amazing views. On a clear day, the silvery strip of the Solway Firth glistens in

KETTLETON BYRE

WALK 22 KETTLETON BYRE & SCAW'D LAW

the sunshine, and beyond, the mountain tops of the Lake District are just visible on the skyline. Looking west, the broad sweep of Nithsdale, a neat patchwork of green pasture and forestry, leads down to Thornhill and Dumfries, while the distant peak of Merrick, the highest point in the Galloway Hills, hovers on the horizon.

Follow the drystone dyke as it turns sharply L over to Little Scaw'd Law and down to Kirkgrain Hass. At a corner point in the wall, just before the springs of Kirk Grain, a new track cuts across the slope to the ridge of Durisdeer Rig and back down to the village. An idyllic scene opens up as the track descends: sheep graze peacefully in the fields below, and across the Nithsdale Valley the grey rectangular outline of Drumlanrig Castle sits within carefully manicured parkland. Across the Kirk Burn and Roman road, the neat, rounded hills of Penbane, Black Hill and Well Hill add a homely touch, while the distinctive 'golf ball' radar station is a conspicuous presence on the summit of Lowther Hill. In the final steep descent you can almost reach out to touch the rooftops in the hamlet, before joining the old Roman road back to the kirk.

Notes: On Sundays from the second week of July to mid-September, afternoon tea is served in the church hall from 2.30 to 5pm. If you have an hour to spare, take the well-signposted footpath from Durisdeer to the Roman fortlet. To shorten the walk, avoiding the stretch along the drystone dyke over Scaw'd Law, descend back to Durisdeer via Blackgrain Shoulder (10km/6.25 miles), instead of turning L up the summit.

DURISDEER

DIRECTIONS

1 From the parking area by the war memorial in Durisdeer (NS 894 037), head S out of the village, turning L just before the cemetery, onto a farm track. After just over half a mile pass through a metal gate and cross a bridge over the Hapland Burn.
0.8km/0.5 miles

2 Ignore turning L, which cuts across Whiteside Shoulder, and ascend steepening track into Glenaggart to reach Kettleton Byre (NS 912 021).
1.6km/1 mile

3 Continue on to Blackhill Moss, ignoring R turn to Kettleton Reservoir by a locked shooting lodge. Continue on the old drovers' road ignoring another R turn after 500 yards, before finally taking a turn L up the W side of Glenleith Fell. Ascend steeply, the track turning sharply back across the slope before skirting round the top of Glenleith Fell, and down to the track running between Blackgrain Shoulder and Wedder Law.
3.7km/2.25 miles

4 At the T-junction, turn L towards Scaw'd Law through a farm gate, and 200 yards further on bear R up to a drystone dyke. Turn L on a faint path running parallel to the dyke, up to the summit of Scaw'd Law (NS 922 038). There is no cairn on the summit.
1.2km/0.75 miles

5 Follow the drystone dyke over undulating terrain to Little Scaw'd Law, before dropping down quickly L then R to Kirkgrain Hass, where a new track cuts across to the ridge of Durisdeer Rig and back down to the village.
4.4km/2.75 miles

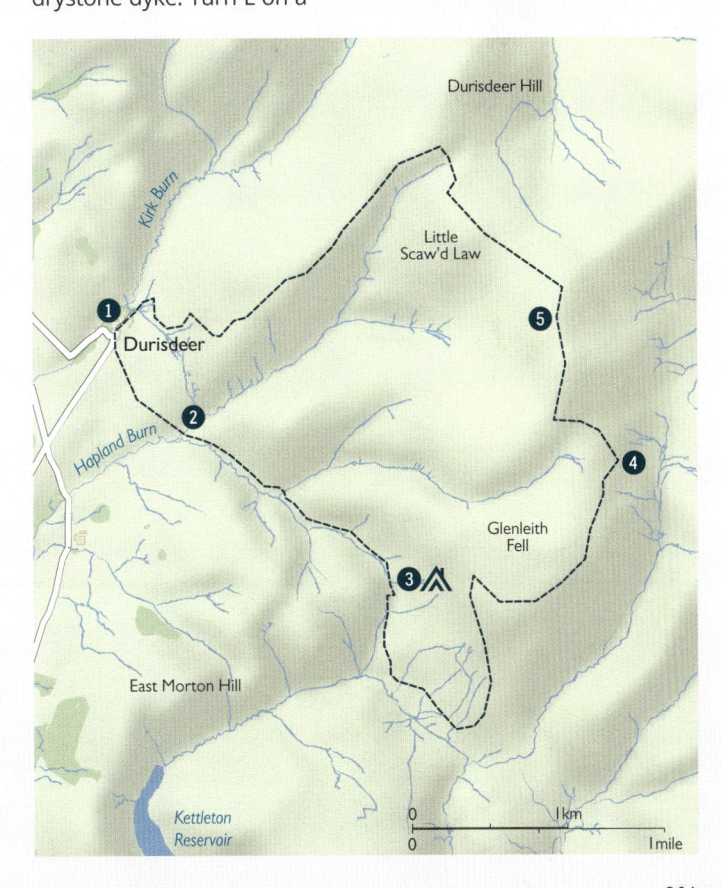

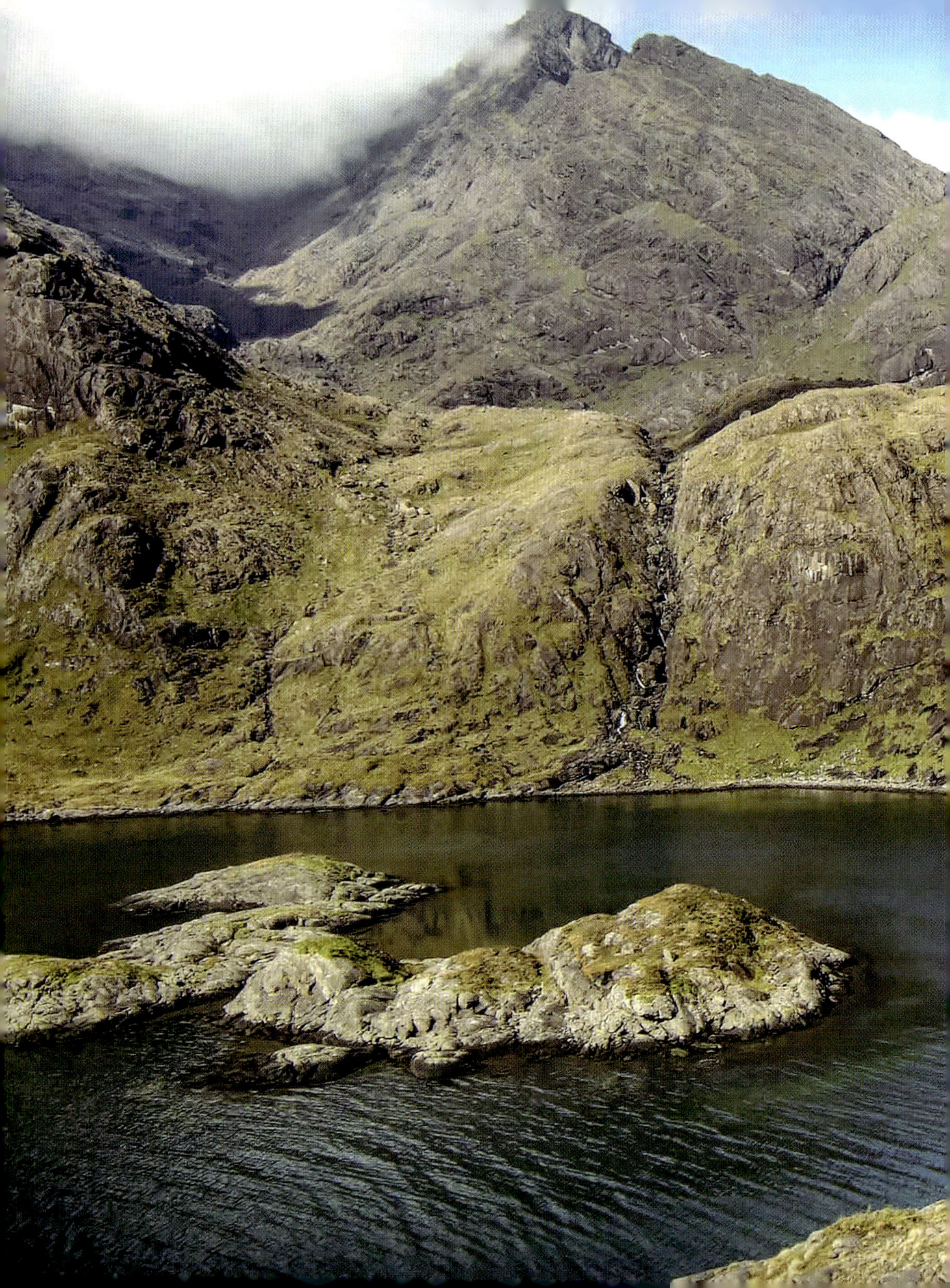

THE ISLANDS

THE OLD MAN OF HOY FROM TUAKS OF THE BOY

WALK 23

BURNMOUTH COTTAGE, RACKWICK BAY & THE OLD MAN OF HOY

Fantastic day trip to the Orkney Island of Hoy, visiting the beachside bothy at Rackwick Bay, before paying your respects to the Old Man of Hoy, a spectacular sandstone sea stack.

Rackwick Bay is the perfect place to linger, breathe in the seaweed-scented air, and marvel at the immense power of the twin master stonemasons, wind and wave. From the teetering sea stack of the Old Man, to the huge, rounded boulders strewn along the beach, the wild Atlantic Ocean has sculpted this extraordinary landscape. Pounded by endless swells, the stack was once a stubborn, solitary promontory but its base was eventually undercut to form an arch, which subsequently collapsed during a violent storm in the 19th century. A 200-foot chasm now separates the stack from the cliff, with a causeway of debris creating a precarious land bridge.

Your first glimpse of the Old Man and the giant, deep red sandstone cliffs on the north-west shoulder of Hoy is on the NorthLink Ferry from Scrabster, but the true scale of the coast only becomes apparent close at hand. Taking a second ferry from either Stromness or Houton, you can drive, cycle, walk or take a minibus to Rackwick. As soon as you make the final turn on the winding single-track road from Moaness, you immediately appreciate why this former crofting community is considered one of the most beautiful places on Orkney. This beguiling bay inspired heartfelt poetry by late Orcadian writer George Mackay Brown, and the composer Peter Maxwell Davies relocated here in the early 1970s, living in a renovated croft high above the shore. Master of The Queen's Music and founder of the St Magnus Festival held every year in Kirkwall, Maxwell Davies wrote many pieces celebrating his life in the islands, including *An Orkney Wedding*, and *Farewell to Stromness*.

INFORMATION

MAPS: LR 7 Orkney – Southern Isles, Explorer 462 Orkney - Hoy, South Walls & Flotta.
START/END GRID REF: ND 202 993. Small parking area at Rackwick.
DISTANCE: 11km/7 miles
TIME: 4–5 hours' round trip (including beachcombing!).
TOTAL ASCENT: 190m
HIGHEST POINT: 160m
NAVIGATION: Easy
TERRAIN: Easy. Well defined path all the way.
DIFFICULTY: Easy
PUBLIC TRANSPORT: ScotRail Highland Line from Inverness to Thurso. Stagecoach North Service X99 Inverness to Scrabster Pier. NorthLink Ferries Scrabster to Stromness. Passenger ferry Stromness to Moaness Pier on Hoy leaves every morning, returning in the evening. On Hoy, minibus to the Rackwick Bay Hostel co-ordinates with the ferry. Vehicle ferry from Houton to Lyness.
SPECIAL NOTES: Bothy is open all year round, no restrictions, and run by the Hoy Community Trust with an honesty box for donations.

WALK 23 BURNMOUTH COTTAGE, RACKWICK BAY & THE OLD MAN OF HOY

1 Before making the steep ascent to the Old Man, it is worth taking a stroll to the heather-thatched bothy and soaking up the special atmosphere of the bay. Burnmouth Cottage is barely 500 yards from the road and surrounded by a low drystone wall. **2** After a peek inside, clamber over the large, rounded boulders that line the beach and enjoy wandering through the dunes back to the car park. Curious seals can often be seen bobbing in the breakers, and you'll hear the mournful notes of oystercatchers and curlews rise up from the marram grass. Once back at the road, take the gravel track (signed for the Old Man) back towards the sea, turning sharp right at the last house, and begin the steady climb out of the bay. **3** Pick one of two turns left up the grassy bank; the second has another helpful sign to the Old Man, and leads up to a kissing gate. From here any confusion is allayed, as the path becomes much easier to follow.

4 If you make the trip in late spring or early summer, you might be bothered by the great skuas (or bonxies as they're known locally) that nest in the heather above the cliffs on Rora Head. As well as harassing other seabirds to steal food, the skuas are notorious for dive-bombing the unwary. Sometimes you really feel the need to duck, they seem so close. Finally at the cliff edge, the Old Man reveals itself – an enormous, drunken construction of sandstone blocks balanced above the waves on a basalt plinth, with a flat, grass carpet at its summit. Fulmars, kittiwakes and puffins nest in the horizontal cracks, while gulls soar above the surf. It is truly an unmissable spectacle. On my last visit I relived the experience of scaling the landward east face that I'd gone through 20 years before, my palms sweating as I traced the line of climbing tat visible at every belay. Retrace your route, keeping an eye out for the bonxies, before wandering back down to Rackwick. If you have time it is worth continuing on the track down to Rackwick Hostel and calling into the Cra'as Nest Museum on the way. The traditional croft house and steading have been skilfully restored, complete with basic furniture and a turf roof.

Rackwick
Let no tongue idly whisper here
Between those strong red cliffs,
Under that great mild sky
Lies Orkney's last enchantment,
The hidden valley of light
Sweetness from the clouds pouring
Songs from the surging sea
Fenceless fields, Fishermen with ploughs and old heroes
Endlessly sleeping in Rackwick's compassionate hills.
George Mackay Brown (1921–1996)

Notes: Burnmouth Cottage is a popular spot with overnight visitors. Many people opt to camp in the grounds of the bothy.

BURNMOUTH COTTAGE

MEL FEA & RACKWICK BAY

WALK 23 BURNMOUTH COTTAGE, RACKWICK BAY & THE OLD MAN OF HOY

THE BEACH AT RACKWICK BAY

DIRECTIONS

1 From the car park at Rackwick, head along a track signposted to Rackwick Beach and Burnmouth Cottage Bothy (ND 205 987), which can be seen 500 yards away. The final stretch passes through a grassy field.
0.6km/0.4 miles

2 Return to the car park via the beach, across the open dunes. Here take the track signposted 'Old Man of Hoy' in the direction of the sea, turning sharp R at the last house above Nose of the Yard.
1km/0.6 mile

3 Continue up the slope, choosing one of two turns L to climb up to the cliffs at Too of the Head.
1km/0.6 miles

4 Contour round the headland, before making your way north across the open moor to the viewing point at Tuaks of the Boy (HY 178 007).
3km/2 miles

5 Return to Rackwick by the same route.

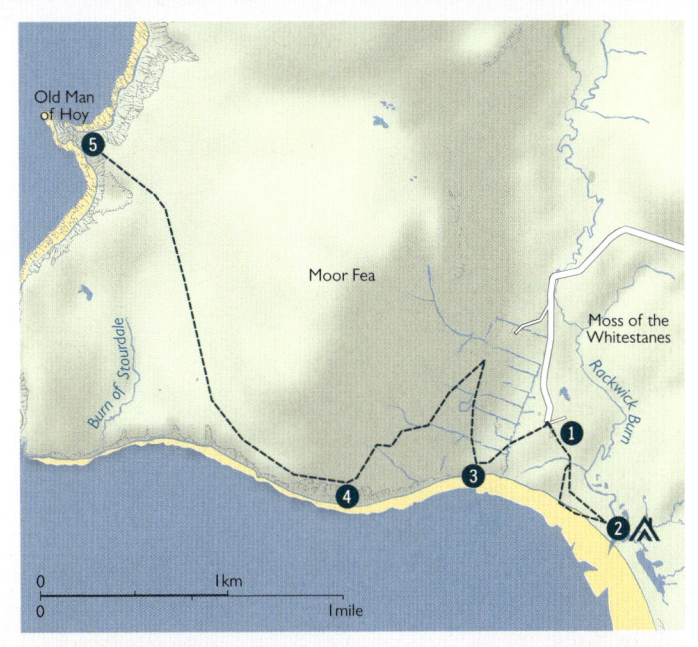

MOANESS FERRY

THE LOOKOUT & THE CLIFFS OF MEALL TUATH FROM HUNISH

WALK 24

THE LOOKOUT & RUBHA HUNISH ON SKYE

An unmissable journey to the northernmost tip of Skye, Rubha Hunish, via the spectacular Lookout Bothy, taking in panoramic views over The Minch to the Western Isles.

Although it may be difficult to believe, there are still a few places on Skye where you can escape the crowds. Rubha Hunish, the designated start of the Skye Trail, now attracts a steady stream of visitors, but the atmosphere is a world away from the coach-filled car parks at the Old Man of Stoer, or the Fairy Pools in Glen Brittle. Go early in the morning, or stay late, and you may be rewarded by the sight of dolphins and whales navigating through The Minch. Between the geos is a good place to spot otters, their territories marked by small, green turf mounds by the shore. Shags and cormorants fly low above the eddies, and gannets circle and dive in a remarkable display of aerobatics. Back at the bothy, the view from the 180-degree bay window, a remnant of the bothy's former life as a coastal watch station, is truly magnificent. Prepare to experience all kinds of weather: shimmering sunlight, castles of cumulus clouds building from the west, rain showers scooting across the water. The canvas changes with every passing moment and it is difficult to tear yourself away.

The cheery sight of a red telephone box on the A855 from Uig marks the turn to Shulista, and the small car park where the walk begins. ❶ Head across a cattle grid, and out onto the open moor, following the vague line of a low escarpment. Across to the west, on a rocky promontory, stand the crumbling remains of Duntulm Castle, former stronghold of the MacDonalds of Sleat, and out in the bay, the pleasing profile of Tulm Island adds to the scene. Once a little height is gained, you begin to make

INFORMATION

MAPS: LR 23 North Skye, Explorer 408 Skye Trotternish & The Storr.
START/END GRID REF: NG 423 743. Small car park just after Shulista turn-off on the A855 North Skye coast road.
DISTANCE: 4km/2.5 miles
TIME: 3–4 hours' round trip
TOTAL ASCENT: 93m
HIGHEST POINT: 116m
NAVIGATION: Easy
TERRAIN: Easy. Well defined path and faint trails, one short scramble down to the headland.
DIFFICULTY: Easy.
PUBLIC TRANSPORT: Citylink coach service 915/916 Glasgow–Fort William–Uig. Stagecoach Highlands bus service 57C Portree–Flodigarry via Uig stops on request.
SPECIAL NOTES: Bothy is open all year round. No fireplace or stove, no drinking water at bothy or on the headland, but water may be obtained at Trotternish Art Gallery, Solitote (NG 428 742). Beware of steep cliff face in front of bothy.

WALK 24 THE LOOKOUT & RUBHA HUNISH ON SKYE

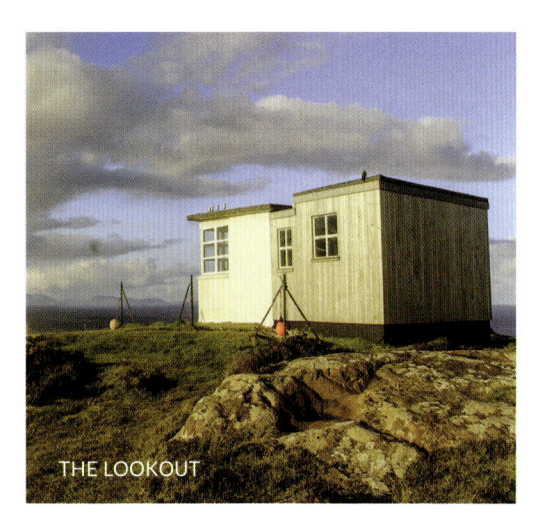

THE LOOKOUT

out the ruins and field system of Erisco. This flat, fertile ground running down to the coast has been occupied since the time of the Vikings. Sadly, their descendants were forced from their homes after the first wave of land clearances during the 19th century, replaced by the landlord for cottars (tenant farmers), who built a line of eight thatched cottages along the old enclosure wall, at regularly spaced intervals.

❷ After half a mile of gentle climbing, pass through a kissing gate in a boundary fence that marks the common grazing land. Head on up the slope, and then follow a vague path to the obvious depression on the horizon between Meall Tuath and Meall Deas. As you approach the gap, the smell of the sea permeates the air and suddenly you are peering down to Rubha Hunish, a bony finger of rock and pasture jutting out into the sea. The name illustrates its intertwined heritage: Rubha is Gaelic for 'headland' while Hunish derives from Old Norse, meaning 'headland of the bear cub'.

The bothy, an easy 5-minute walk up the slope to the right, is a small, boxy building, refurbished by the MBA after suffering storm damage in 2005. The interior was faithfully restored to the original design, and the west-facing panes replaced in the epic bay window.

❸ Energised by the views, go back down to the gap, climb over two stiles in quick succession, to reach a kissing gate. Take a deep breath, and then scramble down a weakness in the basalt cliffs to the grassy bank below. This is less alarming than it looks, though you do need a good head for heights for the first few steps. Once you reach

RUBHA HUNISH

WALK 24 THE LOOKOUT & RUBHA HUNISH ON SKYE

the safe sanctuary of level ground, take time to wander around the intricate coastline, following one of the numerous criss-crossing sheep trails. Three sea stacks and a natural arch reveal themselves as you approach the eastern cliffs, the taller middle stack occasionally scaled by the climbing fraternity. The rocky shelves out by the most northerly point are the best place to look out for whales. I wild camped here and spent an unforgettable evening watching minkes migrate down The Minch, close enough to hear them blowing as they surfaced.

DIRECTIONS

1 From the small car park just after the turn to Shulista (NG 423 743), take the path signposted to Rubha Hunish, along a low escarpment to a kissing gate in the sheep fence.
1.6km/1 mile

2 Once through the gate (NG 414 756), head up to the gap between Meall Tuath and Meall Deas. Turn R up the slope for 300 yards to reach The Lookout bothy (NG 412 765).
0.8km/0.5 miles

3 Return to the gap, climb over two stiles in quick succession, to a kissing gate. Scramble down a weakness in the cliffs to Rubha Hunish. The first few steps are a little exposed, but then the descent is relatively easy. A number of sheep trails criss-cross the headland, one leading to the most northerly point.
1.6km/1 mile

4 After exploring the coastline, return up the rocky staircase, retracing your route down the path to the car park.

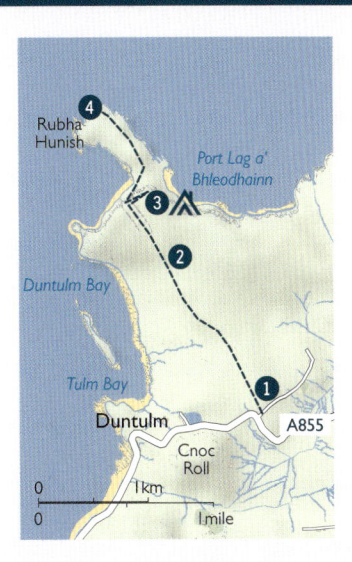

CLIFFS OF MEALL TUATH & MEALL DEAS

THE BAD STEP ABOVE LOCH NAN LEACHD

WALK 25

NEW CAMASUNARY BOTHY, THE 'BAD STEP' & LOCH CORUISK

An epic day's hike in the shadow of Skye's spectacular Black Cuillin Ridge, stopping at New Camasunary Bothy before negotiating the infamous 'Bad Step'. Challenge over, return via the breathtaking amphitheatre of Loch Coruisk.

INFORMATION

MAPS: LR 23 Southern Skye & Cuillin Hills, Explorer 411 Skye-Cuillin Hills (recommended).
START/END GRID REF: NG 488 299. Car park at Sligachan Bridge on the A87.
DISTANCE: 29km/18 miles
TIME: 10–12 hours
TOTAL ASCENT: 670m
HIGHEST POINT: 316m
NAVIGATION: Easy
TERRAIN: Hard. Well defined paths and faint trail, river crossing, rock climbing traverse.
DIFFICULTY: Challenging.
PUBLIC TRANSPORT: ScotRail service from Inverness to Kyle of Lochalsh. Scottish Citylink coach service 915/916 Glasgow–Fort William–Uig stops at Kyle of Lochalsh and Sligachan.
SPECIAL NOTES: Bothy is open all year round, no restrictions. Please respect the privacy of the lodge and old bothy. Strictly no fishing in nearby lochs and rivers. Rubbish accumulation is a problem; please take away everything you bring with you.

Skye offers some of the finest and most difficult ridge climbing in the UK, but you don't need to scale the jagged pinnacles of the Cuillin Ridge, or the prow of Clach Glas on Bla Bheinn to get a taste of the mental challenge needed to traverse these lofty summits. The notorious 'Bad Step', a boilerplate slab of rough gabbro jutting ominously into the cold depths of Loch nan Leachd on the western shoreline of Sgùrr na Stri (Peak of Strife), is a scrambling challenge to test the confidence of any budding adventurer. No harder than classic walking routes on, for example, Arran, Torridon or An Teallach, it is the situation that focuses the mind. You are miles from anywhere, with no easy means of retreat, and the unappealing prospect of a slip-sliding drop into the water below. Once committed there really is nowhere else to go but onwards.

During the late-1960s, local councillors with the support of the landowner and constabulary, put forward a serious but misguided proposal to dynamite the Bad Step. The aim was to improve access from the remote area around Loch Coruisk, principally to evacuate climbing casualties back to the safety of Kilmarie. A track from the Broadford-Elgol road was blasted in to Camasunary Bay, and a suspension bridge erected over the tidal flow of the Abhainn Camas Fhionnairigh. Vigorous opposition from the mountaineering community, however, curtailed the most controversial aspect of the project. The following year the

WALK 25 NEW CAMASUNARY BOTHY, THE 'BAD STEP' & LOCH CORUISK

footbridge was badly damaged by winter gales, and all that remains today are the support struts.

❶ A fantastic panorama greets you on arrival at the visitors' car park, east of the old and new bridges spanning the River Sligachan, as it slows and forms braided channels that flow into the sea loch and out to the Sound of Raasay. Beyond the whitewashed walls of the hotel, the ragged sawtooth peaks of Sgùrr nan Gillean and Bruach Na Frìthe announce the start of the arcing Cuillin Ridge. Across the glen are the softer, less daunting outlines of Glamaig, and the Red Hills. Stepping out south towards Camasunary, the solitary outlier Marsco slowly looms larger, its impressive crags coming into view once you cross the Allt na Measarroch. ❷ Here a jumble of rocks known as the Clach na Craoibhe Chaoruinn (Stone of the Rowan Tree) is a good resting point before heading on, spurred on by the promise of fantastic sea views from Camasunary Bay. A little further, the yawning mouth of Harta Corrie on the far side of the valley draws the attention. Here a huge, 30-foot boulder known as the 'Bloody Stone' marks the spot where fallen warrior from the feuding MacLeods and MacDonalds were laid to rest after many bruising battles.

After four long miles from the road, just beyond the almost imperceptible watershed, a large cairn marks the return route from Loch Coruisk, heading over the bealach on the Druim Hain ridge. ❸ Persevering on, the valley sides begin to tighten through the Srath na Crèitheach. The water flow is trapped in the first of two small lochs, dramatically overshadowed by the imposing profile of Bla Bheinn. Finally the glen widens again, and you catch a glimpse of the sea, the Inner Hebridean islands of Rùm and Eigg seeming to float on the horizon. This is Camas Fhionnairigh (Bay of the White Shieling) Anglicised to Camasunary, its wide expanse of machair, shingle beach, and mudflats presided over by the striking conical hill Sgùrr na Stri. Over the years, many have been drawn to this magical spot and the old bothy, now sadly closed, holds onto memories of summer sunsets and mind-expanding conversations by the fireside. The New Camasunary Bothy, sans stove, opened in May 2016. It has a rather functional feel, but still provides a welcome refuge with fabulous views out across the bay.

❹ After a well-earned lunch, it is time to contemplate the task ahead. The first obstacle is the outflow of the Abhainn Camas Fhionnairigh, just beyond the old bothy on the west side of the bay. At low tide it is possible to cross the stone bed without too much trouble, but if the tide is high you may need to wade through the channel further towards the old suspension bridge struts. Continue round the rocky headland on a faint but obvious trail, cutting inland past the grassy knoll of Rubha Buidhe, and onto the sloping

SGÙRR NAN GILLEAN

BLA BHEINN

NEW CAMASUNARY BOTHY

LOCH NA CUILCE

LOOKING OVER TO THE BAD STEP

shoreline of Loch nan Leachd. This is one of the most sensational spots on Skye, the magnificent peaks of the Southern Cuillins staring down from on high. From this point, it is all about the Bad Step. A sequence of sloping gabbro intrusions block your path to the security of Loch Coruisk, but only one is a serious obstacle. At first, you kid yourself that each little scuttle across the slabs must be the Bad Step, thinking 'Well I don't know what all the fuss is about,' and then bang, the real deal confronts you. Fear not. Once you have climbed into a large notch, and edged out onto the slab, follow the fault line in the rock. Once committed the angle is kind. The secret is to drop down leftward at a small niche in the crack, quickly moving to easier ground, rather than continue on the more obvious line – to an exposed no man's land.

❺ Ah the relief! Within a couple of minutes you are skipping across a sweet little sandy beach, and just round the corner, the magnificent sight of Loch Coruisk – a sweeping rock basin crowned by a towering tightrope of dark crags and sharp pinnacles – where you can finally relax, knowing the worst is over. The long, ambling return follows the southern shore of the loch, taking a zigzag path that rises past Loch a' Choire Riabhaich, and onto the ridge of Druim Hain. ❻ From one of the numerous cairns that mark the saddle, a dramatic panorama of the Black Cuillins unfolds, the entire ridge appearing like a gigantic wall poster. Across the valley, the granite scree slopes of the Red Hills seem tame by comparison. Head down the steep, stony path back to the comfort of Glen Sligachan, hopping across the tributaries of the Allt nam Fraoch-choire below Lochan Dubha, before joining the main track back to the car park. The trek to Sligachan can begin to drag in the dying light, but the thought of a refreshing drink at the hotel bar should speed you along the home stretch.

Notes: Conquering the 'Bad Step' is a popular outing (classified as a grade ½ scramble in an old Scottish mountaineering guide!) and is typically incorporated into an A to B route from either Elgol, Kilmarie, or the tourist boat that lands at Loch Coruisk. The circular route from Sligachan avoids the need to walk back the way you have come, and the logistical problems of needing two cars, infrequent public transport, or reliance on the boat for your return. It follows the route of the Skye Trail from Sligachan to Camasunary. Save this walk for a dry, sunny day; it is desperate if attempted after a period of heavy rain.

LOCH CORUISK

WALK 25 NEW CAMASUNARY BOTHY, THE 'BAD STEP' & LOCH CORUISK

PATH FROM RUBHA BUIDHE

DIRECTIONS

1 From the visitors' car park at Sligachan (NG 488 298), head S through a gate, and out into Glen Sligachan, along a signposted path to Camasunary and Elgol. After just under 2 miles cross the Allt na Measarroch (NG 495 272).
3km/1.9 miles

2 Continue on to a junction of paths marked by a large cairn (NG 502 240). Ignore the R fork, which is the return route from Loch Coruisk.
3.4km/2.1 miles

3 Carry on through Srath na Crèitheach, past two lochans, and out to Camasunary Bay, ignoring a path heading L to Kilmarie just before An t-Sròn (NG 515 211). There are three buildings in the bay: a private farmhouse; the old bothy to the W (now locked); and the new bothy to the E, accessed down a short, boggy path just after crossing a footbridge over the Abhainn nan Leac. At present New Camasunary is not marked on either the 1:50,000 or 1:25,000 maps of the area (NG 517 183).
6.6km/4 miles

4 From the new bothy follow an indistinct path along the shoreline, past the old bothy, to the Abhainn Camas Fhionnairigh. Navigating the river is a serious hazard if the tide is in, or after heavy rain. Once across, turn L, contouring round the coastline on a faint path past Rubha Bàn where you begin to head NW. Cut inland past a rocky knoll, and back to Loch nan Leachd's shoreline. Negotiate a number of rock slabs, before crossing the Bad Step by an obvious crack line (NG 495 192).
3km/1.9 miles

5 A little further on, cross a small, sandy beach. After a few minutes reach the banks of the River Scavaig, and Loch Coruisk. Keep on the S side of the loch, then head up a zigzag path to the saddle on the Druim Hain ridge (NG 501 214).
3.5km/2.2 miles

6 Drop back down to the valley on a steep, stony path, skirting the banks of Allt nam Fraoch-choire before crossing the river and rejoining the main track back to Sligachan. The return from here takes approximately 1.5–2 hours.
9.5km/6 miles

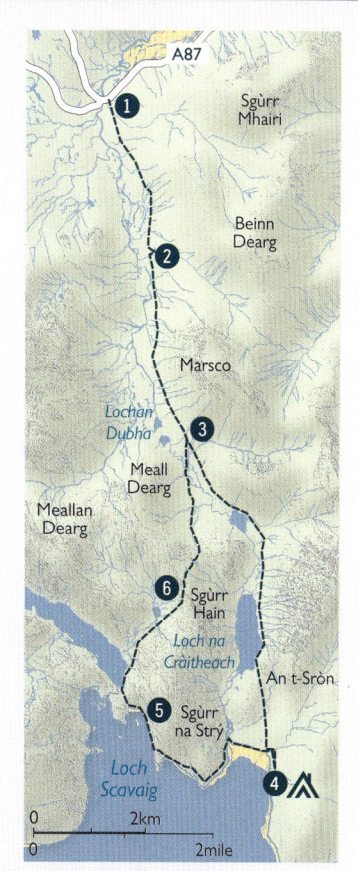

223

LOOKING NORTH ALONG THE RUM CUILLIN TO HALLIVAL

WALK 26

DIBIDIL BOTHY & THE RÙM CUILLIN

Magnificent day's walk skirting Rùm's rugged eastern coast to reach Dibidil Bothy followed by a strenuous circuit of five high peaks, with fabulous views over to the Small Isles and Skye.

The classic round of the Rùm Cuillin is one of the finest ridge walks in Scotland, as well as a thorough test of physical fitness, navigational skills, scrambling ability, and resourcefulness. Far less technically demanding than its sisterly namesake, the Black Cuillin, across the Sound on Skye, the circuit is still a significant challenge, especially if you go off-route in poor visibility. Yet without the enticement of a Munro to draw in the baggers, the circuit is surprisingly neglected, which only adds to its attraction. Hit a good weather window in early summer, or through the autumn after the island's infamous midges have abated, and you will have memories to treasure.

Exposed to the wild Atlantic between Arisaig on the western mainland and Barra in the Outer Hebrides, Rùm, Eigg, Muck and Canna are the four main islands that form the Small Isles archipelago, each with its own unique character and allure. Once known as 'The Forbidden Island', Rùm is by far the most physically dominant, and the Old Norse names of the peaks, Askival (Spear Mountain) and Trollabhal (Mountain of the Trolls), lend it a mystical air. For over a century, visitor numbers have been restricted, first by the Bullough family who ran the island as a sporting estate from the late-1880s to the middle of the 20th century, then more recently by the Nature Conservancy Council (NCC) and the present custodians, Scottish Natural Heritage (SNH). Taking advantage of the lack of human disturbance, these two environmental bodies conducted wide-ranging research into the island's flora and fauna, including the

INFORMATION

MAPS: LR 39 Rùm, Eigg, Muck & Canna; Explorer 397 Rùm, Eigg, Muck, Canna & Sanday.
START/END GRID REF: NM 411 992. New pier at Kinloch.
DISTANCE: 20.5km/13 miles
TIME: 10–12 hours
TOTAL ASCENT: 1900m
SUMMITS: Askival (Corbett) 812m, Ainshval (Corbett) 781m, Trollabhal (Graham) 702m, Sgùrr nan Gillean (Corbett Top) 764m, Hallival 723m.
NAVIGATION: Challenging. Easy to get disorientated in low mist.
TERRAIN: Hard. Well defined path, faint trails, open hillside, scrambling along ridge.
DIFFICULTY: Challenging. Hhillcraft skills required.
PUBLIC TRANSPORT: ScotRail West Highland Line Glasgow Queen St.–Mallaig. Scottish Citylink coach service 915/916 Glasgow–Fort William; Shiel Buses service 500 Fort William–Mallaig (01397 700700). Train and bus co-ordinate with CalMac ferry to Small Isles, five sailings to Rùm per week in summer.
SPECIAL NOTE: No restrictions on access. Stalking activities displayed in Kinloch, or contact Reserve office (01687 462026). Avoid potentially dangerous fissure 100m from bothy, close to coast. No vehicular access.

world's longest continuous study of red deer. Fortunately, a more open attitude now prevails, encouraged by enterprising locals eager to take charge of their own destiny. In 2007 the Isle of Rum Community Trust was established, and residents now greet the incoming ferry offering wildlife tours as well as running a community shop and café.

Rùm has a remarkable array of wildlife, including Scotland's first released pair of sea eagles who patrol the waters of the Sound of Canna beyond the wonderful beach at Kilmory Bay. You can also expect to see otters at dusk from a hide close to the new pier. A large population of red deer still roam the hills, and a working herd of Highland ponies, as well as wild goats and cattle, often gather in the lower reaches of Glen Harris. Rùm is also home to one of the world's largest colonies of Manx shearwaters. Every May the birds nest in burrows high on the mountain slopes, hiding their chicks from predatory golden eagles, ravens and hooded crows.

Anticipation builds as you reach the fishing port of Mallaig and spy the elongated profile of Eigg, the distinctive inselberg of An Stac standing defiantly at its southern shore, merging with the distant, jagged outline of the Rùm Cuillin. The CalMac ferry does a merry dance between the islands but there is no daily service to Rùm, so plan for a two- or three-day visit. There is a free campsite in Kinloch, and an assortment of eccentric pods and cabins in the vicinity, plus a couple of B&Bs. Time on the ferry gives you an opportunity to assess the weather and discuss an itinerary. The tops of the Cuillin are often obscured by cloud, and any deluges run straight down off the peaks. Of the three potentially hazardous river crossings on the six-mile walk round to Dibidil, the most significant is the Dibidil River which is only 500 yards from the bothy.

The journey along the coast from the pier at Kinloch to Dibidil is a fabulous walk, though progress is slow as the muddy, waterlogged route has few solid sections. ❶ A pony path ascends steeply from the straight drive that bypasses the outskirts of the village, and it is not long before the first glorious panoramic view of Skye opens up, with the Sleat Peninsula curving away to the north above Loch Scresort. From here the path undulates beneath the glowering peaks, and soon the isles of Eigg and Muck come into view across the strait. The beautiful play of light on the wide expanse of water is constantly shifting. After crossing the Dibidil River take a little time to rest at the perfectly located and excellent bothy (I am little biased as the current Maintenance Officer!). At this point you may be staring up at the dark

RAINBOW OVER THE BLACK CUILLIN ON SKYE

DIBIDIL BOTHY & BEINN NAN STAC

DIBIDIL BOTHY

ASKIVAL FROM THE SUMMIT OF SGÙRR NAN GILLEAN

buttresses with some trepidation, but once you reach the top of the first dizzying slope crucial momentum is established. ❺ Continue round on the Papadil path, which zigzags above the bothy, gaining height as you go, before striking uphill across the tussocks, aiming for a tiny lochan located just below the ridge up to the summit (marked only on the 1:25,000-scale map). As the slope steepens follow the line of least resistance through the broken ground to the summit cairn of Sgùrr nan Gillean. Here the daunting chain of volcanic peaks snakes away into the distance, the remnants of a giant caldera formed after successive magma eruptions over 60 million years ago. Ainshval and Trollabhal are comprised of fine-grained quartz felsite and Lewisian gneiss which are more slippery underfoot than the super-sticky, coarse-grained gabbro and basalts of Askival and Hallival, especially in wet conditions.

❻ Follow the ridge north-west to a second cairn above Nameless Corrie, before descending steeply down the west side of an exposed ridge to a saddle, and on to the slopes of Ainshval. An easier, grassy climb then leads to the summit. ❼ The next section requires particular concentration. Head north-west above Grey Corrie before descending through the scree and boulders, avoiding the steep north buttress to the west. A faint path becomes clearer as you reach the Bealach an Fhuarain. Clamber up Trollabhal, avoiding the first broken buttress on the right, before negotiating a scree runnel leading onto the blocky rocks guarding the twin summits. The higher top is north of the first summit, connected by a short, exposed ridge.

8 Descending the eastern flank of Trollabhal, the first steep section is disconcerting and difficult to follow before the gradient eases down to the Bealach an Oir (Pass of Gold). If you are short of water, the springs of Glen Dibidil are the only practical refilling spot on the entire round.

9 Next scramble up the west ridge of Askival, before picking up a path to the right up to the summit trig pillar. At 812m this is a fabulous vantage point. Eigg and Muck seem to hover above the horizon, and on a clear day there are spellbinding views out to the Western Isles. Further south you can just pick out the dome of Ben More on Mull beyond Ardnamurchan, and to the west on the mainland the distinct peaks of Beinn Sgritheall and Ladhar Bheinn. (10) The greatest challenge now lies ahead: the climb down east of the impressive Askival Pinnacle to the bealach leading on to Hallival. Descend a short way to a scree platform and look out for cairn further down through the sloping rocks to the right, which marks a faint path. Follow this carefully as it twists and turns through steep terrain. A second cairn provides reassurance before reaching safer ground, where shearwater burrows pockmark the grassy banks at regular intervals. Pause to take in the kaleidoscopic view of the huge, sculpted bowl of Atlantic Corrie before picking a line through the layered bands of basalt on Hallival, the final top of the day **11**. Heading down to the Bealach Bairc-mheall through the boulder field, you are on the home strait. After descending into Coire Dubh you come to a small hydroelectric dam where a well-maintained path leads back down to the village. The path ends at the eccentric Kinloch Castle, an expression of Edwardian opulence built by the Bullough family. Quite an adventure!

Notes: A successful round of the Rùm Cuillin requires a reasonable level of fitness as well as competent scrambling and hillcraft skills. Make sure you're adequately equipped for a long hill day (including an adequate supply of water), and leave a route card in the reserve office. Allow plenty of time: navigating along the ridge is difficult, especially in misty conditions. Except for a couple of short sections on the north ridge of Askival, all the steep rock sections can be avoided, though you still need a good head for heights. The island is prone to flash floods so it is advisable to postpone the walk if heavy rain is forecast. In summer, Saturday is the only time you can arrive at a reasonable hour and leave later in the evening, but completing the ridge within this window is a very ambitious proposition.

LOOKING SOUTH TO BEINN NAN STAC & OUT TO EIGG & MUCK

ATLANTIC CORRIE

DIRECTIONS

1 From the pier, head towards the village. At a signpost just past the school, continue straight on towards Kinloch House, rather than R to the community bunk house along the shore. After 200 yards, a path signposted to Dibidil heads up onto the hillside (NM 404 991).
0.8km/0.5 miles

2 Climb steeply onto the lower slopes of Hallival, and then begin to contour round the Cuillin, following an obvious but often waterlogged path. The first significant ford is the Allt Mòr na-h-Uamha (NM 407 974).
2km/1.25 miles

3 After half a mile cross a second ford, the Allt na h-Uamha (NM 409 968), then continue on down parallel to the coast through gently undulating terrain, eventually dropping down a zigzag section of the path to the Allt nam Bà, beyond Welshman's Rock (NM 409 943).
3.5km/2 miles

4 Once across the burn the path skirts close to steep ground above the cliffs, before turning inland on the approach to Glen Dibidil. Descend to the Dibidil River, crossing with care (this is a serious obstacle in times of spate) and on to the bothy (NM 393 928).
3.2km/2 miles

THE ISLE OF EIGG

5 Continue round on the Papadil path, then ascend the open hillside to a tiny lochan (NM 381 925). Scramble through rocky outcrops to the summit cairn of Sgùrr Nan Gillean (NM 380 930).
2.4km/1.5 miles

6 Follow the ridge NW to a second cairn above Nameless Corrie, before descending steeply down the W side of an exposed ridge to a saddle, and on to the slopes of Ainshval. A gentler grassy climb leads to the summit (NM 378 943).
1.4km/0.8 miles

7 Head NW above Grey Corrie, then descending over scree and boulders, avoiding the steep N buttress to the W. The path becomes more obvious closer to the Bealach an Fhuarain. Scramble up Trollabhal, avoiding the first buttress on the R, then negotiating a scree runnel leading onto the blocky rocks guarding the twin summits. The higher top (702m) is N of the first summit over a short ridge (NM 377 952).
1km/0.6 miles

CROSSING THE DIBIDIL RIVER IN SPATE

WALK 26 DIBIDIL BOTHY & THE RÙM CUILLIN

8 Now descend the E flank of Trollabhal. The first steep section is difficult to follow before the gradient eases down to the Bealach an Oir (455m).
0.8km/0.5 miles

9 Next scramble up the W ridge of Askival, before picking up a path to the R to the summit trig pillar (NM 393 952).
0.8km/0.5 miles

10 From the summit carefully descend a short way to a scree platform looking out for a cairn on R, a little way down the sloping rocks, which marks a faint path. Climb down E of the Askival Pinnacle through steep terrain to a second cairn before reaching safer ground at the bealach (599m).
0.8km/0.5 miles

11 Head to the summit of Hallival (NM 395 962), then descend through boulder field to Bealach Bairc-mheall, and down into Coire Dhu, following the path back to the village.
4.7km/3 miles

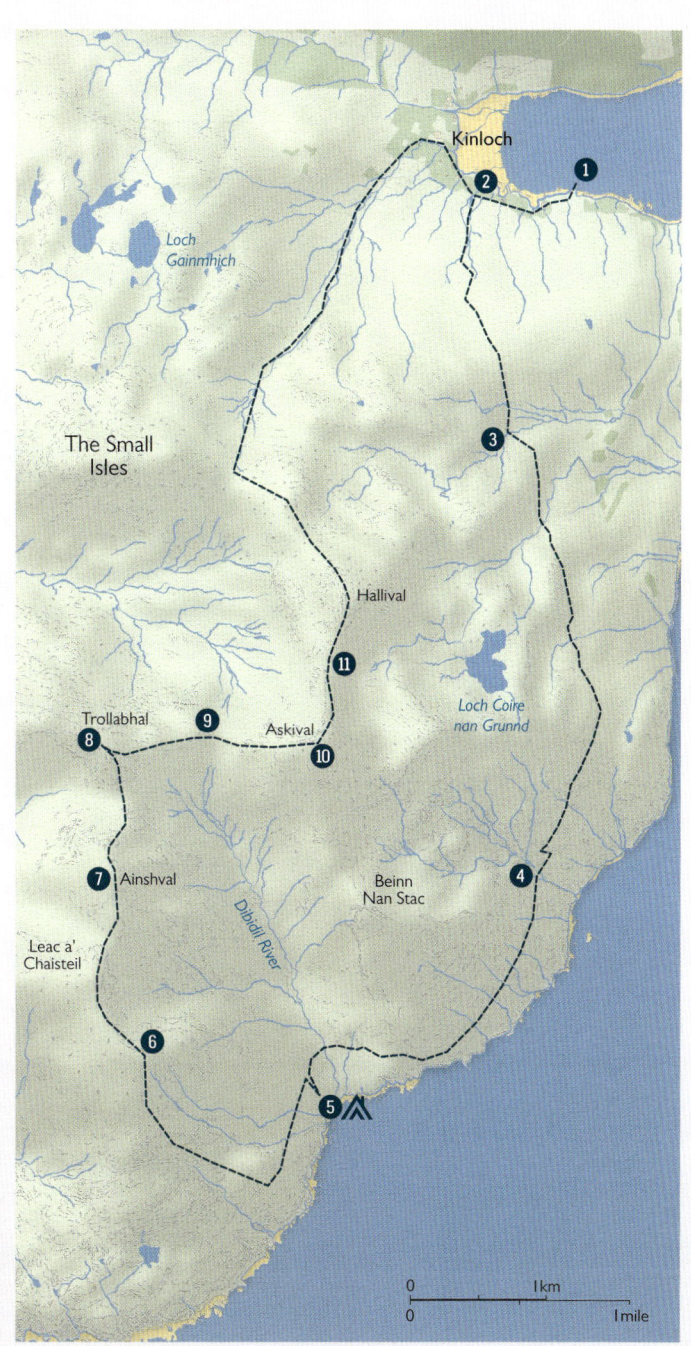

233

BEINN TALAIDH & TOMSLEIBHE BOTHY

WALK 27

BEINN TALAIDH & TOMSLEIBHE BOTHY, MULL

A rewarding ascent of the conical peak of Beinn Talaidh at the head of Glen Forsa with amazing views of Mull's winding coastline and wild interior, stopping off at Tomsleibhe Bothy on the way.

The southern Hebridean island of Mull and its famous outlying isles attract many visitors, drawn by a compelling combination of ancient historical sites, abundant, accessible wildlife, and evocative scenery. Dovetailed into an angular recess of dramatic, sweeping coastline between Oban and the Morven peninsula, the archipelago has something for everyone. Eagle Watch tours on Loch Frisa are a particular draw, while spotting otters at the fishing village of Salen has become almost routine. There are also glorious sandy beaches at Calgary and the southern coast of the Ross of Mull to enjoy, while the spectacular geometric columns of Fingal's Cave on Staffa are another major attraction. Others seek out the spiritual ambience of Iona. At the island's heart lies a chain of rounded basalt peaks, capped by the distinctive flat-topped ridge of Ben More. To the east, the striking profile of Beinn Talaidh dominates the skyline above the tidal strait separating Mull from the mainland. Many hill-walkers are single-minded in an attempt on Ben More, as it is Mull's only Munro. Beinn Talaidh is a worthy alternative, and it is often clear on days when the higher peak is shrouded in thick cloud, brought in on the prevailing, damp westerly airflow.

The most direct ascent of Beinn Talaidh is from the south, but a far more appealing alternative is to scale the northern slopes, approaching from the quiet confines of Glen Forsa.

① A wide gravel access road leads into the glen towards the

INFORMATION

MAPS: LR 49 Oban & East Mull, Explorer 375 Isle of Mull East.
START/END GRID REF: NM 595 427. Small parking area a short way from the turning into the valley at Pennygown, close to Glenforsa Airfield on the A849.
DISTANCE: 18km/11 miles
TIME: 5–6 hours' round trip
ASCENT: 748m
SUMMITS: Beinn Talaidh (Graham) 761m
NAVIGATION: Easy
TERRAIN: Straightforward. Track, well defined path, open hillside.
DIFFICULTY: Straightforward
PUBLIC TRANSPORT: ScotRail train service from Glasgow Queen St. or Scottish Citylink coach service 975/976 from Glasgow Buchanan Street to Oban. CalMac ferry from Oban to Craignure. On Mull, West Coast Motors service 95/495 Craigmure–Salen–Tobermory. Trains co-ordinate with ferries.
SPECIAL NOTES: Open all year. Stag-stalking from 15 August to 20 October and hind cull from 21 October to 15 February. Contact Glen Forsa Estate (01680 300674) for information about access to the hills.

WALK 27 BEINN TALAIDH & TOMSLEIBHE BOTHY, MULL

distant peak, which stares down benignly as you advance towards its lower flanks. Once beyond the cottage at Killbeg and the ruins of an old burial ground, the broad floodplain stretches away into the distance. The track running parallel but a little away from the meandering River Forsa (Old Norse for 'swift-flowing water'). Curious Highland cattle often wander in the open fields that lead down to the bank side. Although far less fearsome than their horns suggest, negotiating your way through them, especially mothers with calves in tow, takes some bravado. Tomsleibhe Bothy is soon visible on the hillside, a small, black dot above the line of spruce straddling the upper part of the valley.

After another mile the track returns to the riverbank, just before the conifer plantations begin to encroach. Passing a locked fishing hut, recently constructed by the estate, you notice the river has been dammed to form fish-holding pens for hopeful anglers. ❷ Once across a wooden footbridge over the Gaodhail River, continue straight on past a ford to the left that leads to some large, metal cowsheds and sheep pens. A few hundred yards further on, the path curves to the right and a poignant war memorial with a damaged propeller comes into view. This commemorates the crew of a Dakota aeroplane that crashed high up in the corrie between Beinn Talaidh and Beinn Bheag during World War II. One airman stumbled down through deep snow to raise the alarm at nearby Rhoail Farm, but alas none of his comrades survived. ❸ Immediately beyond the memorial, ford the Allt na Laith-dhoire (a possible hazard after heavy rain) via

236

LOOKING OVER TO BEN MORE, LOST IN THE CLOUDS

TOMSLEIBHE BOTHY

concrete sleepers lodged in the stream bed, and, as the track forks, take the right turn signposted to the bothy, which is in sight a few hundred yards further up the slope.

④ After resting a while in the homely confines of Tomsleibhe, walk uphill along the muddy farm track, passing through a metal gate before crossing the Allt nan Clàr. Any semblance of a path finally peters out as you climb the steepening slope, which finally levels out at the 450m contour. Turning to inspect your progress, you look back down Glen Forsa out to the Sound of Mull, and across to Ben More. Continue up the boulder-strewn ridge and, with a final effort, the summit plateau is soon within reach. If you are lucky you may be blessed with the sight of a golden eagle, soaring on the thermals above the ridge or patrolling the silent corrie above Gleann Lèan. One telltale sign is the presence of hooded crows, who often gang up to mob their illustrious neighbours. Looking down to the Sound, a flotilla of white sails can often be spied tacking down the strait, and in the afternoon the Western Isles ferry steams into view bound for Oban. A large cairn marks the highest point at 761m, close to a dilapidated trig pillar. The mountain once enjoyed the status of a Corbett, but was resurveyed in 2009 and found wanting by a marginal amount. It now lays claim to be the highest Graham in the arcane world that rules the lives of serious hill baggers! Retrace your steps back down to the valley, and after a final refreshment stop at Tomsleibhe, stride back down Glen Forsa, savouring a fine outing on this very special island.

VIEW DOWN GLEN FORSA

DIRECTIONS

1 From the small car park at Pennygown, head up Glen Forsa on an unmetalled access road. Close to the cottage at Killbeg, pass through a farm gate, and continue across the river floodplain to a locked fishing hut (NM 609 391).
3.5km/2 miles

2 After another 500 yards, cross the Gaodhail River by FB, and continue straight on past a ford to the L. Soon the path curves R, reaching a war memorial (NM 617 377).
2km/1.25 miles

3 Immediately beyond the memorial, ford the Allt na Liath-Dhoire. As the track forks, take R turn signposted to the bothy nearby (NM 618 372).
0.6km/0.4 miles

4 Leaving the bothy, head S towards Beinn Talaidh along a muddy track to ford the Allt nan Clàr. Climb the very steep slope beyond the stream on a faint trail that soon ends. The gradient eases before rising again on the stony ridge at the summit (NM 625 347).
3km/1.75 miles

5 Although you can create a round by returning via Beinn Bheag, the scree slope down to the bealach at the head of Gleann Lèan is very steep, and the pathless terrain over Beinn Bheag is also craggy and demanding. The simplest descent is to retrace your steps.

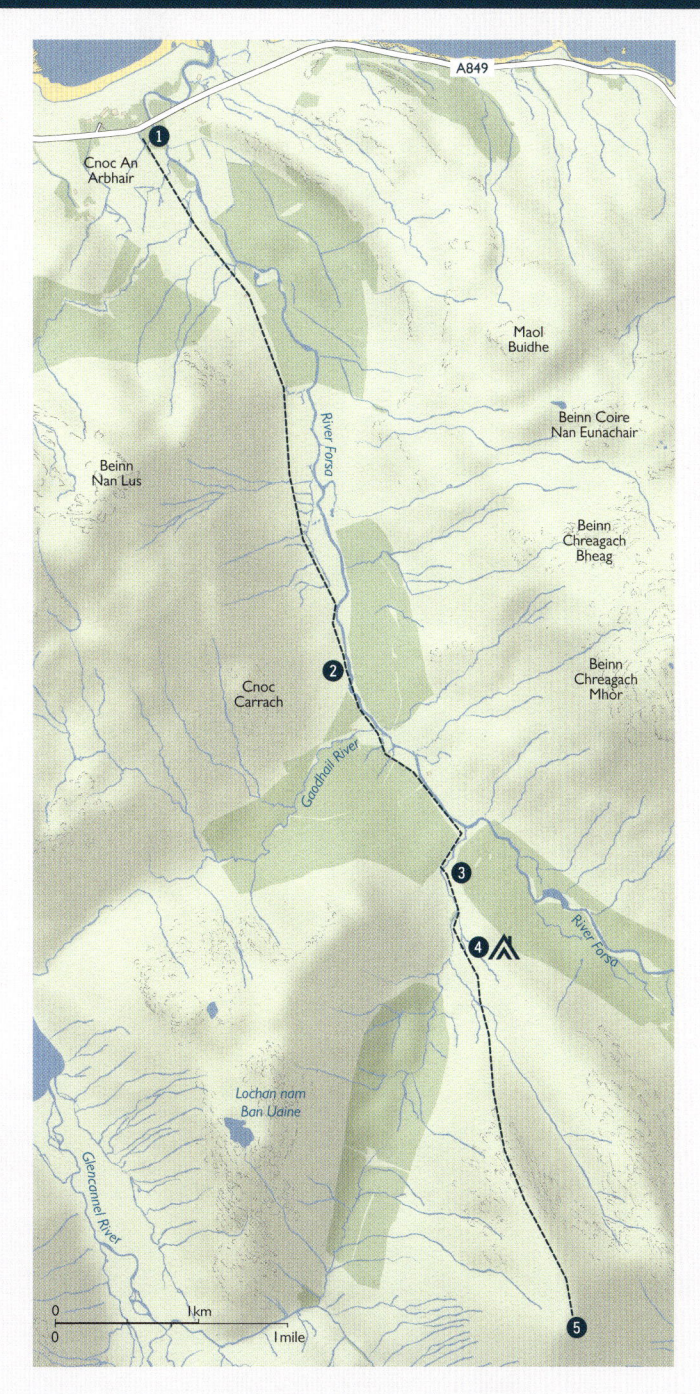

VIEW OF LOCH TARBERT FROM CRUIB BOTHY

WALK 28

JURA'S REMOTE COASTAL BOTHIES, CRUIB & RUANTALLAIN

Exceptional three-day round trip along the uncompromising northern shoreline of Loch Tarbert. A haven for wildlife, this rugged landscape is among the finest in Scotland.

The westward-facing seaboard of Jura has been scoured and sculpted into a procession of quartzite cliffs, sea-stacks, caves and raised beaches that are as remote and inaccessible as any in Scotland. A world away from the metropolis of Glasgow (barely 50 miles as the crow flies), it is home to a large population of red deer and wild goats that roam the open moorland. Golden eagles, hen harriers and buzzards soar above, while along the foreshore otters and grey seals share the rocky skerries with cormorants and guillemots. Only four permanent buildings remain intact along the entire coastline, three of them bothies. For the intrepid adventurer, setting out across this wild, untamed landscape will be a true voyage of discovery, and I could not recommend it more highly.

Jura – from Diura meaning 'deer island' in Old Norse – is home to over 5000 animals descended from a herd of ancient lineage that has been managed for over 1000 years. Deer significantly outnumber the human population of 200, most of whom live in the village of Craighouse, home of the popular Jura Whisky Distillery. The island is neatly cleaved in two by Loch Tarbert and the most eye-catching feature of its southern part is the sensuous line of three domed summits – the well-known Paps of Jura, visible from miles around. The northern half is moody and less defined, empty save for a scattering of properties along the single-track road that hugs the eastern coast, and the estate house at Ardlussa. On the far northern tip beyond the end of the road, lies the cottage at Barnhill, where George Orwell

INFORMATION

MAPS: LR Map 61 Jura & Colonsay, Explorer 355 Jura & Scarba (recommended).
START/END GRID REF: NR 605 828. Lay-by just beyond Tarbert on A846, 12 miles N Craighouse.
TOTAL DISTANCE: 27km/17 miles
DAY 1: 6km/3.75 miles
TIME: 2–3 hours
DAY 2: 15km/9.5 miles
TIME: 5–6 hours
DAY 3: 6km/3.75 miles
TIME: 2–3 hours
TOTAL ASCENT: 140m
HIGHEST POINT: 98m
NAVIGATION: Challenging.
TERRAIN: Challenging. Faint trails, open moor, river crossings, rough walking along coast.
DIFFICULTY: Challenging
PUBLIC TRANSPORT: Citylink bus service 926, Glasgow to Kennacraig. CalMac Ferry Kennacraig to Port Askaig (Islay). Regular ferry on to Jura. Bus weekdays from Feolin Ferry to Craighouse and Inverlussa. Garelochhead Coaches (01436 810200). Easter-September Jura passenger ferry from Tayvallich to Craighouse. Advance booking only (07768 450000). West Coast Motors service 426 from Lochgilphead to Tayvallich.
SPECIAL NOTES: Deer-stalking July–Feb. Call Ruantallain Estate (01496 820287) for information.

WALK 28 JURA'S REMOTE COASTAL BOTHIES, CRUIB & RUANTALLAIN

famously wrote his novel '*Nineteen Eighty-Four*'. To the west, there is gaping wilderness.

Arriving at Port Arkaig, Islay, courtesy of the CalMac service from Kennacraig, the pace of life noticeably slows and no one seems to be in any hurry. From here, a small vehicle ferry chugs back and forth across the fast-flowing Sound with reassuring regularity, and once you have disembarked on Jura, the short journey round to Craighouse follows the only road on the island. Continuing on through the village, past the hotel (which has a useful campsite on its front lawn), shop and distillery, the rock-shattered slopes of the Paps dominate the view. A few miles further on, the road descends steeply to the isthmus at the tiny hamlet of Tarbert, a narrow strip of land separating Loch Tarbert, and the Sound of Jura. One of a number of Tarberts found on the waterways of Western Scotland, from Loch Lomond to Harris, it means 'draw boat' in Gaelic and describes a point of portage between navigable stretches of water. From the time of the Viking settlers, vessels were dragged across this spot on wooden rollers rather than risking the tidal race to south, or the treacherous strait to the north guarded by the infamous Corryvreckan whirlpool.

❶ Setting off west from the lay-by just beyond a stand of conifers above Tarbert Bay, follow a line of white-painted stones leading down to the mudflats at the head of the loch. On the far bank a patchwork of spruce, silver birch and sessile oak hugs the low bluff leading into a narrowing channel marked by navigation pillars. At low tide it is possible to walk straight across to the far shore, negotiating the seaweed and shingle. But if your timing is awry, seek out the stepping stones that cross the Abhainn Ghleann Aoistail and circle back round. ❷ From here walk to the end of a woodland fence, then climb very steeply to the top of the slope and survey the scene. One recommended route across the open moor is to head west-north-west across the undulations of Glac Mhòr to the northern end of Loch na Pearaich ('Parrot Loch') and follow an indistinct line down to Sàilean nam Màireach cove, and round the coast. Alternatively head more directly west, staying on high ground to the Abhainn a' Ghleann Duirch, before hiking down to the salt marsh at Learadail. Numerous deer tracks skirt around the worst of the terrain, but do not be fooled into sticking rigidly to one of them, convinced this is the 'right' path. Before you know it, you are far too high up on the hill, or approaching the coast too early and fighting your way through head-high bracken and dense heather to reach the tideline.

APPROACHING THE HEAD OF LOCH TARBERT

GLAC MHÒR

CRUIB BOTHY

But what reward! As soon as you are down to the flats and over the last low rise to the shore, a majestic view opens up across Loch Tarbert to the southern hills, and a wide-eyed feeling of privilege overwhelms you. There is a certain magic to moving through barely disturbed terrain, a sensation you catch yourself thinking about at odd moments once you have returned home. The water is crystal-clear, the grassy cliff slightly scruffy but pristine, unsullied by the occasional intruder. A little further along the rocky beach, Cruib finally comes into view – a welcome sight and a reward well earned. Expertly renovated in 2012, the bothy's central communal room is one of the most comfortable I have ever stayed in. Along with a bespoke sleeping platform and comfortable chairs, there is a library shelf heaving with reference books and novels, an oil painting above the mantelpiece, and even carpet in front of the fire. On returning after a wander at dusk to collect some cut turf from a peat bank close by, I instinctively went to switch on the light, forgetting I was not in a hostel!

If you have the time, the day trip to Ruantallain is a must, combining a spectacularly located bothy, fixed at a lost moment in time, with an exploration of hidden caves and sweeping raised beaches. ❹ From Cruib Bothy, head round the shore to the outflow of the Garbh Uisge (Rough Water) as it rushes into Loch Tarbert adjacent to Eilean Ard. ❺ Once across, pick up an ATV track heading west, away from the coast through the undulating moor. Skirting to the south of three small lochans, the track leads on to Gleann Righ Mòr. A little indistinct in places, the trail becomes more obvious when the bay comes into view.

❻ Cross the track leading up from the beach to the boathouse on Loch Righ Beag, and continue on to Rubhà an t-Sàilein. The bothy is tucked away in the lee of a low slanting band of rock close to the shore.

This is truly a show-stopping location, the sweet spot of Northern Jura. From the bothy door, two of the Paps – Beinn an Oir and Beinn Shiantaidh – rise serenely above the brooding loch, while out on the headland there is a rare view of Colonsay, the last stop before Newfoundland. You might spot otters in the freshwater pool beyond the bothy's stone boundary wall, and every autumn, female grey seals give birth on this exposed coastal frontier, their tiny pups seeking shelter between the boulders. At the end of the last glaciation 10,000 years ago, the land was freed from the weight of ice and continued to rise long after the sea level subsided, leaving once submerged caves, rock arches and beaches high above the waterline. The most striking feature is the huge stone beach above An Sàilean to the south-east, which you cross on the journey back to Cruib.

Ruantallain is a throwback to a bygone age, before bothies gained in popularity in the 1960s and 1970s. Often, items of furniture and crockery would be left once the property was vacated, and then, over time, would be broken, chopped up or cleared away as visitor numbers increased. Here, antique plates are still piled up haphazardly on shelves, an oval mirror hangs behind the door, and above the fireplace there is a picture of a former laird, partly hidden by a collection of antlers. The darkened, smoke-stained wood panelling adds to the other-worldly atmosphere of the single room, which is lit only by a tiny south-facing window.

❼ Returning by the coast is far more time-consuming than taking the ATV track, but is much more rewarding. Skirting the massive raised beach above Rubha Buidhe, gain the rock platform at Creag nan Seabhag, and weave your way through the gaps in the rocks formed by basalt dykes. There are numerous caves to poke your nose into, the most startling being Uamh Righ (King's Cave) just before you reach Bàgh Gleann Righ Mòr. According to legend, the bodies of ancient kings were transported here, en route to their final resting place on the sacred island of Iona. Deep within the gloom at low tide, you can just make out the ghostly outlines of overlapping crucifixes etched into the undercut rock.

❽ Faithfully following the deer tracks from the bay, pick your way over the rough terrain of Aird Reamhar, through the broken dykes, and round to the next curve of pebble beach at Rubha Liath. ❾ Once round the next headland at Rubha Gille nan Ordag, look out for two white-painted obelisks (navigation beacons), before heading inland. Within 500 yards the ATV track comes into view, heading back down Sàilean a' Gharbh-Uisge and onwards to Cruib. (10) After a second night at the bothy make the slow journey back to Tarbert.

Notes: The terrain across the northern part of Jura is challenging, and the route to Cruib is much more complex than it appears, even on the 1:25,000-scale map. There are numerous well-established deer tracks that criss-cross the slopes and linking these together can aid progress. It is important to allow twice as much time as you think you will need so that you can pace yourself accordingly.

RUANTALLAIN BOTHY

LOOKING EAST TO RUBHA BUIDHE

DIRECTIONS

Day 1
Tarbert to Cruib

1 From a small lay-by (NR 605 828) follow a line of white stones down to the mudflats at the head of Loch Tarbert. Walk across at low tide or use the stepping stones across Abhainn Ghleann Aoistail (NR 598 834), close to a weir marked on the 1:25,000 map, and circle back round.
2km/1.25 miles

2 From here walk to the end of a woodland fence, and climb to the top of the steep slope. At this point you can either: A) Head WNW across the undulations to the N end of Loch na Pearaich and follow a rough line down to Sàilean nam Màireach, and round the coast to the salt marsh at Learadail (NR 572 834). Or B) Set off more directly W, staying on high ground. Once across the Abhainn a' Ghleann Duirch, head down to the salt marsh at Learadail.
2.8km/1.75 miles

3 Pick up a faint track round the shoreline, up over a small rise and down to the shore or strike uphill 40 yards to an ATV track that leads down an indistinct ridge to the trees. The bothy (NR 567 829) is hidden between the water and a low grass cliff and does not come into view until the very last moment.
1.2km/0.75 miles

Day 2
Round trip to Ruantallain

4 From Cruib, head for the outflow of the Garbh Uisge adjacent to Eilean Ard (NR 557 824). An ATV track leads straight up from the bothy to Chriostail, along a little ridge and down to the burn, but it is difficult to pick out in places. The alternative is to pick your way along the coast, although it is still heavy-going. The Garbh Uisge is a serious obstacle in times of spate, and is very difficult to cross at any point up to the Loch a' Gharbh Uisge – the water from the slopes is channelled into a narrow glen. If you are in any doubt about crossing, it is best to head back to Cruib.
1.25km/0.75 miles

5 Once across Garbh Uisge, pick up an ATV track leading W over the moor away from the shoreline, skirting S of three small lochans and on to Gleann Righ Mòr. The track becomes more distinct as you come into sight of the coast again.
4km/2.5 miles

6 Cross the track that heads up from the beach to the boathouse on Loch Righ Beag and continue on to Rubha an t-Sàilein. The bothy is hidden below a low bluff and only comes into view minutes before you reach it (NR 505 832).
1.75km/1 mile

7 To return to Cruib via the coast, descend past the small lochan below the bothy, cutting across to the raised beach at Rubha Buidhe. Continue along rocky coastal fringe to Bàgh Gleann Righ Mòr (NR 520 826).
1.5km/1 mile

8 Cross the bay and resume over rough terrain to the promontory of Aird Reamhar and round to the pebble beach at Rubha Liath.
3km/1.75 miles

9 At the next headland, Rubha Gille nan Ordag, look out for two white obelisks before heading inland. Within 500 yards pick up ATV track heading back down Sàilean a' Gharbh-Uisge and on to Cruib.
3.5km/2.25 miles

Day 3 Cruib back to Tarbert

10 Return to road following the route via Loch na Pearaich or across higher ground.
6km/3.75 miles

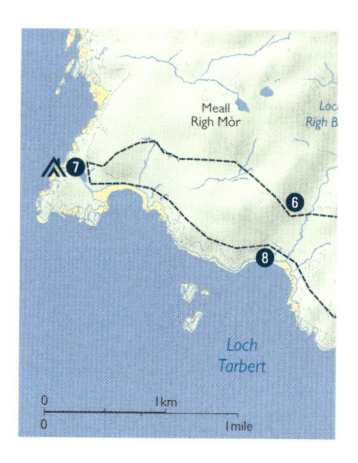

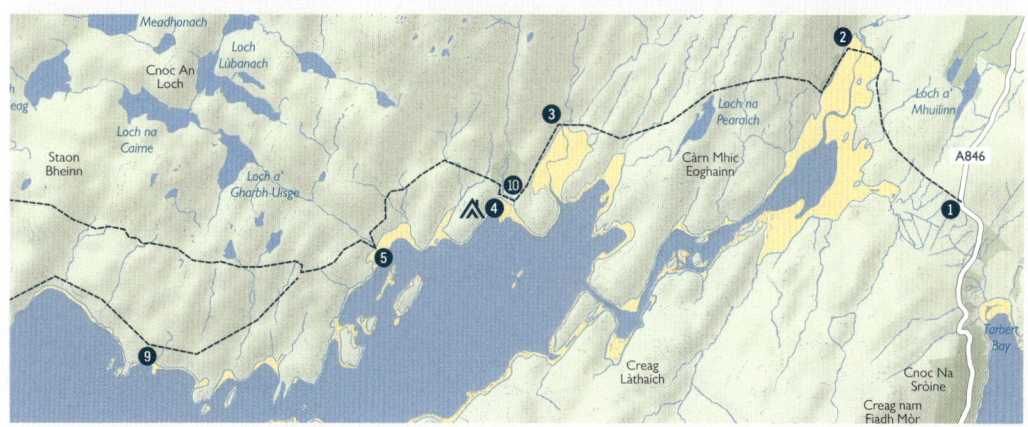

WALK 28 JURA'S REMOTE COASTAL BOTHIES, CRUIB & RUANTALLAIN

MUNROS, CORBETTS & GRAHAMS

MUNROS

Scotland's highest mountains are named after Sir Hugh Munro, who listed peaks that he judged to be over 3000 feet (914m) in a book of tables in 1891. His total of 236 separate summits has been superseded, thanks to modern survey techniques, and with a couple of more recent revisions, stands at 282. There is also a concept of a Munro top, which is a peak that is not regarded as a separate mountain, but is within the height range. Tops are applicable to each of the other lists below; it is a little subjective, but has been agreed by all participants. The highest is Ben Nevis (4411ft/1345m), the most southerly Ben Lomond (3196ft/974m).

CORBETTS

These Scottish mountains are over 2500ft (762m) and below 3000 feet (914m) compiled by John Rooke Corbett in the 1920s. The definition of a Corbett is based on there being at least 500ft of ascent on all sides. In total there are 221 Corbetts.

GRAHAMS

These are summits between 2000 and 2500 feet (609 to 762m) with a drop of at least 150m all round. They were first published in '*The Relative Hills of Britain*' (1997) by Alan Dawson, but later attributed to the late Fiona Torbet (née Graham) who had compiled a similar list at around the same time. There are 219 Grahams in all.

DONALDS

Finally there are the Donalds which are a collection of hills in the Scottish lowlands over 2000 feet (609m) compiled by Percy Donald in 1935. The definition of a Donald has been open to debate and follows a complicated formula, a prominence of at least 30m is automatic, but in various cases ones with a relative height of 15m have been accepted if they are of 'sufficient' topographic interest. There are currently 89 Donalds Hills and a further 51 Donald Tops.

GAELIC GLOSSARY

Many landscape features and place names in the book are in Scots Gaelic. Also included below are Scots words that are frequently used in the descriptions.

A
abhainn river
ailean field, grassy plain
aird height, promontory
allt stream
àth ford

B
bàgh bay
beag small
bealach saddle pass
ben/beinn/bheinn mountain
buidhe yellow
burn stream
byre shed or barn for cattle

C
càrn cairn
clach stone
cladach beach, shore, coast
coire hanging valley
cnoc knoll
crannog ancient fortified lake/marsh dwelling
creag crag, rock, cliff
croft tenanted smallholding

D
damh deer
dearg red
dreich dreary
druim spine, ridge
dubh black
dun fort

E
eas waterfall
eilean island

F
feith bog, underground stream
fionn fair, white

G
gaoith wind
garbh rough, stony
geal white
ghillie hunting/fishing guide
glas grey-green
glen/gleann valley

H
howff rough-and-ready shelter

L
laird owner of an estate
lairig pass, saddle
liath grey
lochan small lake, tarn

M
machair coastal grassy plain
mam breast
maol bare, bald
meall/mheall round hill
mòr/more/mhor big, great

R
ruadh reddish
rhubha point or headland
runrig landholding divided into strips belonging to different owners

S
sgòr/sgorr jagged peak
sheiling shepherds' shelter
stane stone
strath wide valley
stravaig wander, roam

T
traigh beach

U
uaimh/uamh cave
uaine green

BIBLIOGRAPHY

Rab Anderson and Tom Prentice. *The Grahams and The Donalds: Scottish Mountaineering Club Hillwalkers' Guide*. Scottish Mountaineering Club, 2015.

Dan Bailey. *Great Mountain Days in Scotland: 50 Classic Hillwalking Challenges*. Cicerone Press, 2012.

Dan Bailey. *Scotland's Mountain Ridges*. Cicerone Press, 2006.

Donald J. Bennet. *The Munros: Scottish Mountaineering Club Hillwalkers' Guide*. Scottish Mountaineering Club, 2006.

Alastair Borthwick. *Always a Little Further*. Diadem Books, 1983.

Dave Brown and Ian R. Mitchell. *Mountain Days & Bothy Nights*. Luath Press, 2008.

Hamish Brown. *Hamish's Mountain Walk and Climbing The Corbetts*. Bâton Wicks Publications, 1996.

Irvine Butterfield. *A Survey of Shelters in Remote Mountain areas of the Scottish Highlands*. Ian Mackenzie, 1979.

Irvine Butterfield. *The Call of the Corbetts*. David & Charles, 2007.

Irvine Butterfield. *The High Mountains*. BCA, 1986.

James Carron. *A Ceiling of Stars: The Remarkable Life of a Highland Hermit*. CreateSpace Independent Publishing Platform, 2012.

Mike Cawthorne. *Wilderness Dreams: The Call of Scotland's Last Wild Places*. The In Pinn, 2007.

Graeme Cornwallis. *101 Best Hill Walks in the Scottish Highlands and Islands*. Fort Publishing, 2009.

David Craig. *On the Crofter's Trail*. Birlinn, 2006.

Jim Crumley. *The Nature of Winter*. Saraband, 2017.

Peter Edwards. *The Hebrides: 50 Walking and Backpacking Routes*. Cicerone Press, 2015.

Peter Edwards. *Walking on Jura, Islay and Colonsay*. Cicerone Press, 2010.

Keith Fergus. *Fort William and Lochaber: 40 Favourite Walks*. Pocket Mountain Ltd, 2016.

Paul Gannon. *Rock Trails: Scottish Highlands*. Pesda Press, 2012.

Affleck Gray. *Legends of the Cairngorms*. Mainstream Publishing, 1988.

Andrew Greig. *At the Loch of the Green Corrie*. Quercus, 2010.

Iain Harper. *The Cape Wrath Trail*. Cicerone Press, 2015.

Eric Langmuir. *Mountain Craft and Leadership*. Mountain Training Boards of England and Scotland; 4th edition, 2013.

Robert Macfarlane. *The Old Ways: A Journey on Foot*. Penguin, 2013.

Graeme Macrae Burnet. *His Bloody Project*. Saraband, 2015.

Cameron McNeish. *The Munros: Scotland's Highest Mountains*. Lomond Books, 1996.

Cameron McNeish and Richard Else. *Wilderness Walks*. BBC Consumer Publishing, 1998.

Alistair Moffat. *The Hidden Ways*. Canongate, 2017.

John Murray. *Reading the Gaelic Landscape*. Whittles Publishing, 2014.

W.H. Murray. *Scotland's Mountains, (Scottish Mountaineering Club Guide)*. Scottish Mountaineering Club, 1987.

W.H. Murray. *Undiscovered Scotland: Climbs on Rock, Snow & Ice*. J.M. Dent & Sons, 1951.

Desmond Nethersole-Thompson and Adam Watson. T*he Cairngorms: Their Natural History and Scenery*. HarperCollins, 1974.

Neil Oliver. *A History of Scotland*. Orion Publishing Co, 2010.

W. A. Poucher. *The Scottish Peaks*. Constable and Co Ltd, 1964.

G. Scott Johnstone. *The Corbetts & Other Scottish Hills: Scottish Mountaineering Club Hillwalkers' Guide*. Scottish Mountaineering Club, 2002.

Nan Shepherd. *The Living Mountain: A Celebration of the Cairngorm Mountains of Scotlan*d. Canongate, 2011.

Phoebe Smith. *The Book of the Bothy*. Cicerone Press, 2015.

Ralph Storer. *100 Best Routes on Scottish Mountains: Revised and Updated*. Sphere, 2012.

Chris Townsend. *Scotland*. Cicerone Press, 2013.

Paul and Helen Webster. *Aviemore and the Cairngorms: 40 Shorter Walks*. Pocket Mountain Ltd, 2009.

Paul and Helen Webster. W*ester Ross and Lochalsh: 40 Coast & Country Walks*. Pocket Mountain Ltd, 2010.

Nick Williams. *Central Highlands*. Pocket Mountain Ltd, 2004.

Nick Williams. *Northern Highlands*. Pocket Mountain Ltd, 2004.

Nick Williams. *Southern Highlands*. Pocket Mountain Ltd, 2004.

Nick Williams. *Southern Uplands*. Pocket Mountain Ltd, 2004.

Nick Williams. *The Cairngorms*. Pocket Mountain Ltd, 2004.

Nick Williams. *West Highlands*. Pocket Mountain Ltd, 2004.

Ken Wilson and Richard Gilbert. *Classic Walks: Mountain and Moorland Walks in Britain and Ireland*. Diadem Books, 1982.

Ken Wilson and Richard Gilbert. *The Big Walks: Challenging Mountain Walks and Scrambles in the British Isles*. Diadem Books, 1980, 1989.

Ken Wilson and Richard Gilbert. *Wild Walks: Mountain, Moorland and Coastal Walks in Britain and Ireland*. Hodder & Stoughton, 1988.

Ken Wilson, Dave Alcock and John Barry. *Cold Climbs: The Great Snow and Ice Climbs of the British Isles*, Diadem Books, 1990.

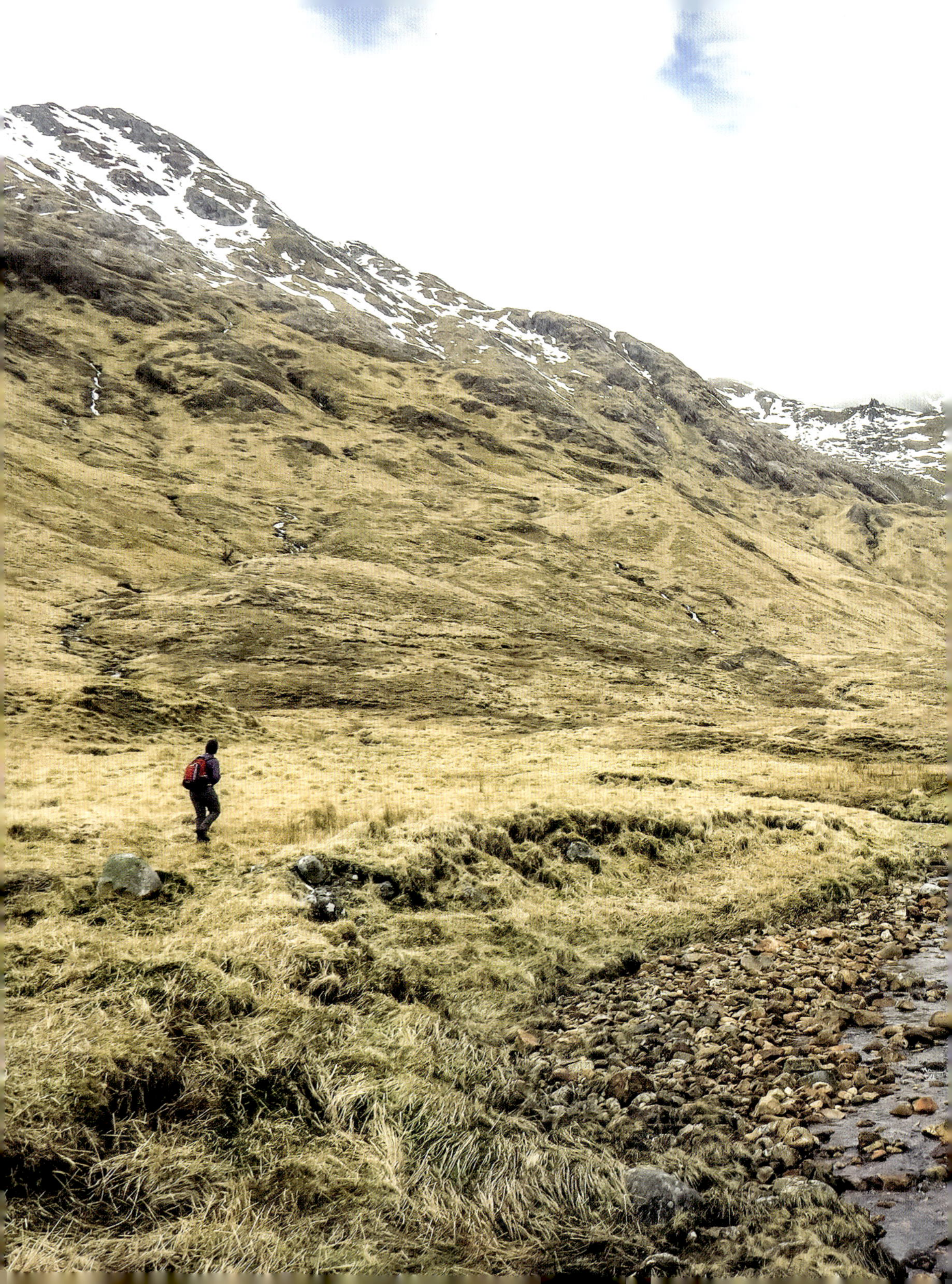

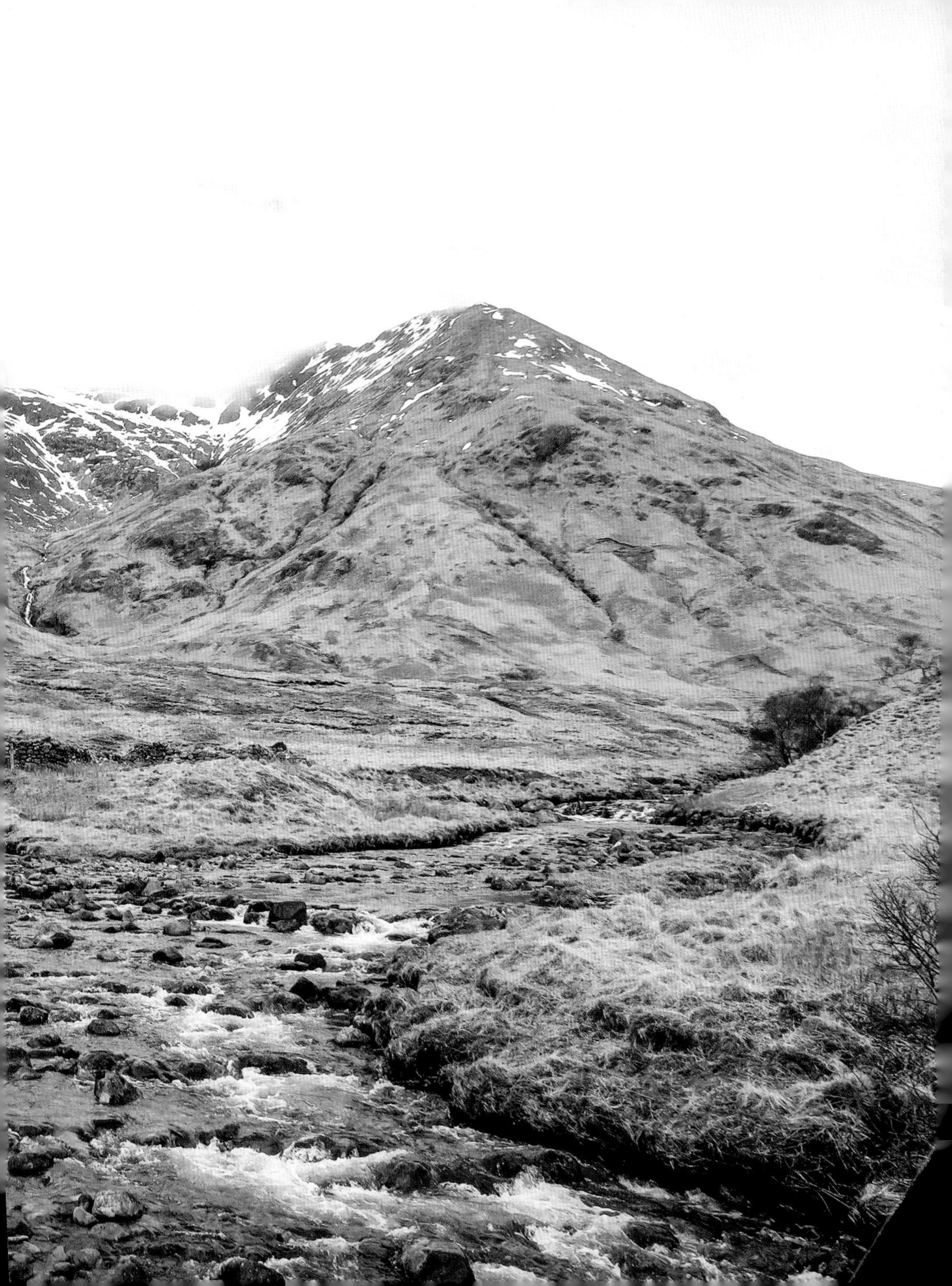

Scottish Bothy Walks: Scotland's 28 Best Bothy Adventures

by Geoff Allan

www.geoffallan.co.uk

Editor
Anna Kruger
Design and layout
Tania Pascoe and Amy Bolt
Proofreading
ProofProfessor

BE SAFE!
While every care and effort has been taken in the preparation of this guide, conditions can change quickly, materially affecting the seriousness of a mountain walk. Therefore, except for any liability which cannot be excluded by law, neither Wild Things nor the author accepts liability for damage of any nature (including damage to property, or personal injury or death) arising directly or indirectly from the information in this book.

Published by
Wild Things Publishing Ltd
Bath, BA2 7WG,
United Kingdom
wildthingspublishing.com

COPYRIGHT, PHOTOGRAPHY & MAPS

First edition published in the United Kingdom in 2020 by Wild Things Publishing Ltd. ISBN 9781910636190. Text and photography copyright © 2020 Geoff Allan. The moral rights of the author have been asserted.

All photography © Geoff Allan except p11 Emma di Gleria; p164 (top) Anthony Tomlinson. Maps designed and produced by Lovell Johns Ltd. Contains Ordnance Survey data © Ordnance Survey and OpenStreetMap.org data © OpenStreetMap contributors, CC-BY-SA.

AUTHOR ACKNOWLEDGEMENTS

This project has been a massive team effort and I am blessed to have had the help and support of my family and a wide circle of friends to get over the finishing line. I would especially like to thank my sister Hil who invested countless hours in the editing process, and offered sage advice and insight about how to pull this guide together, Dave Rosenthal, who listened patiently over extended library coffee breaks as I de-stressed during the writing process (and cast an experienced eye over some of the intricacies of the text), and my loving girlfriend Imelda for continuing to believe and keeping me on the straight and narrow. Heartfelt thanks also to my mum and sister Ruth who have been steadfast in their positivity, and my niece Mia who is continuing the family hiking tradition, and joined me on a couple of the walks.

Over the last three years my long-suffering friends have tolerated cringeworthy bouts of bubbling over-enthusiasm and lengthy periods of total self-absorption, loyally cheerleading from the sidelines. It gives me great pleasure to mention them here. Thanks, one and all, and I wish you continued good health and happiness. Anthony Tomlinson, Caroline Piercy, John Irving, Katherine Lawlor, Phil Matthews, Elly Danak, Adam Campbell, Alison Dickson, Frances Priest, Mervyn Drever, Jo Scott, Chris Minty, Valerie Thornber, Colin Hattersley, Nick Wallerstein, Suzanne Mcgowan, Graham Holden, Simon and Jana Jackson, Dave and Jo Walker, Struan and Karen Macnee, Kat Jones, Rueidi Nager, Jamie Andrew, Anna Wyatt, Bridget McGill and Joe, Mark Taylor, Kerstin Hinds, Brad and Heidi Carroll, Jo and Sam, Eileen Allan, Al Brightman, Pete and Juliette Jennings, Steve and Katherine Matthews, Phil and Ruth Levack, Doug and Sarah Shephard, Hanna, Isabel, George and my fabulous god-daughter Phoebe, Pam Shephard, Greg Hacket, Emma and Max di Gleria, Paul Tomkins, Mark Ryle, Jacqui Austin, Kay Johnson, Donald White, Diarmid Jamieson, Finlay Bennet, Ricky Mellon, Tom Legendre, Allyson Stack, Janet Christie, Chris Rigby, Alan Grieve, Dan Bailey, Alan Rowan, Fiona Russell, Alan Little, Ralf Groothuizen, Jonathan Andrew and Jon Haber. The Irish connection: Tina Reynolds, Carmel and Carlos Capelet, Ethan and Jamie, Orlaith and Barry Hopkins, Aoibhinn, Róisín and Daniel, Aoife Reynolds, Tania Flynn, Marion Gilsenan, Michael Irwin, Tom Grealy, Frances Moylan and Daniel Soler Fontanet. The team in Braemar: Sue Harper, Steve Rennie, Al and Sarah Hubbard, Julian and Katy Fennema. And finally my friends and neighbours in Temple, with a special shout out to Tam and Kerry Bell who live next door! I'd also like to thank Simon Birch and the trustees of the MBA, plus my fellow MO's in the Western Highlands and Islands Area (keep up all the good work!), the staff at the National Library of Scotland, Martin Quinn and the gang at Craigdon Mountain Sports, Edinburgh, JP Cameras, Davie and the mechanics at Station Garage, Gorebridge, my happy campers on last summer's Walkabout Scotland tour: Chris and Geoff, Vicki and Larry, Liliana, Suzanne, and Jessie, and last but not least Tania Pascoe and Daniel Start at Wild Things, for their enthusiasm and expertise.

Other books from Wild Things Publishing:

The Scottish Bothy Bible	Wild Guide - Lakes & Dales	Wild Swimming Italy
Bikepacking	Wild Guide - London & South-East	Wild Swimming Spain
Lost Lanes South		Wild Swimming Sydney
Lost Lanes Wales	Wild Guide Wales	Wild Swimming Walks
Lost Lanes West	Wild Guide Scotland	France en Velo
Only Planet	Wild Guide Scandinavia	Hidden Beaches Britain
Wild Garden Weekends	Wild Guide Portugal	
Wild Ruins & B.C.	Wild Swimming Britain	
Wild Guide - South West	Wild Swimming France	